Lindsay Simpson and Sandra Harvey have written two other bestselling books, *My Husband, My Killer* (1992) and *The Killer Next Door* (1994). Lindsay is an ex-journalist and the author of *The Australian Geographic Guide to Tasmania* (1997) and *To Have and To Hold* with Walter Mikac (1997). She is currently the coordinator of Journalism and Media Studies at the University of Tasmania.

After collaborating with Lindsay, Sandra Harvey's first solo effort, *The Ghost of Ludwig Gertsch*, was published in 2000. Sandra is a former journalist for the *Sydney Morning Herald* and is currently senior media adviser to the NSW Minister for Police.

Though they may not always be handsome, men doomed to evil possess the manly virtues. Of their own volition, or owing to an accident which has been chosen for them, they plunge lucidly and without complaint into a reproachful, ignominious element, like that into which love, if it is profound, hurls human beings.

JEAN GENET *The Thief's Journal*

BROTHERS
IN ARMS

SANDRA
HARVEY

LINDSAY
SIMPSON

ALLEN & UNWIN

To Elliot, who fought his own battles

First published in 1989
This edition published in 2001

Allen & Unwin
83 Alexander Street
Crows Nest NSW 2065
Australia
Phone: (61 2) 8425 0100
Fax: (61 2) 9906 2218
Email: frontdesk@allen-unwin.com.au
Web: http://www.allenandunwin.com

National Library of Australia
Cataloguing-in-Publication entry:

Harvey, Sandra.
   Brothers in arms.

   ISBN 1 86508 501 4.

   1. Bandidos Motor Cycle Club. 2. Comanchero Motor Cycle Club. 3. Mass murder—New South Wales—Milperra. 4. Trials (Murder)—New South Wales. 5. Motorcycle gangs—New South Wales. I. Simpson, Lindsay. II. Title.

364.1523099441

Printed by Australian Print Group, Maryborough, Vic.

10 9 8 7 6 5 4 3 2 1

Contents

PREFACE

Lindsay Simpson and Sandra Harvey are two journalists from the *Sydney Morning Herald* and *Australian Associated Press* who met when they were assigned to cover the court case of 43 men charged with seven counts of murder after a shootout at the Viking Tavern in Milperra on September 2, 1984.

Through the two years of court proceedings, they came to know some of the bikies in the dock. The tales of the individual men proved far more interesting than the court case. A week after the first evidence unfolded, the women made a pact to tell the story of the struggle between two men and their gangs which ended in a cold-blooded shootout in a quiet western suburb of Sydney.

All the material in this book is either from their own observation, from official court or medical records or is the result of hundreds of interviews conducted over three years with the persons directly concerned. Many people have understandably asked not to be publically acknowledged as sources.

The authors would like to thank Leanne Walter's family for their considerate help, the NSW police force, specifically Chief Superintendent Ron Stephenson and his team of detectives, Detective Bruce Demmery and Detective Aarnie Tees in particular.

They would also like to thank the lawyers, from both the defence and the prosecution, who gave their assistance and the handful of bikies and their families who agreed to give their versions.

Lindsay Simpson would like to thank her husband Bruce Miller who believed in the book from the beginning and for his contribution to the photographs.

BANDIDOS

Bear: Stephen Roberts
Bernie: Bernard Podgorski
Big Tony: Tony Cain
Bull: Phillip Campbell
Caesar: Colin Campbell
Charlie: Charlie Sciberras
Chopper: Mario Cianter
Davo: William Littlewood
Dukes: Greg McElwaine
Gloves: Mark McElwaine
Hookie: Steve Owens
Junior: Mark Shorthall
Kid Rotten: Lance Purdie
Knuckles: Phillip McElwaine
Lance: Lance Wellington
Lard: Tony Melville
Lout: Rick Harris
Lovie: Lewis Cooper
Opey: Stephen Cowan
Peter: Peter Melville
Pig: Grant Everest
Ray: Ray Denholm
Roach: James Posar
Roo: Rua Rophia
Shadow: Gregory Campbell
Snake: Geoff Campbell
Snodgrass, Snoddy: Anthony
Mark Spencer
Sparksy: Gerard Parkes
Steve: Steve Hails
Tiny: Graeme Wilkinson
Tom: Tom Denholm
Val: Vlado Grahovac
Whack: John Campbell
Zorba: George Kouratoras

COMANCHEROS

Andy: Andrew Thomas
Blowave: John Bodt
Bones: Scott Dive
Chewy: Rick Lorenz
Dog: Tony McCoy
Foghorn, Foggy: Robert Lane
Glen: Glen Eaves
JJ: Robert Heeney
Jock: William Ross
Kraut: Kevork Tomasian
Leroy: Phillip Jeschke
Littlejohn: John Hennessey
Morts: James Morton
Pee Wee: Garry Annakin
Snow: Ian White
Sparrow, Sparra: Ivan Romcek
Sunshine: Raymond Kucler
Terry: Terrence Parker
Tonka: Michael O'Keefe

Chopper (Mario Cianter),
Bandido, shot dead.

Leroy (Phillip) Jeschke,
Comanchero, shot dead.

Dog (Tony) McCoy, Comanchero,
shot dead.

Foghorn (Robert) Lane,
Comanchero, shot dead.

Shadow (Gregory) Campbell,
Bandido, shot dead.

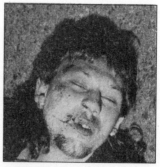

Sparrow (Ivan) Romcek,
Comanchero, shot dead.

Leanne Walters, shot dead.

Snodgrass (Anthony Mark) Spencer, suicided in jail.

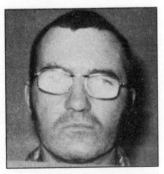

First photo of Jock taken after the massacre, his head shaved because of surgery.

Jock two years later.

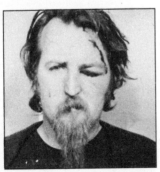

Tonka (Michael) O'Keefe after the battle.

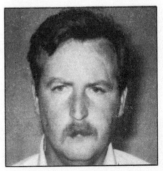

Tonka after some time in jail.

Gloves (Mark) McElwaine after the battle.

Gloves later.

Morts (James) Morton after the battle.

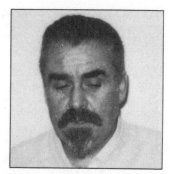

Morts later.

Sunshine (Raymond) Kucler after the battle.

Kucler later.

Glen Anthony Eaves after the battle.

Eaves later.

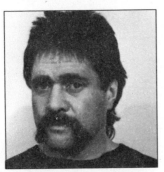

Roo (Rua) Rophia after the battle.

Roo later.

Lance Wellington after the battle.

Lance later.

Lard (Tony) Melville after the
battle.

Lard (after prison fare) later.

Bull (Phillip) Campbell after the
battle.

Bull later.

Kristine Duffy (Comanchero JJ's
'old lady') was the only woman to
be charged after the massacre.
She was charged with affray but
later no billed.

*All photographs by courtesy of
the New South Wales Police
Department*

1

Shots at the clubhouse

Mrs Lesley Proudman's eyes opened wide in her darkened bedroom. Jolted from a heavy sleep, she held her breath.

Then she heard it again—a deafening explosion outside her bedroom window. This time she knew exactly what it was.

Pulling back her tapestry bedspread, she leapt up and ran slipperless to the bedroom door.

Clad only in her long winter nightie, she was halfway into the loungeroom before she realised she was running. Curiosity propelled her towards the large front window, where she knew the blind would be up. Here, standing in the dark, her presence as an observer would be undetected.

Peering into the night, she picked out the figure clearly. He stood isolated in a pool of light from the street lamp in the empty turning circle. Across his groin cradled horizontally in both hands was a pump-action shotgun.

The figure, in a bulky black leather jacket, seemed frozen, staring, as if towards her. She gazed back at him, transfixed. For a moment they seemed linked in an unspoken conspiracy.

He broke the spell, turning quickly, the shotgun dangling awkwardly from a strap in his right hand. She noticed the car parked behind him, and two other men. One climbed into the driver's seat and the other slammed the door on the passenger side.

Mrs Proudman blinked and they were gone, disappearing up Louisa Road, rounding the first bend with a resonating crunch as they changed gears.

No, she didn't get the registration number, she couldn't see—it all happened so quickly. "And, no, I didn't really hear anything else, but wait, there could have been shouting."

Later, Mrs Proudman would curse herself because she left her glasses sitting on her bedside dresser. Was it a Holden or a Valiant? Well, it was pale coloured she had thought an hour later, standing in the the cold street in the company of two uniformed policemen.

She turned from the window, released from her spell. Skirting the large mahogany coffee table, she made for the front door, hurtling down the outside stairs and almost colliding with the dark figure coming up them.

"David! Did you see? That was shooting again . . ."

"Yes, yes, I know, I was flat on the floorboards. Are you okay, Lesley?" His breathing was quick and shallow.

"I saw him out of the window . . ."

"You did what, Lesley? What were you doing at the window, woman? You could have been killed."

"I saw the man with a gun, it must have been the same fellow as last time . . ."

"What on earth were you doing looking out . . .come upstairs. I'm ringing the police."

Back in the loungeroom again, Mrs Proudman talked excitedly.

"There were three of them . . ."

"Yes, I heard them all shouting. I was reading in bed when they drove up."

Reverend Connolly switched on the lamp next to the phone and began dialling. It was the second time in two days he had rung Balmain police station. He remembered the number from the night of the first shooting.

"I heard the racket as the car sped up, Lesley, I was expecting—ah, yes—it's Reverend David Connolly here, from Louisa Road, I'd like to report another shooting. No, no-one hurt . . ." But the trembling in his free hand was a telltale sign that the Reverend was clearly shaken.

"The police are on their way, Lesley. Now, where's your gown? Put it on or you'll catch a death of cold. I'd like to know exactly what's going on around here." The Reverend's words made Mrs Proudman realise just how cold she was, and just how foolish she'd been standing by the window with the blind up and the gunman opposite. She imagined the gunman hadn't seen her.

Back in her bedroom, she pulled on her dressing gown and found her glasses on the dresser. How silly can you be? she thought to herself.

Constable Peter Blinman had convinced himself some hours earlier that 11 August 1984 was going to be a bugger of a day. Earlier that morning, during an unexpected downpour, the police car in which he was a passenger slid off the road sideways into the gutter. He spent the day filling in paperwork.

Now, at 2.31 am, already into August 12, just when things were quiet and he and Constable Barry Powter were patrolling the narrow back streets of Balmain, the call came over the radio: "Shots fired at Louisa Road, Birchgrove. Nearest car in attendance."

Powter was not impressed. He was working a double shift because his replacement had rung in sick. But Blinman radioed back to confirm their attendance.

"Address, please. This is car 48, VKG over."

"Number 150," Blinman repeated after the crackling radio had responded. "That's not the bikies' place is it?"

The two constables had seen exactly two years' service in the police force. Blinman, a tall young man with a deep voice, was two months senior to Powter. "Shit, just our luck, you and me and a pack of bikies," Powter rejoined. "We'll look real good."

Counting the numbers down Louisa Road, Blinman was sure he was correct. Powter dropped into second gear as they crawled along. Yes, there was 150, the large old wooden house with the red tiled roof at the end of the street—the bikie clubhouse.

It was in darkness. The redbrick side walls had eerie shadows cast by the street lights leading down to the Long Nose Point ferry. Powter stopped in the turning circle at the end of the street. Neither man was in a hurry to open his car door.

The bikies had been in the upstairs kitchen when the shooting started, drawing in turn on a carved bamboo bong, inhaling lungfuls of sweet–smelling marijuana, and staring with drug-addled introspection around the place they called their home.

On the grey and white laminex table someone had spilt tomato sauce. Dirty plates stood piled around the sink and on the table. The remnants of Big Tony's leg of lamb, yesterday's feast, lay congealed on some of the plates in thick, white grease.

Charlie Sciberras, a diminutive figure with a woolly goatee beard and fuzzy black hair, was telling jokes. The laughter that followed was infectious.

Some time after midnight, a few of the men crawled into the bedrooms off the kitchen, bedrooms of sorts—bare rooms with double mattresses and little other furniture to be seen.

Seven men were there that night, all of them Bandidos. Four men lived there permanently. Rua Rophia, a tall, handsome Maori known to his brothers as Roo, Stephen Cowan, whose club name was Opey, Big Tony Cain—another New Zealander with a neanderthal-shaped head, and Chopper, one of six Campbell brothers in the Bandido Motor Cycle Club.

The upstairs kitchen, where the seven men now lay shaken, cowering on the floor, was used by the clubhouse residents. It was here their enemy had attacked, smashing the kitchen window and spattering shotgun pellets through the shabby, fibro sheeting around its frame.

When the first shot was fired, Charlie was standing, leaning up against the wall underneath the window, his black droopy moustache framing the wooden stem of the bong. Without warning, a pellet sliced the air above his head and lodged in the kitchen cupboard. Charlie gasped, and then laughed, partly from disbelief and partly from the effects of the marijuana.

Roo had a hangover. The Bandidos had been partying all day Friday and all day Saturday. The shooting made Roo sober. He was impressed enough to whistle in disbelief.

"Boom, boom, smash . . .man, that's what I heard," Charlie said, making the most of his brief flirtation with death.

"You'll never believe this, man," he said later to Roo. "Look at this . . .the fuckin' thing whistled through my hair like this." He ran his fingers through Roo's black shiny mane. "Hell, brother, if I'd been any bigger . . ."

Chopper took control of the situation as soon as the first shot was fired. He switched off the kitchen's single electric light and ran downstairs into the bar, where the club shotgun lay across the carved wooden bartop. Upstairs again, he took up position to the right of the shattered window.

He strained around to the left and saw the gunman in the turning circle opposite. He recognised his scrawny frame and lifeless long hair. Chopper took aim and fired one shot.

He turned and looked at Rick Harris, whose club name was Lout. "I got the bastard."

"Fucking idiots," Roo said. "They're crazy, man, they're really trying to fuckin' kill us."

"I'll bet the woman next door rings the cops. The whole neighbourhood'll know about it."

"We don't want the fucking pigs inside here swarming all over the place," Chopper addressed the men in the kitchen. "I'll handle it, I'll do all the talking."

The men laid low in darkness until they heard the car roar off down the road. Then Chopper went downstairs with the gun, opened the front door and looked gingerly up the street before venturing out to the top of the front steps.

"The Pres" should be told right away. They couldn't afford to slacken off on guard duty. Next time someone would be killed. Those bastards meant business.

Chopper, whose real name was Mario Cianter, was a somewhat hot-blooded Italian, used to being in charge. Although not an office bearer, he was one of the the club's older and more influential members. And as a Campbell, albeit an adopted one, he assumed a natural authority. Out of the seven people in the house that night, he felt he was the most responsible.

"Keep inside," Chopper motioned to the two men behind him. "I'll do the talking."

At least, Reverend Connolly thought, this time the police had been quicker. Standing at the loungeroom window, he heard the patrol car approach and saw the lights sweep the turning circle. He secured the cord of his dressing gown before going outside to meet them.

"Good evening. Yes, Reverend David Connolly, the man who rang you. I'm a visitor to Sydney and I'm staying here at number 148, Mrs Proudman's house. Mrs Proudman stood behind him, her hands deep in the pockets of her winter dressing gown.

Glancing to his right, the Reverend saw several men emerge from the house next door. They looked a ferocious lot. He was momentarily struck by the bizarre situation. Big, scruffy men standing around in sloppy joes and jeans, he and Mrs Proudman in their night attire, and the two uniformed young policeman going through the motions, emulating experienced detectives. This time, he was sure, the bikies were angrier.

Another police car pulled up and three more officers, and another neighbour in a dressing gown, joined the odd assortment of people in the middle of the road.

"I was terrified out of my wits," the Reverend continued. "I was downstairs reading when I heard a car speeding down the road towards us. It was just like the other night."

The uniformed constable scratched away in his notebook.

" . . .Next I heard was doors slamming, lots of shouting and then the gunfire started. It was then, as I lay face down on my bed, I heard shots returned from the house next door."

Chopper ignored the Reverend's last comment. He told the police his name was Cooper Lewis (Louie Cooper was one of the Bandidos still inside the clubhouse). "I don't know why anybody would shoot at us," Chopper lied. Behind him, the other men stood silent.

"I don't know who it could possibly be . . .imagine if my lady was making a cup of coffee at the window, she could have been killed . . ." said Chopper, anger still brewing.

Constable Blinman, Powter and Chopper walked to the rear of the house where they looked up at the smashed second floor window.

Powter returned to his police car, then started to search the roadway under the No Standing sign. He was rewarded. Bending down, he picked up a red coloured shotgun cartridge lying about 30 centimetres from the kerb. Back in the police station at Balmain, he placed the find in his locker.

The bikies, or bikers, as they preferred to be called, moved in on a Sunday afternoon in late August 1983. At that time, they were members of the Comanchero Motor Cycle Club. The lease was signed by "Mr S.J. Curtis" on 26 August 1983, rent stipulated at $300 a week.

"Mr Curtis" (in reality Stephen Cowan, known to his brothers as Opey), provided two references to the manager of the real estate agency in Darling Street Balmain. He gave the name of an employer—J & B Fencing—from which a certain "Mrs Ross" described him as "reliable".

The other comment on the application form under reference checks came from a Mrs King, named as his last real estate agent. It was a little more effusive: "Tremendous, always on time paying his rent."

On the day he inspected the house, "Mr Curtis" was dressed in a cream coloured sports coat, his long hair neatly plaited at the back. He appeared to be a reliable if somewhat unusual tenant. After all, it was not easy to rent out a house at $300 a week with $1530.45 required in advance, particularly as both the inside and outside of the house badly needed a paint and some of the carpets were stained. But Opey had been on the look out for "something with a bit of style", preferably near the water and close to the city.

On that Sunday afternoon in August 1983, Mrs Proudman and a friend were sitting on her lounge suite sipping a cup of tea when they heard the utility trucks pull up.

Mrs Proudman, a kindergarten teacher nearing retirement, was the widow of a clergyman who died fifteen years earlier from multiple sclerosis. Quiet and thin, her olive-brown skin showed signs of middle-age but her body was still trim and agile. She had a quiet way of speaking, almost subdued, but occasionally she permitted herself to laugh like a schoolgirl.

From her loungeroom Mrs Proudman had a bird's eye view of Long Nose Point Reserve, the turning circle opposite, and the house next door.

She stood at the window facing north, astounded at what she saw.

"Just look at this!"

Three utility trucks completely blocked the turning circle. The white wooden gate leading up to the steps of number 150 swung open as three men in leather jackets laboured under the weight of two poker machines. They struggled up the front steps. "That fellow there with the long plait is the one who came down with the real estate agent," she explained to her visitor.

As she spoke, her friend read out loud the insignia on one of the men's jackets, the lettering embroidered in gold in a horseshoe shape: "Comanchero Motor Cycle Club".

Behind the three who disappeared into the house with the poker machines, two other men struggled with a large neon sign with the same club name in red and yellow letters.

"But, Lesley, poker machines aren't legal are they? I mean they can't be serious, moving things in like this in broad daylight . . ." The two women watched, unnerved by the spectacle.

"Space invader machines? No, I don't believe it . . .and no furniture that I can see." Mrs Proudman, always practical, looked back to the utility trucks.

Two days later Mrs Proudman still felt uneasy about her new neighbours. She had been marking exercise books when she heard the sound of hammering and decided to investigate. The first thing she noticed when she walked past the old garage was a series of little white lines painted diagonally across the garage floor and in between each a Harley Davidson motor cycle was neatly parked. She crept under her balcony around to the back of the house. As she peered through the downstairs window, she cupped her face with her hands in astonishment.

A large wooden bar had been erected across the middle of the main downstairs living area, straddling the room under an archway. Next to it, on the wall, was a blackboard with prices chalked up. "Jack Daniels 75c a nip, Fosters and Tooheys $1 a can." Then she noticed the photos pinned around the bar, snapshots of men standing next to motor bikes. It looked like a Hall of Fame.

"It's a clubhouse, for goodness' sake! They're turning it into a bikie clubhouse . . ." she said out loud to herself.

Never in the history of Louisa Road had the residents seen such occupants as the members of the Comanchero Motor Cycle Club. The street was a mish-mash of expensive double-storeyed homes. Its residents included a famous Australian author, a playwright, a pop star of the 1970s and various people from the wealthy fashionable set of Sydney society. The winding, narrow roadway ran the length of a peninsula that jutted into the sprawling Parramatta River.

Number 150 is one of the prime pieces of real estate in the street, standing as it does overlooking the river and the Long Nose Point Reserve. Perhaps it needed a little renovation, but the structure was sound. Built in 1910, it was typical of the grand houses of its time, with high white stucco ceilings upstairs and down, double windows facing the foreshore and a large cool sandstone wine cellar in the basement. Its gardens, deteriorated from neglect during the years the house had been up for rent, were built in layers with sandstone walls like military parapets facing the river. Square holes were drilled in the stone, as if ready for cannons.

To the right lay Long Nose Point Reserve, screened from the house by the large Moreton Bay fig trees leading down to the water and the public wharf. From here, large tub-like blue and cream Urban Transit Authority ferries carried commuters to the city in 45 minutes. After the bikies moved in, patrons of the ferry were greeted by the large neon sign in the window facing the water: Comanchero Motor Cycle Club.

Picnickers came to the Reserve on weekends, dangling their legs over the sandstone rocks and looking out over to Greenwich in the west and Balls Head Reserve to the east, casting their eyes down the wide river that eventuallly lost itself in Sydney Harbour.

The bikies' arrival in Louisa Road slipped into Birchgrove folklore with surprising ease. Every Saturday they would "party", and far from everyone's expectations, the doors of number 150 were not kept closed. Everyone was invited to Saturday parties, everyone that is who happened to bump into the Comancheros on their weekly drinking sprees to the local pubs in Balmain: the Sir William Wallace, The London Hotel and then down to the Commercial by the wharf. After a suitable interlude in these pubs which the Comancheros would take over like an army laying siege to a small town, their President, Jock Ross, an aging Scotsman, would give the orders that it was time to grace the clubhouse.

Steak, chops and salad at $3 a plate were served on these nights. The steak would be barbequed with each bikie serving time as the cook. Another would be on duty to collect invitations and guide bikes past the turning circle to park on the reserve.

Rock bands, specially chosen for the parties, would set up in the late afternoon in the back garden by the water's edge, where occasional wet t-shirt competitions would also take place. On those days, the bikies would crowd around and watch as one of them turned a hose on the women who lined up and waited to be sprayed, clad in white t-shirts and jeans.

Stories materialised around Balmain. The women in the real estate office would giggle when Kid Rotten (or Lance Purdie, as his parents christened him), a 38 year-old Vietnam veteran, came in to pay the rent. Shadow, another Campbell brother who at twelve years old had one day brought Chopper home from school with him, also tried his luck with the local women. He asked one of the real estate office workers out to dinner, saying he would even bring his car and leave his bike at home.

Stories began to circulate about bikie initiations and rites, like red wings, little badges sewn onto the arms of leather jackets, reportedly awarded to men who had had oral sex with a woman who was menstruating. But nobody knew if the stories were true.

One local who came to a party at Louisa Road reported that a large red heart, about two feet high, was painted in one of the upstairs bedrooms. The red glossy paint had run down the purple walls giving it a bleeding look. This was "the Virgin's Converting Room".

But somehow, among the contrasting conservative Balmainites, the Comancheros won their place. On big party days, delivery vans would pull up in the turning circle: Buttercup Bread vans delivered white rolls and white toasting loaves which the boys would get at a reduced price because one of their brothers, Tony Melville, or Lard, worked there. Then there would be the meat delivered, kilos of sausages and t-bone steaks, carted up the front path and into the house.

Phillip McElwaine—Knuckles to his brothers—the appointed club-house barman, would arrive on party days, his van loaded with cartons of Tooheys, bottles of Jack Daniels and Black Label Scotch. Chivas Regal was reserved for club members only. Customers with a penchant for Scotch were served Johnny Walker. Knuckles was one of three McElwaine brothers who were all Comancheros. Their father Bob, a retired publican, was an honorary member of the club. He brought up his boys to be boxers. Knuckles was a champion, an asset to Australia, his father always said, a Commonwealth and Olympic boxing medallist. That was before a bike accident ended his professional boxing career.

Party supplies were the only shopping Mrs Proudman ever saw her neighbours do, she would sometimes remark to friends (who had become increasingly interested in Balmain's latest residents). "And you know, I never see any washing on the line. Well, there's the occasional t-shirt, but never any sheets or towels or anything. You wonder how they manage . . ."

Life next to the bikies was not all novelty and wonderment. At some parties, Mrs Proudman would see them urinating on their front lawn, and sometimes, during her days off in particular, she would become irritated by the dull thud, thud, thud of their rock and roll music. Just occasionally, however, she would find herself humming along to the less aggressive tunes they sometimes played.

One day she confronted one of them in the garden. "Would you turn that down please? I'm trying to work. I feel like a bit of quiet."

The man (she was surprised at how old he was when she got up close, perhaps only 20 years her junior) merely grunted, but disappeared inside the house and turned the music down. It was the first of a few "meetings" she attempted to have with her neighbours. Some complaints were successful, some were not.

Other days, she would feel claustrophobic, hemmed in by row upon row of Harley Davidson motor bikes, presumably club members visiting. She would knock on their door and one of them would come directly over and move the offending bikes so she could drive her own car out.

One cold winter morning when her car wouldn't start, one of the men came over and got it started for her. She had been particularly grateful, but the mechanic merely said, "No worries, lady".

Mrs Proudman's nine-year old grandson would make up names. "That's the boss," he would say pointing at one of the black-leathered figures from the safety of her wooden balcony at the rear of the house.

On another occasion, a Thursday night, Mrs Proudman's daughter, Jackie, was having trouble getting her car out of her mother's garage because of the obstructing bikes. She was furious and stormed across to the house next door. As she put her hand up to knock on the door she saw them through the window. They were standing in a circle, each man holding a raised glass. She heard them toast a dead brother before one of them spotted her waiting at the door. Jackie was ushered back down the front steps and away from the house.

Life for the varying number of residents at 150 Louisa Road was reasonably mundane. In the mornings, the bikies would watch cartoons on the commercial television stations. Some mornings Colin Campbell—Caesar—the oldest of the six Campbell brothers, would practise with his bull whip, striding up and down the garden cracking it, adopting a ferocious look on his wrinkled face, his thinning hair ruffling in the breeze from the harbour. He had lost his teeth twenty years before.

The front door bore a cryptic sign: a fat turkey with a thick line through it: No Turkeys. Inside to the right, a pool room was set up. It adjoined the bar with a skull and crossbones in the corner and a Mr Juicy machine, churning orange juice.

The downstairs kitchen was used for dispensing food on party nights. Upstairs was strictly residents only.

Three months after her neighbours moved in, Mrs Proudman noticed they were no longer sporting the word "Comanchero" on their backs. Instead, a fat Mexican with a sword and a gun in his hands sat across their leather jackets with the words "Bandidos Australia" replacing the old insignia. She saw that the neon sign in the bay window announcing the Comanchero Motor Cycle Club had disappeared.

If she had looked a little closer, she would have seen on the same window, in black gloss paint, the following lines:

"If it's white sniff it,
If it's female or if it moves fuck it,
If it narks—kill it."

Mick, the local gardener, also noticed the bikies' name change. One day while he was cleaning out their front garden, he saw a new sign up. It was near one of the sentinel walls, on a rope attached to the street light in the back yard. It read: BANDIDOS ONLY PAST THIS POINT.

He asked Opey, "the gentle giant" as he called him, what had happened. "How come you haven't got 'Comancheros' on your backs any more?"

He half expected a rebuke, but Opey was accommodating. "Oh, some of our blokes went to America and met this club called the Bandidos—they're the best—and we decided to join them as the Australian Chapter. When we go there they look after us, and when they come over here we look after them. We're brothers."

"So, you're not Comancheros any more?"

"No, mate, no more."

Mick received this information in silence, not fully understanding, but not wanting to ask any more questions. He realised from the start he could not be taken into their confidence. That was their rule.

When Mick knocked off around 3.30 pm Opey would give him a lift up to Balmain. Sometimes in the mornings, when Opey would be returning from breakfast at the Squash Centre, not that he ever played squash, he would tell Mick with a grin, but it was "a good feed", he'd give the gardener a lift down to the bottom of the street.

Opey often had Hulk with him, a large, slobbering German shepherd cross, the guard dog for the clubhouse. It was the only guard the bikies had in their early days at Birchgrove.

Mick was a tall, lanky man approaching 50. He was strong and took great pride in keeping the reserve "real nice looking". He had an easy, friendly nature, grinning from underneath the brim of his green felt sun hat. He spoke slowly, with an Australian drawl, using his big bony hands to embellish his stories.

He came to be accepted by the club, sometimes being invited inside to sit cross-legged on the floor cracking a can of beer and nodding at the boys. Sometimes he would find shotgun cartridges in the backyard. Shooting practice, the boys would tell him.

One day in the backyard Mick struck up conversation with one of the boys. "See these lovely chokos here?" he pointed to the large green fruits hanging from the vine on the back fence and spilling over the lawn, "Why don't you boys collect them and cook them up?"

"Can you eat them?" the bikie had asked.

Mick laughed long and hard. He thought every Australian lad knew what a choko was. He would have to tell the wife.

Another day Knuckles appeared at the door of Mick's shed in the Reserve carrying his baby, Harley. "Can you look after him, mate, while I go into the clubhouse? I've got a meeting there see, and I don't want to take him inside."

Mick's sun-hardened face softened as he took the tiny baby in his carry basket and placed him on the garden shed seat down by the water. Harley's father returned twenty minutes later.

Mick had a soft spot for Knuckles. He had followed his career as a champion Australian middle weight boxer. He wouldn't hurt a fly, Mick always said.

Not long after this the Comancheros split and the group left at Louisa Road starting calling themselves the Bandidos. Knuckles and Snodgrass (Anthony Spencer) the new Bandido President, came down to visit Mick, who was sitting in the small wooden shed near the ferry wharf.

"Listen, if there's anything we can do for you, we will," Snodgrass told him, adopting a serious tone. "You look after us and we'll look after you."

Snodgrass, a smaller man than most of the other men, was built like an overgrown jockey, a small neck, large shoulders tapering to a small waist. His long hair was a reddish mousey-brown, rarely combed and usually tied back with an elastic band. He had watery pale blue eyes. "Snoddy" seemed to have a permanent feeling of uneasiness about him. He was their leader, he made decisions, but leadership did not sit easily on his shoulders.

To Mick, however, in the days approaching Christmas 1983 Snoddy and his men were new found friends, if perhaps a little unorthodox. They were the sort of blokes he had grown up with, rough and ready, and loyal.There were only a few he felt he could not like.

On Christmas Day the Bandidos, as they were now known, had a party. Davo (William Littlewood) dressed up as Santa in the full regalia, his ginger beard peeking out from behind the white cottonwool. His bag was full of presents collected by the boys a few days earlier for the 40 or so Bandido children. Davo's parents—Mummsie and Daddy Cool—always cooked Christmas dinner for the boys without families. It was a traditional biker Christmas.

Aside from tending to the garden, Mick used to carry out the empty bottles. Each Monday there was a cache of glass amassed from a weekend of serious drinking and partying. Mick never ceased to be amazed at the amount of liquor they would consume each weekend.

Tequila was a favourite after the boys became Bandidos. He would collect cases of empty bottles of the potent Mexican spirit. He noticed the red sombrero-shaped bottle caps. Just like the bandit on their jackets, he thought. Every week three bikies would hand over the empty beer cans in large green garbage bags. They were nominees, he was told.

"The crime rate's dropped around Birchgrove," Mick would tell his old retired mate Alan. "It's since those boys moved in—you know that? It's those bikies that keep the weirdos out of the park, mate. That's for sure."

Alan, a retired Louisa Road resident, would join Mick each morning for a yarn and a cuppa as they sat in the cool of the shed by the wharf. Mick would take out his cut sandwiches and boil the jug in the tool shed.

Once, Mick came to work on a Monday morning to find skid marks from a motorbike on the grass.

"Listen mate," he said to Opey. "Can you pass the word around to tell the boys to keep of the grass with their bikes."

"Oh, it wouldn't be us, mate," the bikie had explained. "See, we have these other clubs that come down here to party and we can't control them." It was the only time Mick had cause to complain.

Six months passed happily enough. But in early August 1984, Opey began to ignore his gardener friend, as if he was permanently preoccupied. Mick sensed a change in the easygoing atmosphere in the clubhouse. No-one spoke to him any more and there were always one or two of the men on duty guarding the bikes.

Reverend Connolly first noticed the fortification of the clubhouse, as he described it, the night after the first shooting. That night bikes had choked the turning circle, spilling on to the pavement and blocking Mrs Proudman's driveway. He guessed it was a full-scale meeting. Guards, some armed with baseball bats stood watching the Harleys and the house. He tried to fix his mind on "Rumpole of the Bailey", the programme he and Mrs Proudman were watching, aware the events next door contained more drama than anything the ABC, the national broadcasting station, could produce.

Now, there was a permanent guard who skirted the grounds day and night. The Reverend noticed furniture being moved too, forming crude barricades against the windows, both up and downstairs. It worried him. He expected more trouble.

2

Two leaders

The second shootout was almost abortive. Five and a half hours before, Jock Ross, the President of the Comanchero Motor Cycle Club, was riding through West Ryde on his blue 81 Electraglide Harley Davidson with ten of his men. They were Jock's main pack. Only big, bearded Morts (James Morton) had been left behind to guard the new Comanchero clubhouse at Harris Park, which had been set up in February 1984, after the Comancheros split into two groups.

Word reached Jock as he led his men down Victoria Road towards the city that his rear guard, the last two bikes travelling abreast in standard formation, had fallen behind. After signalling to his men something was wrong, he rode back up Victoria Road until he reached the corner of Hermitage Street. It was there he spotted them and pulled off the road into a Mobil petrol station.

Jock took in the situation quickly. Foghorn (Robert Lane), his Vice President, was still sitting astride his Harley on the footpath at the corner of the intersection. Directly in front of Foghorn was a police paddy wagon. Two police officers, notebooks in hand, were interrogating Foghorn and his passenger.

Senior Constable Darryl Lane and Constable Glenn Dein had been out on patrol in West Ryde, heading for suburban Meadowbank, when Lane spotted Foghorn's M1 carbine rifle strapped across his back as he sat at the lights. The constable didn't like the look of it—the gun and the petrol station—with armed robberies on the increase. He decided to stop.

Lane asked the inevitable: "Have you got a shooter's licence?" Foghorn had many aliases and he produced one now, a shooter's licence with the name John Simon Carlton, D.O.B. 19.3.54.

At 30 years of age, Foggy was becoming wiser in his dealings with the police. You did not argue. Just produce the necessary legal paraphernalia and play their game.

He was a thin, sallow man with a gingery moustache and goatee beard, dwarfing a pencil-thin mouth. His sunken eyes were lacklustre brown, masked by dark eyebrows and accentuated by sagging skin under his eyes, making him look older than his years. He gave the appearance of being in perpetual mourning, bearing the stamp of a man whose life had beaten him down to a state of resignation.

Foghorn's hobby, which had become a major part of his life by his early twenties, was building motor bikes. He owned four bikes, one of which was at that time in pieces on the loungeroom floor of his State Housing Commission home at Heckenberg, in far western Sydney.

His two roles in life—Jock's Vice President and right hand man, and a single father of twin girls—made him a sort of Jekyll and Hyde character. In the eyes of his leader, he was "a hellishly brave man".

Two years before, Foggy had tried to outride a constable who chased him for a traffic infringement. When the officer finally confronted him, Foggy punched and kicked—put up a hell of a fight—before he was subdued and taken to Fairfield police station. They searched his car and found a .303 rifle, a double barrelled shot gun, a bandolier of bullets and a sledge hammer. He had told the police that the sledge hammer was to smash the bikes of their then rivals, the Gypsy Jokers.

Foggy loathed the cops, but he knew on this particular occasion he had to be cool.

"Where are you off to, mate?" asked Constable Lane.

Foggy hesitated, but only briefly: "Forest Lodge Hotel at Glebe."

The other Constable, Glenn Dein, spoke up, digging into his knowledge of the legality of firearms. "Where do you leave the guns when you go inside the pub?" he said.

"There's always a guard on them."

Constable Lane noticed another rifle in a scabbard, strapped to the side of the Harley Sportster, on which Foggy still sat, a composed expression on his face. "Do you own both guns?" Lane asked.

"No."

"I own that one." Foghorn's passenger spoke for the first time.

He pointed to the M1 Carbine rifle, which now lay boldly on the police van bonnet. "I haven't got a shooter's licence for it so he's carrying it for me." Dein seized on this new information, taking the man's name, date of birth and address.

While Lane went to the police radio to check on the particulars, Dein switched his attention to the pump action shotgun on the side of the bike.

"Is the second gun loaded?" asked Lane.

"No, you can check if you like."

"Are you carrying any ammunition for the gun?"

Foggy stared straight at him. "Yes."

He lifted his jacket to reveal a ring of shotgun cartridges attached to a black leather belt around his waist.

When Constable Lane returned, Dein heard the familiar sound of Harley Davidson engines. Looking up, as he returned the shotgun to the scabbard, he noticed a large group of bikes pull up at the Mobil service station across the road.

The police officer began to feel nervous.

Several men dismounted. One of them, a wirey looking figure in black leathers, with a thatch of thick greying black hair and glasses, crossed the road to where they stood.

"What's the trouble here?" he asked in a Glaswegian brogue. He was calm, efficient and, Dein thought later, an obvious leader.

"I'm not real happy about the way the guns are being carried," the constable replied.

"It's all right. I'll get them put in the car." Jock knew all the answers.

"Who'll drive the car?"

"I'll get someone with a shooter's licence to drive it. No worries."

Lane liked the Scottish man, he thought to himself as Jock turned and crossed the road back to the bikes, carrying the two guns. He had been pleasant and cooperative, when Lane had been expecting trouble. Dein had much the same reaction. He had never encountered an incident like this in his short span in the police force, but then bikies were bikies and if shooting trips were what they were into, he was not going to question it.

He and Lane climbed back into the wagon. The law had not been broken. They were satisfied they had done their job.

He watched the bikers move out in formation, heading east along Victoria Road, their Comanchero colours noticeable under the street light.

The constables thought nothing more about them. They did not know that more of the bikies who had parked at the service station had been armed. They did not hear about any shooting incident later that night at 150 Louisa Road, Birchgrove. The next time they heard of the Comanchero Motor Cycle Club was three weeks later on Father's Day, September 2.

Mangrove Mountain lies inland from the sea, not far from the Pacific Highway, the main tourist road along the New South Wales coastline north of Sydney. It is part of a green belt of sub-tropical forest, sparsely populated, as much of the land is unsuitable for farming. Only the rivers really know the interior. Silver-grey eucalypts struggle for survival at the top of the plateau that gives Mangrove Mountain its name, the saplings occasionally gaining a foothold on the higher rocks, leaving their elders to dominate the safer ground below. They form silhouettes against the pure blue sky 500 feet above the dirt road, bare grey rocks scattered between them.

It is old land, land the locals say was settled by convicts, land which barely tolerates humans. It is a land which held a fascination for Jock Ross. Along Mangrove Creek Road, the houses are confined to the flats down by the creek, the green pastures cultivated over the last century, reminiscent of the old country. Cows graze on the flats and maize grows down by the river.

Orange trees are laid in neat rows in the fields off the road snaking down the mountain to Mangrove Creek Valley. In spring, acres of flowers stir in the breeze. In the green salty depths of Mangrove creek, bream, ocean perch and flathead can be caught.

Jock Ross, apprentice blacksmith, former soldier, owner truck driver and leader of men, first discovered Mangrove Mountain in 1971 when he left his home at Terrigal on the New South Wales central coast, bought a caravan and became a landowner.

At 26, William George Ross—William to his mother and Wally or Jock to his mates—had moved to Australia from Glasgow. It was 1966. His first home was in a flat on the New South Wales central coast, where he lived with his family. From there he moved to Point Clare near the Entrance, a sprawling seaside resort choked with used car yards and hamburger bars. In 1971 Jock, with his then wife Sandy and baby Deirdre, bought land along Mangrove Creek Road before the real estate boom that followed a few years later.

In 1974, Mangrove Mountain became the fashionable place to live for the upper middle class from Sydney, people lured by the magnet of the bush. Locals abandoned their orchards and sold out to property developers caught up in an eager scramble for land.

Slick, wealthy inhabitants—people such as a political cartoonist, the descendants of the Lloyd Jones family, founders of the luxury chain store David Jones, and a general manager of a commercial radio station in Sydney—moved in. Along the riverbank of Mangrove Creek Road, avant garde, newly-varnished log cabins sprouted, with round windows and sundecks looking out over the creek, the properties of weekenders and hobby farmers.

In one hollow the Yoga Assram, an eastern religious cult, claimed a hold on the land, building low huts, setting up headquarters and nurturing organic vegetable gardens. Dreamy followers worked diligently with the red earth, turning it into rockeries, planting flowering cacti and meditating on the newly planted green lawns.

Jock's 25-acre plot was cheap land, bought for a song at $800 an acre. It was a rocky plot set on the side of a hill. A dirt road separated it from the lush land near the creek. Here the land had already started to slope upward to reach the escarpment. Bottlebrush trees, wattles and eucalypts claimed the soil leading down to the road.

But Jock, an Australian resident of seven years whose previous homes stood in the grimy factory-bound cities of Scotland and England, loved the rocky block of land. He loved the bush. He liked the anonymity, the feeling of estrangement, of being unaccepted. He liked the challenge it gave him to tackle the land, subdue it and make it his home.

He started by hacking a dirt track leading from the road up to the only flat area next to a large, silver-white gum tree. It was to this spot he towed his caravan, parking it underneath the gum's outspread branches which provided shade after midday. He bought a jeep, the sort of vehicle needed to conquer this kind of territory. He bought a calf for Sandy, the tall, lanky girl he had married and who was to bear him two children. She used to feed the calf by hand from a plastic bucket.

Then he invited his men to the Mountain, a handful of labourers, some ex-servicemen, men with time on their hands who were happy to swap their family life for riding motor bikes.

Jock's club had then been in existence for two years. Up until then, he and his men rode around the central coast on Harley Davidson motor cycles, adopting drinking holes, often on the look out for a fight. He called his boys the Comancheros, after an Indian tribe he saw in a John Wayne western movie.

Jock's land at Mangrove Mountain became one of their first projects. With a handful of blue-jeaned, flannel-shirted men, he set to work on the area to the right of the caravan. They cleared and flattened it, sealing their victory with a concrete foundation.

To the right of his new home's foundations, he erected a corrugated iron water tank, water being a prime consideration. In summer, the land that lay away from the river flats was parched and dry, the scrub turned brown and yellow, and even the eucalypts' branches became grey and brittle.

Up above the caravan, Mangrove Mountain rose at a 90 degree angle, dominating Jock's land and marking his boundaries.

A large boulder balanced on the edge of the plateau was a reminder of the might of nature, silently threatening to fall and crush Jock's tiny aluminium home.

He planned one day to get to the top of the mountain.

Ross first met his new neighbour, Peter Armstrong, a month after he moved in. Jock and six of the boys had been having a bit of a barbeque combined with some shooting practice down by the riverbank. Peter Armstrong was the owner of the Lazy-B ranch, as proclaimed by a wooden signpost at the top of the driveway. He too had invited a few of his friends over for a barbeque.

The Armstrong party was standing over the steaks when the first bullets were fired above their heads. Peter Armstrong, solidly built, with well-sculpted muscles from his profession as a stunt man, did not hesitate. He strode across to the hedge separating him from the shooters.

"What exactly is going on here?" he demanded.

One of the group of six came towards him. Armstrong saw he was scruffily dressed in jeans and unshaven with thick granny glasses, but he sensed something about the man which spoke of authority.

The two stared at each other across the hedge calculating the other's worth, weighing each other up—two fighting men bristling with anger.

"I've got friends here. We're having a few drinks and a pleasant barbeque. I don't want any accidents," Armstrong spoke first.

Jock met his cold glare. "There'll be no accidents. I'll get my men to stop."

Armstrong felt the tension leave his face. He knew the men were part of a bikie gang and he knew this was their leader, the dark shaggy-haired man he'd seen toiling on the property across the road. The rest of the men he saw were unimpressive, an untidy gaggle standing passively in the distance as their leader sorted out the problem.

Peter Armstrong and his wife Heather had moved to Mangrove Mountain in 1969, when they bought an old wooden house overlooking the flats. They were fulfilling their dream to create a stuntfarm, the first of its kind in Australia.

Sandy eventually struck up a friendship with Heather, a resilient woman with red hair, striking blue eyes and a hardened face, who was learning stunts herself. They were the same age. They would go to macrame lessons together, sit and chat over cups of coffee in Heather's kitchen, an escape for Sandy from the one-roomed old-fashioned caravan.

Jock and Sandy started going to the Lazy-B for dinner. Heather would cook a stew on a camping primus stove with one gas ring, set up in her makeshift kitchen. The guests would sit in the loungeroom, talk and drink beer. On these occasions, Jock would wear a clean shirt and jeans and comb his straw-like hair, which fell almost to his shoulders.

Peter Armstrong, a tall man with a ruddy complexion and fair hair dulled by approaching middle age, was a man Jock could respect. As a mark of his friendship, Armstrong invited him to join in the stunt classes. On Sunday mornings or Saturday afternoons, he would wander across to the Armstrong's 40-acre paddock with some of his men.

Down in the paddock, he took orders from Peter Armstrong. Despite a lisp, Peter's voice, a low-pitched rasp, commanded authority.

"Jump!" he would order in a voice that was controlled but compelled the listener to obey. It was a tactic Jock was to emulate later with increasing success.

"Run—now, roll!" and Jock would roll along with the other novices, jumping over the tables and crates set up in the paddock and rolling on the other side. He never graduated to the real stunts—bouncing over the tops of cars travelling at five or six miles an hour. But he learnt other things, like how to act on his feet in combat training. He tried out one of the movements in a local pub brawl one night, throwing himself on one of his opponents, who moved, and left him flat on his face.

One night, sitting in Lazy-B ranch, Heather relayed local stories. "Funny things happen around here," she said as the four sat in the loungeroom, balancing plates of stew on their knees. "There's a graveyard down the road, you know, hidden from view."

Jock stopped eating, his fork, which he used like a shovel, still in his hand.

"They'd bring the coffins up and put them in off the creek in the old days. They weren't allowed to go through the land."

Heather told them about the legend surrounding the rock on Mangrove Creek Road, where one night a truck driver had lost control and crashed, his truck bursting into flames and incinerating him. "His ghost's still there."

Sandy laughed to break the tension. She recognised the look on her husband's face. "Oh, it's just a story. Look at you, Wally Ross, like a kid believing that!"

But that episode signalled the start of Jock's uneasiness. From then on he would ask Sandy to walk him up to the Lazy-B ranch or Heather would walk him back. He would not walk home at night alone. "It's the ghosties," he confided to Heather, and she laughed, not convinced.

One night, as they walked up his dirt track towards the caravan, he told her of his fear of the dead. "I used to take the gold out of dead mens' mouths on the war fields, see?" he said. "When I was fighting in the British Army, you know. I'd go back onto the field and take the gold out of their teeth."

She looked at him swiftly to see if he was teasing. But he showed no signs of it.

"Sometimes," she continued with her infamous Mangrove Mountain legends, "in the heat of summer we'll find wet patches in our front room—you know—the one facing the river that no-one sleeps in.

"Where does the damp come from?"

"Well, it's not mildew. It's Fred, our ghost. The room's haunted. He passes through the house like a cold thing touching you on the shoulder."

Jock shuddered involuntarily."Where did he come from?"

"They say he drowned in the creek and they pulled him out just there, where the house was later built. That's why he won't leave."

But none of Jock's phobias were known to his men, who followed him with a devotion and loyalty that went far beyond the usual respect shown for the president of a motor cycle club.

The structure of the club was much the same as that of other bike clubs. He appointed his office bearers. As new members joined, he would record them in the club book as nominees. "Noms" served their due time, at least three months, before they were allowed their first badge of office.

The strip of material with the word COMANCHERO was the first official sign of membership. After a minimum of three months and if the member was accepted, he was rewarded with a Horseshoe, a gold embroidered arc to be stitched on to the back of his riding leathers.

It was compulsory for members to attend the Saturday club meetings and to keep their Harley Davidson motor cycles—another prerequisite for membership—on the road at all times. At a cost of around $10000, and exorbitant insurance rates, the bike was the prospective member's first substantial sacrifice for his new lifestyle. Then there was the cost of keeping the machine roadworthy. Factory-built Japanese bikes were uniformly despised and labelled "Jap shit". The old British bikes such as Nortons and Triumphs were fit to be ridden, but Harleys—1966 Shovel Heads with multi-coloured tanks and elaborate insignias showing the individuality of the owner, or 1946 Harley Davidson Knuckleheads, a Harley trike, the 1966 Harley Davidson Hog-Slayer—they were the real bikes.

Jock carefully chose the men on whom he bestowed the honour of an office in the Comanchero club. He looked for loyalty and strength in his Sergeant-at-Arms, the man who sorted out disputes between club members or other clubs. The Vice President had to be brave and display a degree of leadership, but not so much as to challenge Jock's authority.

Each Comanchero had the club tattoo on his biceps, a sign of eternal devotion to the club.

On "runs", trips into the bush or along the New South Wales coastline, the Comancheros would show themselves to the outside world, their leader riding up front, the rest in formation according to rank behind. They sat low in the saddle. In the early days Skol, Foggy, Snow, Animal, Rat and Branco would ride up front, out to do battle with society, putting up the highway, brave in numbers.

Fights were part of the biker way of life. During the early 1970s on the central coast, the Knights were the Comanchero enemy. The Knights once awarded their "Dog of the Month" trophy to a club member who had sexual intercourse with a dog on heat.

Both groups could not survive in the same area. In May 1973 Jock put a plan into action. He heard the Knights were drinking at the Tall Timbers Hotel, a wooden double-storeyed establishment on the main road at Ourimbah, a hotel the Comancheros called their own.

Jock drew them out into open ground by sending an emissary to the pub to tell the Knights about a big keg party in one of the paddocks in the backwoods. The Knights took the bait and when they arrived Jock and his men pounced. Battered, the Knights retreated, but Jock would always bear his own battle scar in the form of a limp. A Knight on a Chopper, a cut-down Harley Davidson, dropped into low gear during the fight and ran straight over him. Jock retaliated later with guerilla tactics, hiding in the bushes along the coastal roads and firing at bikes ridden by Knights. At that point, the police intervened.

Jock Ross had by then built an aura around himself. Even the police with whom he had his earliest dealings spoke of him with respect. He was the sort of man police admired, a man with a fearsome reputation, someone to be reckoned with. He picked on a "pug" (a professional fighter) one police officer told another—at a pub on the coast. Jock came off the best.

But open feuding in the quiet country streets around the central coast could not continue. Sergeant Max Lamond from Newcastle police was appointed to have a meeting with Jock at a tiny shack at Phegans Bay, where he'd taken temporary refuge from doing battle with the Knights. Lamond explained to Jock why it would be better if the Comancheros cleared out of the central coast.

Shortly after, Jock and his band left the area and Max Lamond never saw any of them again.

In the mid-1970s Snodgrass Spencer, or Anthony Mark Spencer as he believed his real name to be, was in the navy. He joined at the age of seventeen after a life spent in and out of institutions for homeless children. His life in the navy was symbolised by the tattoo on his right upper arm—a florid ship sailing on the high seas. Underneath, a sailor looked out to sea through a spy glass. The tattoo on his left forearm displayed an anchor, a common tattoo for the men of the sea. When Spencer joined the bike world he had the words "No More" inscribed under the sailing ship severing his ocean-going connection forever.

Snoddy's flirtation with the seas was a short-lived adventure, a sort of test he set himself to try and overcome his deep fear of drowning. If he could sail on the very waters he feared, he believed he could conquer his phobia. As a boy familiar with institutions, it was not a difficult thing to pick one of the armed forces for a career. If anything it was expected.

His fear of drowning stemmed from an incident when he was living at an Anglican boys' home in western Sydney. He was having a bath in the concrete and green tiled room when some boys kicked open the swing door and stood over the steaming water. Snoddy remembered one face, leering, saying "Little runt, little runt . . ."

One held his head, one gripped his arms and the other lunged at his legs. Snoddy gasped for air, as the boy at his head—fat, greasy, with large white hands—spread his sausage-like fingers over his face. Bubbles rose to the surface and he tried to wriggle from their grasp, squirming like a flathead on the end of a line. But the boys stiffened their grip. He opened his mouth to breath but a finger was pushed down his throat and he was forced under again.

He felt his strength ebbing and he ceased struggling. The world became bathed in red. White spots exploded before his eyes. Then there were voices, faint in the distance. He tried to focus on what they were saying, tried to concentrate, but the darkness beckoned.

When he woke up he was in sick bay, tucked into a pair of crisp white sheets, his head on a starched pillow with the words "Government Property" stamped in red on the underslip. He lay looking at the ceiling trying to recall what brought him there.

Snodgrass was used to neglect. He endured the well-dressed couples who arrived at the home at the weekend to select their child to take home. Freckled, with hair an indeterminate colour—not a fiery red but the colour of dirty sand—he would return to his dormitory and exercise books, where he would record his feelings in a half-print littered with spelling mistakes. It was a habit he never gave up.

The navy was much the same experience, a constant trial to be borne. Snoddy was prone to burst into tears if something stirred him emotionally, yet he could be stoic under the worst of hardships, accepting his fate as a boy to be despised.

As he progressed through puberty, Snoddy retained something of a child's high-pitched voice. It failed to deepen to the mature tone of the other boys. When he joined the navy as a young man, his face, which still bore the scars of the acne he suffered in his early teens, would occasionally be wet with tears, over an act of kindness. Sometimes without apparent cause, he became maudlin and fell into fits of depression. In his navy days he found solace in booze and dope the sailors shared on their long trips at sea.

Snoddy was nineteen years old when he met Jock Ross, twelve years his senior. Ross had a place for Snoddy, who was stumbling around in the real world after the navy, unable to settle down into any job. Jock had a family to offer him too, rough and ready boys, the type that Snoddy was used to. For the first time in his life he was accepted. He had found something he liked doing, in an institution which did not spurn him.

Jock, with his matt of thick dark hair, his tales of his time as a soldier (he told Snoddy he fought in Vietnam) and above all, his camaraderie, became the father Snoddy never had. Jock's voice in particular held him in awe. It commanded when merely commenting. It was a voice never to be disobeyed, a melodious and at the same time harsh sound, which spoke in a vernacular he often did not understand. It cast a spell over Snodgrass that was to last for the next decade.

3

Tale of two clubs

The first Sydney clubhouse for the Comancheros became an integral part of Jock's power base. His domain was the western suburbs, and the clubhouse, although small and unattractive, was his castle. It was a fibro building wedged among the smoking chimneys of Granville, an industrialised suburb lying almost 28 kilometres to the west of Sydney. Granville's claim to world fame was a commuter train crash on 18 January, 1977, when 83 people died.

The houses in George Street, with their empty yards, corrugated fences and dogs chained to kennels, formed a dismal backdrop for the Comancheros, compared to Mangrove Mountain.

Engineering companies and milling specialists sprawled on either side of the four-lane F4 Freeway, which swilled cars westward from the city. Graffiti on cement walls facing the highway read: "Vote Socialist Workers for a Labor Government with Social Policies." It is doubtful Jock ever read this graffiti. Despite his working class background, the group of men he now surrounded himself with were not men who aspired to following a socialist leader.

In 1980, Skol, Jock's Vice-President and Branco, his Sergeant-at-Arms, had left the club with five other Comancheros. Thirteen men were left under Jock's leadership. Skol had also married Sandy, seeking permission from Jock to do this while still a Comanchero.

However, over the next three years membership grew to 40 full members and five prospects.

Jock's self-appointed title was the Supreme Commander. On his leathers, he fastened army badges to symbolise his strength. He told his men he was a former member of the crack squad to enhance his reputation for being ruthless. Most of his followers believed him, others dealt with idiosyncrasies by ignoring them.

Inside the clubhouse he erected a Nazi flag. With the appropriate solemnity, all new members swore allegiance to their Supreme Commander and to the Comanchero Motor Cycle Club. Military parades were set up when each man was awarded his colours and became a full member. A strict code of laws was pinned on the wall and his men were forced to obey them.

Jock ruled on the principle of divide and conquer, encouraging animosity and competitiveness between his club members, who as a result would squabble among themselves.

He set up a strike force—his army elite. They wore a special patch on the front of their leather cut-offs displaying a dagger with a lightning bolt running through it, the words "Strike Force", written across it. Sheepskin, JJ, Tiger, Leroy and Foghorn were the chosen members of this inner sanctum. They were his most loyal subjects, men to "take care of any trouble" if it developed with other clubs or organisations.

At club meetings the members would line up like soldiers on parade to be checked by their Supreme Commander. Jock began teaching battle tactics, manoeuvres he learnt in military textbooks.

The men lined up and awaited his orders. "First line!" he screamed like a sergeant at parade drill.

"First line ready, Sir!" his Sergeant-at-Arms shouted back.

"Second line!"

When the second line was ready Jock gave the order "It's a hit!" The men would remain in line formation and run towards the back fence, the first line wrestling with an imaginary enemy. The second line, which contained the taller men, was ready to beat the enemy with bats or gun butts and render them senseless.

Nominees were rostered on sentry duty, sometimes from the roof of the clubhouse.

When the boys went on a run to the bush for two days of partying or pig shooting, 40 men would pull out from the Granville clubhouse and ride out, two abreast in formation behind their leader, a formidable sight to the docile motorists on the F4 freeway.

Even at their isolated campsites, Jock ordered the nominees to guard the bikes through the night. There was always an enemy as far as Jock was concerned.

Shortly after coming to Sydney Jock had his head split open after taking on another club.

In June 1983, he took on the Loners, a small city based club. They had incurred Jock's wrath after a brawl at the Lone Star hotel in the city where one of their members threatened several Comancheros with a shotgun.

Jock attacked their clubhouse and three of their members were bashed.

He then employed one of his old tactics. He invited the Loners to the Melton Hotel at Auburn for a drink, supposedly to sort out their differences.

It was the same trap the Knights fell into in May 1973. Two carloads of Comancheros armed with baseball bats attacked the eight Loners using the tactics Jock had taught them during their backyard military drills. They surrendered their colours. When the police arrived, the Loners said they did not want any charges laid. They recognised they had been wiped out as a club.

Jock invited Bernard Podgorski, the Loners' Vice-President, to start up another club—the Bandileros—a sister club which would work as a nominee club for the Comancheros. It would be good training for the new men.

Podgorski had ridden up to a Comanchero campsite at Wiseman's Ferry near Mangrove Mountain, to meet Jock, the Supreme Commander of the Comancheros. They had partied all weekend and the former Loners had passed the test. Jock gave the orders they were to be given Bandilero colours.

The ceremony was formal. Jock stood in military splendour astride a large barbeque plate in the backyard of the Comanchero clubhouse. He ordered his Master Sergeant-at-arms, Sergeant-at-Arms Caesar, and Sheepskin Mick, the Strike Force sergeant, to bring up the ranks, and the backyard was transformed into a military parade ground.

The eight bewildered Bandileros stood in line in front of three ranks, each controlled by a sergeant. One by one, Jock handed them their Bandilero colours and in return each swore allegiance to the Comanchero club and its Supreme Commander.

"Fuck, who is this guy?" one of them asked when they finally left the party.

"If I'd wanted to march around the fuckin' backyard, I would have joined the fuckin' army!"

But march they did, and show subservience to their Supreme Commander.

Jock's favourite magazine was *Soldier of Fortune*. He was proud of his notoriety and conquests, keeping newspaper clippings of his skirmishes, including one which spoke of a rock band called Grand Junction who developed a deep fear of the Comancheros. One of their roadies was beaten up, and a patron in the Bateau Bay Hotel, where they played, was thrown through a plate glass window.

A banner was erected to dead Comancheros inside the clubhouse, giving them full battle honours.

"To Lost Brothers" it read.

An eagle sat on top of a yellow shrine, which had a gold cotton fringe on the bottom. On one side were the names of Lost Brothers, brothers who died in bike or road accidents. The list in 1982 stood at three. Bull Spackman, Johnboy, and Spoon.

Once a member joined the Comancheros, he was a member until death. All nominees signed a photocopied form pledging their bodies to their brothers. Families had little place in the funeral rights.

The form stated:

I, being a nominee of the Comanchero Motor Cycle Club, do hereby being of sound mind and under no mental or physical pressure, agree that in the event of my death, regardless of circumstance, the following will be abided by:
1. I am to be taken to the Palmdale Crematorium;
2. Transported by sidecar attached to a Harley Davidson Motorcycle;
3. The Cortege is to be made up of my fellow Comancheros, as laid down in Comanchero tradition;
4. I am then to be placed in the Comanchero garden along with my other brothers.

Johnboy Burston's funeral had been one such funeral. His 23-year-old body was taken by sidecar north from Sydney to the coastal town of Ourimbah to be buried in the Comanchero garden next to Bull Spackman. Channel Seven television cameras filmed the cortege as it moved up the highway, capturing footage of bikie women standing in rows on the back of a truck at the rear.

Johnboy had died in a car accident in Woodville Road, Granville, near the clubhouse. His body was taken from Sydney in the early hours, one Saturday in May 1983.

Jock defied the law, which prohibited transport of a dead body by sidecar, thereby attracting the publicity from the Gosford Star and the television station. His face, which flashed on the screen after footage from the cortege was as fierce as he could make it.

"The unions tell us when we can have power, when we can have petrol . . ." he snarled. His eyes, exaggerated by the thickness of his glasses, were slits of hatred. "The unions will not tell us when we can bury our dead, or how to bury our dead." He signalled the cortege to move off.

At the funeral site he ordered seven of his men into a line, all before the cameras. "Attention! Weapons up!" They stood in military formation by the grave site, double-barrelled rifles raised for the soldier's salute. As Jock reeled off the numbers each man fired a shot. When Foggy, sixth in line, fired his rifle, he jerked, stumbling under the force of the gunfire.

Bull Spackman's funeral had been 15 months earlier in November 1982.

Bull, a former RAAF ground worker in Western Australia, died when his tow truck collided with a cattle truck near Molong, outside Orange in the central west of New South Wales.

His brothers placed his body on a makeshift platform strapped to a bike's sidecar. Bull's own bike was carried on another makeshift platform.

That day, R.H. Creighton's chapel in Gosford was transformed. Part of the script from "Stone", an Australian bikie movie of the 1970s, the same film for which Peter Armstrong had directed the stunts, was read to the mourners. Then 30 bikes and more than twenty cars travelled north to Palmdale Crematorium.

Bull's wake at his property in Wyong lasted two days. His black Fairlane utility, much admired by many of the Comancheros, was passed on to club membership. Foghorn Lane took a particular liking to it and eventually bought it from the club. It was to become his trademark.

A plaque was erected to Bull Spackman on the side of the road, a five minute drive west out of Molong. The Comancheros rode out in formation and erected it on the site where Bull met his death, as further tribute to their dead comrade.

The Supreme Commander's first job after he moved to Sydney was as a bus driver. Later he worked as an owner truck driver and started a fencing contract business. He found himself a new bride—Vanessa Eaves—plump-faced, trim and girlish looking, with pale skin and wavy light brown hair. Jock perceived her correctly as having "a bit of fire", but also as willing to accept he was the boss.

Jock also found himself a new home. While the clubhouse in George Street, Granville, wallowed in its setting of industrial squalor, Jock's new red brick house, set back from the main road running through West Pennant Hills, was a badge of affluence, his entrée into the world of comfortable middle class suburbia.

It was in this city bushland setting Vanessa Ross took up residence as Jock's wife. She was already a single mother and shortly after she and Jock married, she gave birth to Jock's second daughter, Holly-Anne.

They had met like many biker couples—in a pub. Vanessa had been to a rock concert and had turned up with a girlfriend for a drink. The bikies were at the bar and one of them gave her girlfriend a Comanchero calling card with the Comanchero arc and "Comanchero Extraordinaire" printed opposite the club's GPO box number. Vanessa first saw Jock leaning against the bar. They argued playfully, Vanessa flirting with the man she had guessed was President.

After their initial meeting, she saw Jock working on a bridge close to her home in Parramatta. He had a casual job sandblasting. One of the other boys, who held up the stop and go sign, would make an exception for her when she was late for work, halting the cars coming the other way. She would exchange waves with Jock. Vanessa and her girlfriend, used to drive down to the bridge at weekends looking for the road crew. Then they received an invitation to the new home of "Mr Pres" as she and her girlfriend used to call him.

Jock and Vanessa would talk on the phone for hours. "I'm really not interested," Vanessa told Sue, but she was flattered by the attention. Her son Shayne was then six years old. Jock told her he had two children, Deirdre and Jordie.

He was a strong man, a leader, and she slipped easily into wedded life wth him. She was a good wife and proud of her new home. She took Holly-Anne home from hospital to the new address, a home she had not dreamed possible during her days of single parenthood. "The nurses were asking if she was coming home in a sidecar," she had giggled to Jock who had caused something of a stir at Westmead Hospital where Holly was born.

In Comanchero terms, women were disposable property. "Your lady" could be given to another brother if you thought she would make him happier than she made you. Comanchero men owned their women.

Vanessa accepted this. Just as she accepted Jock's bike club brothers and Phillip "Leroy" Jeschke's continued presence in her new home. Jock had saved Jeschke from prison, providing $4000 bail when Jeschke appeared in Brisbane magistrate's court on three counts of armed robbery in Queensland. In paying for Leroy's release, Jock had bought himself a loyal supporter.

Leroy was popular among the men, tall and thick set, with dark curly hair, cut short, his meaty biceps and almost all his upper torso covered in intricate blue tattoos.

Vanessa busied herself establishing her own foothold among the Comanchero women. She became their leader. If the women had a problem, they went to Vanessa. If the boys were in trouble, Vanessa summoned the women to her side with a phone call. They came without question.

In the middle of summer in 1983, three men from a local swimming pool company arrived at the Pennant Hills address to begin work on a swimming pool. Three days later Jock, dissatisfied with the standard of work, sacked the men on the spot.

The following weekend Jock decreed it was part of the nominees' duty to serve time working for their leader. He and Snow dug the hole and seven Comanchero prospects were ordered to lay concrete. Pig, a "nom" of just two months, was disillusioned, but, like the others, he didn't complain.

Labouring was the last thing he felt like doing in the scorching January heat, but orders were orders.

The photographs from this episode looked incongruous, almost ridiculous. Large bearded men, overdressed and uncomfortable in jeans and leather jackets, standing around the pool drinking beer. There was not a swimming costume in sight.

But Holly-Anne could now be seen from the lounge and dining room windows learning to swim, and the Rosses had joined their Pennant Hills neighbours in the swimming pool stakes.

Jock could never pinpoint the exact time he realised his leadership was under threat. But by the middle of 1983 he was well aware of a division in the club, led by his then Sergeant-at-Arms, Caesar Campbell.

Jock was jealous of Caesar, the oldest of the Campbell brothers, a man of his own age with thinning brown hair and a face like an ageing bulldog. He assumed authority for the whole Campbell clan—Shadow, Chopper, Bull, Snake and Whack Campbell—all brothers and all Comancheros.

The Campbells had a special bond between them, but it extended to their club brothers. If any of the men had problems, particularly the younger members, Shadow often became their confidante. And Chopper's "love to party" made him popular with everyone. To Jock, however, they were more the Scottish clan, the Campbells, joined by ties of blood.

Foggy warned his leader the Campbells had been complaining about the military drills. "They're not into it," he warned Jock. "Some of the noms have been whinging too."

The bubble burst at the last July club meeting in 1983, when Jock and Caesar had a stand-up row. Caesar stormed out of the clubhouse, followed by nine others, including Snoddy, one of Jock strongest devotees.

Jock's leadership was badly shaken.

The Campbells meant business. They disliked Granville and anyway, the building was due to be demolished. They did not like the drills in the backyard. They wanted style. Jock was forced to put the idea of a club move to the vote. The majority opted to move to bigger premises.

Jock thought over his tactics. He could not force the men to stay, he knew that. Let them find a better clubhouse. He could handle that. As a warrior and a soldier he knew his strength was waning. To oppose such a combined front would be suicidal.

The lot of finding a new clubhouse fell to Opey. "Somewhere close to the city, somewhere with lots of style" was his brief.

150 Louisa Road, Birchgrove, did more than fulfill his orders. There was

no problem securing the lease. He provided Jock's fencing contracting business as a reference and Vanessa Ross answered the telephone when the agent called.

The Comancheros packed up the military relics from Granville and made the move to Birchgrove.

But Jock was not happy there. He withdrew three weeks after the Comancheros laid claim to their new headquarters. "I've some decisions to make," he told the men.

It was early spring. Jock took Vanessa, Deirdre, Jordie and Holly-Anne and camped by a creek in the bush near his old favourite haunt, Mangrove Mountain.

Out in the open, he mulled things over. Whichever way he looked at it, he had to be prepared to test his reputation as a leader. He had three options: to stay with the club, split the club, or leave. He felt uneasy about staying at Birchgrove in a foreign environment, away from the western suburbs, in a place he had not chosen. But who would be prepared to leave with him? He realised many of the men were taken with the mansion on Louisa Road. For Jock, it was an intolerable situation, a real threat to his supreme power.

He returned to Sydney and at the next Thursday night meeting at Birchgrove he announced he was going back to Parramatta. He was splitting the club into two chapters—the city chapter and the western chapter. "Anyone who wants to join me can go out to the bar."

There was silence following Jock's announcement. Then Leroy said he would follow Jock. Jock had counselled him before the meeting. Eleven others followed including Foggy, Snow—his longest standing member, Sparrow, JJ, Noddy, Dog, Kraut and Sheepskin Mick—all Jock's stalwarts. But 30 men decided to remain at Birchgrove. It was the first time implicit loyalty to Jock was overruled.

Jock had nowhere to go in Parramatta. For the time being, the twelve men who followed him met at his house in Pennant Hills.

Relations between the two Comanchero chapters deteriorated rapidly. Jock no longer had overriding influence. The city chapter had their own meetings and they made their own decisions.

In September 1983 Jock and Vanessa got married. Holly was five months old. Snodgrass, who had been elected leader of the city chapter, called his men to another club meeting. "Jock and his chapter went to the Cross to celebrate his buck's night. While he was up there, he got into a blue with some of the bouncers and he got bashed. He wants our chapter to go up there and pay them back."

"We want nothing to do with it," Roach spoke up. It was a decisive move away from Jock's authority.

Jock had been "iron barred"—smashed over the head with an iron bar. He and his western chapter had tried to tackle some of the most formidable bouncers on the main street of Kings Cross—the Tongans and Maoris who guarded the doors of "Les Girls", the famous transvestite show.

Jock had spent his wedding day in severe pain. Vanessa had held him up during the ceremony.

Snoddy had not been invited to Jock's wedding, even though he had known Jock longer than any of the other Comancheros.

Vanessa was firm about which guests she wanted at her wedding and for once Jock had concurred.

"I can't have the boys running wild and stupid," Vanessa said to him. "You can't trust them when they're off their faces. Snoddy's always stoned and you know how stupid he gets. I'm not going to have them ruin my wedding."

One evening at a hotel in Rose Hill, a Comanchero from the western chapter told three of the city chapter members, Snake, Bull and Roach, that Tonka, one of Jock's stalwarts, was having a party.

They decided to attend. The reception from Jock had been cool. Bull noticed some new faces. "How come these blokes have got their strips and horseshoes so quick?" he asked Jock.

"None of your business," Jock snapped.

When Snake had asked him a similar question Jock had answered, "You're not welcome here and you'd better leave before you're bashed."

The following day Snoddy rang Jock. "Why were these Comancheros treated that way at Tonka's?"

"Well that's the way it is," Jock said.

Snoddy was surprised the insult did not hurt him as once it would have. Jock, in a new, weaker position, was aware for the first time that he was not strong enough to maintain his usual hold on Snoddy. Instead of cultivating him, he chose to treat him with disdain.

After Jock's withdrawal from Birchgrove, the Bandileros chose to join the city chapter of the Comancheros, handing their Bandilero colours to Snoddy. They mistrusted Jock and his plans to take over control of all bike clubs in Sydney.

In October 1983, both chapters took part in an informal run. It was to be the last time the Comancheros rode together as a club. Jock had told the city chapter to meet him at an appointed destination. He rode with the city chapter for an hour then Jock and his men went on their own way.

Shortly after the Comancheros split into two chapters, Snodgrass and

Charlie Sciberras left for the United States to buy Harley parts for the club. It was a mission that had long been planned.

When he and Charlie boarded the plane for Los Angeles, Snoddy had no idea what this trip to America would come to signify.

For Snoddy, the United States was the land of the sci-fi thrillers, hamburgers and the easy life.

The two men found their way to Albuquerque, a small southern city sandwiched between New Mexico, Arizona and Colorado, west of Las Vegas. It represented an awakening to Snodgrass, whose experience until then had been restricted to New South Wales and the southern part of Queensland.

The United States was big, bold and exciting. It overpowered him. And it welcomed him.

He met other brothers, in a bike shop, another family who welcomed him with open arms, just as Jock had done many years before. The Bandido Motor Cycle Club, also known as the Bandito Nation, had been formed in Houston, Texas in March 1966. They were named after the Frito Bandido, a Mexican food television commercial popular in the 1960s.

Ronnie Hodge, their National President, was appointed in May 1974, after their previous President was convicted of murdering two people suspected of having ripped off the Bandidos during a drug transaction. By the time Snodgrass and his Comanchero brother met Ronnie Hodge in Albuquerque, the Bandidos had 28 chapters spread throughout the country.

At his first handshake with the drawling overweight Ronnie— Stepmother to his men—Snoddy's allegiance was already switching. Hodge was a former marine, so the two men talked about the sea. Soon Snoddy found himself talking about his dissatisfaction with Jock's leadership. "I dunno, he seems to be mad on all this military stuff. You know, bikes are a thing of the past. He wants to train us like army men, like his soldiers . . ."

Hodge found he and Snodgrass had more than sea life in common. The Bandidos were already well established in the secret manufacturing, distribution and sale of amphetamines, according to the FBI, which had begun surveillance on the group. P2P, a necessary chemical for the manufacture of amphetamines, was legally available in Australia.

On the long flight back to Sydney, Snodgrass was already thinking of setting up the first Australian chapter of the Bandidos. He flipped through the Bandido by-laws, trade-marked on the right top corner with a fat Mexican bandit wearing a snarl and a sombrero, and holding a knife and a gun:

Each Chapter will consist of a President, Vice-President, Secretary, Treasurer, Sergeant-of-Arms, and a Road Captain.

Prospective new members must be sponsored by an old member and will have a six month probation period. If the probationary is voted out of the club, his sponsor will be advised of the decision.

Much the same as the Comancheros rules, Snoddy mused. Wives or girlfriends were allowed to be honorary members, and could wear jackets proclaiming them "Property of Bandidos", but they were not permitted to wear the fat Mexican.

Snoddy's thoughts switched momentarily to Lee—his lady with the husky voice, green eyes and long blonde hair. She told him earlier that day she was missing him, to hurry home. "Hon, I am, I love you, can't wait to have you babe, I'll be there soon," he'd said before the last of his American quarters ran through the public phone at LA airport, disconnecting the call.

Snoddy read on. "Any member found using the needle will lose his colours and everything that goes with them." That was Jock's policy too. He hated hard drugs.

Snodgrass saw an Australian courtesy card in his mind's eye. It would be the new club's calling card: "1%er" in the left hand corner in red print— signifying the new Bandidos were the 1 percent of the motorcycling public who were not law-abiding citizens. Then in bold print, BANDIDOS, separated by the fat Mexican bandit with the sharp knife and AUSTRALIA written underneath him.

"We are the people our parents warned us about" would be written underneath the bandit. Then more slang, like their American brothers: FTW, or Fuck The World, and on a line at the bottom: If You Can't Be Well Liked, Be Well Hated.

Snoddy was being adopted again, but this time by a much stronger group than that of Jock Ross. He had worldwide connections, and, who knows, he later told Lee, one day he could be putting around Texas and living out on a little farm with her and Joel, Lee's son, whom Snoddy adored.

What Snoddy didn't know as the 747 touched down at Mascot airport in Sydney was that the FBI was already at a high level of investigation into the US Bandidos. His visit had already been noted.

The FBI's interest in the Bandidos was triggered by three unsolved cases. These were the attempted assassination in San Antonio, Texas, of assistant US attorney James Kerr on 21 November, 1978; the murder of a Federal court judge also in San Antonio in May, 1979; and the murder of a police officer in Louisiana in July that year.

Inevitably, what Jock Ross most feared happened. Snoddy rang Jock after he returned from the United States and told him he no longer wanted to be a Comanchero. Jock responded by sending three emissaries to the clubhouse in Louisa Road. They were expected as they drove up to the small white gate.

Half a dozen of the former Comancheros stood around watching. Snodgrass opened the safe to get six sets of Comanchero colours, a few horseshoes and a couple of unused strips. Comanchero colours painstakingly removed from leather jackets and Comanchero wristbands were duly handed over. The ceremony, if it could be called that, was carried out in silence.

Snoddy waited until a week had passed before he visited Jock in his home at Pennant Hills. "I'm starting up a new club, the Bandidos," he told the man he once feared. "I've got a charter from the guys in America—Albuquerque," he felt relief as he spoke.

"I'll have all the colours that are outstanding to my club," was Jock's gruff reply.

Snoddy rode down Pennant Hills Road a free man on his shiny, new red 1982 Harley. He felt good inside.

Two weeks later the Comanchero emissaries arrived again. This time they left with eighteen sets of colours.

"Where's the rest?" Foghorn, speaking softly, understating the tension, asked Snoddy.

"There won't be any rest. I want to send the rest to the States to show them we've finished with the Comancheros."

Foghorn shrugged his shoulders. "We'll see about that."

Jock phoned Snoddy later that night. The discussion was terse. "All right, after the Christmas run in January," Snoddy said, "we'll burn the rest of the colours."

Snoddy began to consolidate the first Australian chapter of the Bandidos. His first decision as leader was to send his and Shadow's colours to the United States to show their new brothers that they had finished with their old club.

Caesar was appointed Sergeant-at-Arms, Shadow was Vice-President and the Comanchero rules under which the club had previously functioned, were revised. Meetings were changed to every second Wednesday night and were compulsory. Three missed meetings within a year, and colours were automatically suspended. Each meeting ended with a toast to the Bandido emblem and a toast to lost brothers.

Runs were planned for each long weekend and two runs a year were compulsory.

Club fees of $5 a fortnight rose to $6, to supplement the $300 weekly rent. Bar profits provided the remainder. The clubhouse opened seven days a week and all facilities were available to the members. Each full member had his own key.

No heroin is allowed in the club, instant dismissal and a bashing if anybody is caught using it or associating with anybody who uses heroin.

Everybody's woman is to be treated with respect, as you would want your own woman to be treated.

No woman is allowed in the clubhouse unless her old man is there. (This is to stop dissension among members so nobody roots anybody else's missus.)

If a fight occurs between members, the offending member is suspended for a period which is worked out by other members at the general meeting.

If a member is set upon or becomes involved in a fight with an outsider any member who does not back his brother will be bashed and thrown out of the club.

If a member wants to become involved with another member's missus or girlfriend, and the woman's old man agrees, the member and his brother in question may decide if they can go together.

If another member's old lady or girlfriend puts in on you, tell her old man and let him deal with her, otherwise severe punishment is dealt.

The new rules were noted in the minutes book at the first Bandido meeting. Caesar, as Sergeant-at-Arms, was to enforce them.

Bandido nominees, after being introduced to the club, were assigned to an old man, a full club member whose duty it was to acquaint the prospective member with the rules and his duties as far as the bar and cleaning up was concerned. The old man also had to make sure his prospect didn't discredit the club in any way.

After six months, if 50 percent of members voted in favour of a nominee and he had not broken any club rules, he received his top rocker, BANDIDOS, which he could sew across the top of his jacket. After twelve months, if 75 percent of members voted the nom was doing the right thing by the club, he received a bottom rocker, AUSTRALIA. Three months later, after fifteen months as a nominee, he would be voted upon at a full club meeting, where he must receive 100 percent vote in his favour before he was entitled to have the patch showing full colours, the Mexican bandit.

Bernie Podgorski, formerly President of the Bandileros, was allowed the privilege of only three months probation because he had been in other clubs beforehand. In that time he was expected to get to know his 30 new-found friends.

He soon became a full member and was raised to the office of club treasurer.

"Big Tony" Cain and Hookie, also formerly Loners and Bandileros, slipped happily into the Bandido lifestyle. The 23-year-old New Zealander lapped up the male companionship, the bike runs and the shooting trips. It reminded him of the hunting trips his father and his eight farming uncles used to take him on in lush New Zealand grazing country from as early as 12 years old.

Big Tony had experience with guns. At sixteen he bought his own firearms—a rifle for deer and pig shooting, and a shotgun for ducks and rabbits. At eighteen, he worked for a pet food company travelling around the countryside shooting sick, old and injured livestock, loading carcasses onto a truck and transporting them back to an abattoir.

Shadow, Bull, Whack and Pig shared Big Tony's love of pig shooting, and together they often took off for a couple of days on a shoot.

Early in January, two Comancheros arrived at the Bandido clubhouse with an inventory on the outstanding colours. They also came armed with a list of the Bandilero colours still in possession of the newly formed Bandidos. The night the outstanding colours were burned, as far as Jock was concerned, signalled the end of the city chapter of the Comanchero Motorcycle Club.

JJ (Robert Heeney), a Comanchero of three years, and his offsider had been sent to witness the symbolic ceremony.

JJ was solemn for his 27 years. He moved with the wariness of a caged animal, pausing deliberately before he spoke: "Jock sent me."

He followed two Bandidos down the front stairs and around to the back of the house. He studied the new identity displayed on their leathered backs, the paunchy Mexican dwarfed by his sombrero, carrying a sickle-like sword in his right hand and aiming a shotgun in his left.

JJ had been sent to exercise the right of his club to honour their discarded colours and ensure they were respectfully burned, even if the men who once wore them, men who had sworn an oath to the very patches that now crinkled and buckled in the heat of the drum, had betrayed them. He hung back slightly from the men who stood around, spilling into the garden. Twenty sets of colours had been collected and shown to him before being dropped into the fire. Snodgrass, Caesar and Kid Rotten stood closest to the ritual, their faces lit up by the flames. To Snodgrass, it was the end of an era, perhaps one of the few times in his life when he made a decision that was openly supported and popular. He felt strong, immensely strong, severing a symbiotic tie with the 43-year-old Scotsman, the tie established long before his rebirth as a Comanchero.

Half an hour later, the deed was done. Money owed to Comanchero club funds, $5000 in all, along with two bikes which belonged to a brother who had died some years earlier, were given back.

Then the two Comancheros, carrying the colours Jock specifically asked to be returned to him, rode off in silence, leaving the traitors behind to celebrate.

4

Leanne

Leanne Walters first ventured into the seedier side of life on the streets of Liverpool by climbing out of her bedroom window after dark. She was nine years old. Her initiation into the night world away from her fluffy toys and pastel-coloured bedroom walls was through her sister Cheryl, four years her senior.

Liverpool, where Leanne had grown up, was once an outer-lying town graced with old buildings and elegant farmhouses. By the mid-1980s it had become a sprawling city. Heavy industry had been introduced, followed by cheap housing. Before long, Liverpool had a reputation as a tough western suburban neighbourhood with a high crime rate and equally high unemployment among its youth.

By thirteen years of age, Leanne Walters knew every inch of Liverpool, but Scott Street, which ran from the shopping centre to the railway station, was her main hang out. At the far end, opposite the railway lines, stood two hotels where she and her best friend Melinda would meet.

The Railway Hotel advertised chilled kegs and a disco on Wednesday and Thursday nights. The Commercial, opposite, was a favourite with bikie groups in the area. The sign on the hotel wall above the driveway leading to the carpark read: "No Jap bikes allowed on these premises whatsoever by order of the licensee."

Just up from the hotels was the Las Vegas pinball parlour, another favourite place, squeezed between the Videobiz shop advertising Greek, Italian and Yugoslav movies, and the British and American Bike Spares shop. At the Las Vegas, Melinda and Leanne would order a $1.20 strawberry milkshake and spend 40 cents on a computer video game of Terra Cresta. Sometimes they would drift out to the back room for a game of pool, nodding to acquaintances as they went.

Vic Farr, the tattooist two doors down from the pinball parlour, was one of Leanne's adopted friends. Since she was ten years old, Leanne had admired the faded photos in his front window. She used to gaze longingly at the tattooed bodies.

Leanne was a likeable kid, Vic thought. He knew she could look after herself. She had no hesitation in telling his customers to "Get fucked" if they teased her. Vic, a small man, his parchment face wrinkled from years of smoking Winfields and drinking beer, grunted his approval. And he would laugh sometimes at her dirty jokes.

Leanne and Melinda used to stand and watch Vic work on the men who regularly came into the parlour. The men would take off their leather jackets and offer their muscular arms for Vic's surveillance.

Leanne would lean on the counter, her jeans tight around her thighs, her Triumph t-shirt proclaiming her interest in the bike world, which she professed to know. Mostly, these tough men would ignore her, tolerate her eager looks and that was it. Occasionally one would make a pass at her, and Leanne would respond with the over-enthusiasm of a child wanting admission into the mysterious world of adults.

She used to pester Vic for tattoos, and he would repeatedly answer she was too young. But her skin was already scarred with coloured ink. "Sweet" and "Sour" were tattooed on her left and right breasts, above her nipples, in blue ink, a job she had engineered from a more accommodating tattooist in Kings Cross. The nickname "Shorty", which she inherited from Cheryl, who, by 1983, had left the streets of Liverpool for more respected circles, was inscribed in large, ornate lettering coiled around her right ankle. Sometimes, when she wore a singlet, a tattooed bunny rabbit, his paws clutching his belly, would show on her lightly freckled arm. "A.C.A.C", proclaimed her sexual preference, not either way—just men.

The first signs of Leanne's illness appeared one Sunday night in September 1983, when she returned home from a day's trail-bike riding. "The bike fell on me leg," she complained to her mother. "It's sore, it hurts."

Pamela Walters was used to Leanne's ploys with imagined illnesses, although two weeks previously Leanne had been diagnosed as having severe tonsillitis. "Leanne should stay in bed for a few days and make sure she finishes the course of antibiotics," Dr Geoffrey Edelstein advised. He was concerned it could develop into glandular fever.

On Tuesday night Leanne still complained of pains in her legs and Pamela Walters took her daughter back to the surgery. The locum doctor suggested her condition was caused by bruising of the muscles in her leg from the trail bike.

Pamela was a big woman, with thick red-brown hair layered around a plump face, her skin loose with age. Her eyes were violet blue. She had been attractive once, but since her husband left her seven years before she had let herself go a bit. Her chin, always prone to drooping a little, had become double. Her arms showed the pale flecks of age spots and her left eye had developed a slight squint, which became more pronounced when she was angry, hurt or upset. When Rex Walters walked out on her, she found a job emptying sanitary bins at Liverpool's Grace Brothers department store.

"I've got pins and needles in me legs, Mum," Leanne called from her bed the morning after the doctor's visit.

"Have a warm bath then, that'll be the go," her mother replied. But the bath didn't help.

That evening, Mrs Walters prepared her daughter's dinner, mashing mince and potatoes like she used to do when Leanne was a baby, because she had difficulty swallowing with tonsillitis. After a few mouthfuls Leanne started to vomit. "I can't move my legs, Mum. I can't walk!" she screamed.

Mrs Walters carried her daughter to the car and drove to casualty at Liverpool Hospital where an intern admitted her immediately.

That was at 7pm. By 1.30am, after transferral to intensive care, a lumbar puncture and a variety of tests, Leanne's condition was diagnosed.

Mrs Walters was sitting in the waiting room staring blankly at a smiling Princess Diana on the cover of the Australian *Women's Weekly* when two doctors emerged. They had allowed her to see Leanne, in between tests. This had reassured her. She seemed normal.

"It's a condition known as Guillian Barre's syndrome, as far as we can tell," a bespectacled man explained to Mrs Walters. "It's a virus which attacks the nervous system. Has she had diphtheria recently? That is often how it develops."

Pamela Walters shook her head. "No, she had all the needles when she was a baby. She had tonsillitis, and I took her to the doctor. She's been taking antibiotics. I had to mix her food up, you know, mash it up, and then this happened," Mrs Walters wanted to show the doctors how much she had tried to help.

"It often starts from an infection," the doctor continued. "The virus would have attacked the antibiotics. It attacks the nervous system and paralyses you."

"So what does that mean?" Mrs Walters was frightened and confused.

"I very much doubt if she'll have the use of her legs or her hands for the next six months," the doctor said. Mrs Walters drove home alone.

The next day, Thursday, the hospital gave Leanne something to eat. She vomited it up and a thin trickle of brownish bile came through her nose. The virus had affected her breathing. The paralysis had crept into her lungs. It was a severe case, particularly for a girl so young, the doctors agreed. She was put on a ventilator, and a specialist was called.

"I don't want this tracheostomy thing, Mum," Leanne begged her mother, "I don't want a scar on my throat. Tell them not to do it." But, by this time, Leanne could barely talk.

When Rex Walters first came to see Leanne in the intensive care ward at Liverpool Hospital, the same hospital where she was born, she weighed less than six stone.

Rex was a burly man with the face of a club comedian. His brown hair was carefully restrained with bryllcream. On that first visit he stood looking at his child, now a young woman, whose body seemed to sink back into the bed and waste away into the mattress. He was filled with fear and remorse.

"She can't lift her arm, can't move her fingers," he sobbed later to Lorraine, the blonde-haired woman for whom he left Pamela Walters and his three children. "She can't talk, can't move her mouth even. She just laid there."

Rex first saw his daughter two days after she was admitted. Every visit, he would expect to be greeted with bad news so he would shy away from the men in white coats or suits who moved impersonally around the wards.

Leanne had a tube placed in her throat which was slit and bandaged directly under the centre of her chin. It was a tracheostomy, one nurse explained, to help her breathe.

Rex's mother managed to find a book with a description of this strange disease threatening her granddaughter's life:

> . . .an acute infectious neuronitis of unknown etiology characterised by widespread peripheral and cranial nerve involvement. Most common between the ages of 30 and 50. A mild upper respiratory infection or less often gastroenteritis usually precedes development of the syndrome. The initial neurological symptom is usually weakness of the lower extremities then after 24 to 72 hours the weakness extends to the upper extremities and facial muscles . . .the paralysis reaches its maximum within a few days of the onset . . .cranial nerve paralysis frequently occurs and may cause facial paresis and difficulty in swallowing, talking and mastication . . .
>
> About one fourth of patients require a mechanical respirator . . .if death occurs it most commonly results from respiratory failure or intercurrent infection . . .the mortality rate is between 15 and 60 percent . . .

The medical terms frightened her and her son. Rex Walters wondered whether Leanne would die. Gradually, they reassured him, Leanne would improve, but she was slow to recover. He could never see it as he stood there confused, wanting to help this girl, his child, wanting to see her respond, to be normal again. He would see her more often if she got better, he'd make sure of that.

"A wild one," he called her, "pretty wild". He could still see her standing in front of him—11 years old and caught shoplifting at one of the Liverpool stores.

"They shoved this bikini top down my front, Dad. It wasn't my fault. Joanne had the bottoms on and they didn't arrest her. "Only me, they pick on me. They took me for a ride . . ."

He believed her then. She'd become mixed up with the wrong crowd. But soon after that incident, she'd been expelled from school. He knew she had been wagging. Pamela Walters rang to tell him Leanne's latest ploy.

"She kicked a teacher," Pamela told him when he questioned her as to why she had been asked to leave Liverpool Girls' High School. Her school report to a social worker described Leanne as grossly insolent, violent, persistently disobedient, exhibiting profane and immoral conduct. Her interests were listed as vodka, bikes, bikies, drugs, sex—in no particular order of preference.

Leanne drifted into a girls' home and was put on a bond. By the time of her illness, she knew what it was like to stand before the magistrate at the nearby Children's Court at Minda. Two weeks before Christmas in 1980, aged eleven, Leanne was arrested and charged with stealing a watch. That first time, she was admonished and discharged, but two months later, she appeared before the court again, this time for stealing the $17.50 swimsuit her father found out about. The magistrate was more severe.

"You will be released on probation," he told her. "For 18 months you are to be of good behaviour. You are not permitted to shop without your mother."

In 1982, Leanne was committed to her first institution for stealing a packet of cigarettes valued at $1.13. Seven months later, she was arrested for stealing again and the female magistrate sentenced her to enter into a recognaisance, forfeiting $100 if she failed to behave for two years.

In May that year Leanne underwent psychiatric tests to see if she could be re-admitted to high school. She was found to be emotionally and socially immature with a very low self esteem.

During a school walkathon through the streets of Casula later that year, the stream of Liverpool High School students passed a brewery delivery truck parked outside a hotel.

Leanne climbed to the top of the pile of cartons, tore one open and ripped the ring pull off a can of beer.

"Leanne Walters, what do you think you're doing—get down from there immediately!" a teacher yelled as the crowd of children stood watching, spellbound by her antics.

"Whaddaya think I'm fuckin' doin'?" Leanne retorted. "I'm havin' a beer!"

But what of that spirit now, Rex thought as he stood, hands gripping the steel frame of the bed.

He was remembering the night in April 1976, not long after he packed up and left the family home in Alderton Street.

He had met Lorraine in September 1975, the week before his birthday. He had taken a busload of skiers down to the Snowy Mountains, New South Wales' skiing area.

At that time, Lorraine worked for Crown Corning Glassware, making glass bottles for medicines. She joined the bus with a group from work. She and Rex got talking over a port at the Royal Coachman Lodge at Smiggins Hole. "I might be back in two weeks," she said at the end of the night. "Coachway Tours have announced there are a few vacant seats for the next trip to the snow."

Rex enjoyed her company. He found it relatively easy to escape the family home and take her out to dinner.

In March 1976, six months after he met Lorraine, he left Pamela. When he returned on that memorable evening in April to pick up the rest of his belongings, Pamela's brothers were waiting for him. Standing in the driveway, they set upon him, punching him, giving him the biggest thrashing he had ever received.

Just before the bashing, Rex remembered seeing the faces of his three children at the raised venetian blinds in the loungeroom window.

Rex knew Leanne loved him, in a way that was different to his other two children. At seven years old, when her father left, Leanne, like many children brought up by their mothers, had a firm image of Rex as her saviour, the man who would take her away and make something of her life—she knew not what.

Another memory of her came to him—Leanne exhausted, after a twelve kilometre walk from Liverpool to Leppington. She was ten, and after fighting with her mother she had stormed out of the house. "I'm going to Dad's, you bitch. And I'm not coming back!"

Rex remembered his daughter standing hot and angry on the front step of his parents' house at Leppington, where he and Lorraine lived in a caravan in the back yard.

He had not been the perfect father, he realised that.

On October 21 Leanne was transferred to Royal Prince Alfred Hospital near the city for plasma pheresis, a new blood filtering treatment. There, Rex Walters saw more of his daughter. Calabros, the Italian Liverpool-based bus company where Rex worked, allowed him to operate in the city. He would drop off his coach in the afternoons and, still in his uniform, he would climb the stairs to the intensive care ward.

"She's feeling pins and needles in her toes," a nurse told him after her first week there. She had been lying motionless with weights attached to her feet and a machine with tentacles like an octopus standing next to her bed.

"That's a very good sign," the nurse told him.

Initially, recovery was slow. Leanne had wasted away to little over four stone. During one visit, she began crying, her face immobile, tears streaming down her cheeks. "Dad, I'm going to end up a vegetable," she whispered, her voice sounding as though it had returned from the grave.

"No you won't, love. It's just your body working its way back to normal," he had tried reasoning, speaking to her as he remembered speaking to her when she was not yet seven years old.

"But it's not normal, dad. It'll never be normal. I can't stand it. I can't stand it. Why did it happen, Dad, why?" And there had been more tears.

When Leanne was returned to Liverpool Hospital, she created a problem for the staff. She was too old for the children's ward, and although old for her years in some ways, she was not yet an adult.

In her medical files at Liverpool Hospital she was listed as "Sexually promiscuous", and someone had further noted, "Smokes, drinks, tattoos."

Leanne became the youngest patient on B wing, in the hospital's older section. The other beds were occupied by stroke patients, all well into their declining years.

Nurse Karen Brennan was lonely. Already thin, she was in danger of becoming anorexic. Her frame underneath her white uniform was tiny, her face pale and waif-like, accented by her short, coal-black, crimped hair.

She seemed continually anxious, and compensated by smoking too many cigarettes, flicking the ash nervously.

Karen was particularly moved by Leanne, this rebellious fourteen year-old paralysed by a disease many of the doctors had only previously seen in elderly patients.

One day she would be a child throwing a temper tantrum, the next an adult, coping stoically with intense pain and suffering. As a long-term patient she exerted her authority over the nursing staff demanding "not to be put in with any of them wogs" and gaining special treatment from nurses who gave in to her for a little peace and quiet.

At other times, she could remind the nursing staff of her maturity, handling her illness with resignation and manipulating the doctors and student doctors who clustered around her bed to study her disease. As the weeks passed Leanne became increasingly important to Karen. She was more than a patient, she was someone whose company Karen enjoyed and looked forward to seeing when she arrived at work each day.

Leanne's bed faced the door in the four-bed ward. As Karen approached, her shoes squeaking on the grey-flecked linoleum tiles of the long hospital corridor, she would see Leanne briefly before the girl became aware Karen was there.

She was usually sitting propped up on pillows, her hair, parted in the middle, hanging listlessly, framing her pale freckled face. Her eyebrows, faint light brown brush strokes from constant plucking, were usually drawn together in a look of boredom. Most week days, Leanne would be absorbed in an afternoon re-run of the American television show "Happy Days". Fonzie was her hero, she told Karen. He was a rebel who took no shit from anyone. He knew what life was all about.

Other days Leanne would lie listlessly staring at the ceiling, listening to Billy Idol's "Rebel", the Angels and ACDC—loud rock music the other patients complained about.

Leanne had no control over her bowels. She would lie waiting for Karen to clean her up, helpless, forced into this humiliation by the nature of the disease. Karen would bathe Leanne last in the mornings, knowing she liked to sleep in. That way, too, she got to spend more time with her. Even then, Leanne would scream when Karen put her in the wheelchair to take her to the showers. "It's sore. It hurts. I can't stand it!"

Karen introduced her own brand of discipline to her new charge, knowing the idea was foreign to her. She meted it out, using the authority the uniform gave her, taking away the television when Leanne misbehaved and putting it into another ward until she received an apology. But she softened sometimes, rewarding her with pocket money or sneaking her into the bathroom late at night so she could have a cigarette, knowing full well that if they got caught Karen's job would be on the line.

Leanne had few visitors. Her grandparents, who lived at nearby Leppington, would visit as often as they could, as would Pamela Walters. There was also Rex or the occasional friend, but most of the time Leanne was alone. Cheryl, the sister who introduced her to the darker world of adulthood, a fairer version of Leanne with prominent cheekbones and a plump face, visited with second-hand copies of *Easy-Rider* bike magazine.

The fluffy toys she loved as a child were brought in and propped around the head of her hospital bed—a pink panther, a bunny in electric pink and white and a baby hippo.

The week before Christmas on 19 December, 1983, Leanne stood on a tilt table for the first time during physiotherapy. After ten minutes, she became dizzy, her pupils constricted and she broke out in a cold sweat before blacking out and being wheeled back to her ward. The next day, however, she lasted twenty minutes with no side effects.

Her diet at that time consisted of egg flips, 80 millilitres per hour fed through a naso–gastric tube leading from her nose to her stomach. She would take three-quarters of an hour to eat a packet of crisps, but time aside, it was a victory for her.

On Christmas Day Nurse Brennan was rostered on morning shift. She brought in Leanne's gift, a size eight black t-shirt with the words "Harley Honey" and three pink roses screen-printed across the front, wrapped in red and white Santa paper.A few times on Christmas morning, Leanne got up in her wheelchair and pushed herself around the ward.

Pamela brought her daughter silver-plated dangling earrings and a digital watch. Leanne accepted the presents, but refused to go home for the rest of the day.

Nurse Brennan would help Leanne endure the stifling hot January heat by wheeling her to the hospital kiosk, where she would buy her favourite foods—Bubble O'Bill icecreams and salt and vinegar crisps. The nurse would manoeuvre the wheelchair down the ramp past the flowers for sale to the faded, pink-striped umbrellas, where visitors sat drinking cans of Fanta and Coca-Cola and smoking cigarettes. Then they would proceed to the row of overhanging camphor laurel trees, the wheelchair clicking rhythmically over the neatly paved, red brick footpath.

One day as they were walking near casualty, a man with tattoos and long hair came towards them. "Watch out for the fucking hole," Leanne said in a loud voice for the man's benefit, enjoying his brief glance. Karen reached forward putting on the brakes of the wheelchair and walked off towards casualty.

"Hey, where are you going Karen? Come back here. Come back . . ."

She ignored the girl's plea. She was furious. Nurse Brennan sat inside the waiting room and lit up a cigarette.

"I didn't mean it, Karen. I'm so sorry," Leanne was full of apologies when the nurse returned five minutes later. "Don't you ever do that to me again." Karen was partly mollified. "Don't you be rude to me."

On her rostered days off, Karen would take Leanne to the hairdressers, or home to her flat for the day.

She would carry Leanne to her cream utility truck and sit her in the front seat. Once they drove to Karen's hair salon in Mount Pritchard where Leanne had a wash, cut and blow dry. Her dark blonde hair was styled long at the back with front side fringes she would flick back away from her eyes, a popular style among Liverpool teenage girls. Twenty minutes in the hairdresser's chair was difficult for Leanne, but the compliments that followed at the hospital later compensated for her pain.

For Leanne's first visit to Karen's Glenfield flat, Karen hired a video. Leanne lay on the vinyl lounge, a blanket draped over her legs, as she marvelled at "Raiders of the Lost Ark", the movie she had asked Karen to hire. They feasted on Big Macs and French fries. Leanne savoured the break from hospital food. At Karen's she could also smoke to her heart's content.

As Leanne's strength returned, her bad temper intensified. She became restless and anxious to quit the hospital. One evening in late January, a nurse confiscated a packet of cigarettes hidden in her bedside drawer. "You stupid fucking bitch. Give 'em back, they're mine!" she screamed, halfway out of the bed, grabbing at the junior nurse. "I'll fucking smoke if I want to. It's not your fucking lungs, you cunt. I'm sick of youse lot telling me what to do. Fucking bitches. I hate it here! Where's Karen?"

Karen was not on duty, and as the nurse leaned over the bed and attempted to calm her down, Leanne punched her in the face. She let loose—kicking, yelling and spitting—two orderlies were called to assist the stunned nurse.

In the first week of February, Karen decided it was time Leanne started to walk again. After signing on at half past three, Nurse Brennan went straight to Leanne's bed. "You're going to walk today, Leanne."

"Bullshit, I can't and you know it."

"Well, there's no harm in trying," Karen said as she cupped her arms underneath the girl's wasted legs and swung them over the bed, sliding her onto the floor. Karen deftly held an arm around Leanne's bony shoulder and the two staggered together, stumbling towards the door, where, with one final wobble, Leanne's legs collapsed underneath her weight.

Karen saw the triumph, laced with exhaustion, in Leanne's eyes. "I knew you could do it, mate," Karen said.

By February 13, Leanne could stand, albeit shakily, with the aid of crutches. On February 18, she slipped unnoticed out of the ward. Her parents, security guards and the police were notified. She returned at 11.25pm, refused to say where she had been, and went straight into a deep, unbroken sleep for the rest of the night.

Two days later, when Pamela came to visit her daughter, Leanne said she was leaving, and at 3.45pm she signed herself out. Her mother carried her to the car.

By July, Leanne weighed more than seven stone. She had had her hair restyled, cut short around her face and left long at the back. Then she had her photograph taken at a booth that advertised four instant black and white photographs for $2. She pasted one of the photos on to a "sex licence card" someone had given her from a sex shop.

In the black and white photo she kept in her wallet, her lips were pursed, her eyes flirted with the hidden camera. "This is to certify that the person named and described on the reverse side has been licensed to enjoy sex anytime, anywhere, anyway."

Leanne was not sure what "erogenous zones" meant, so she left that space blank. Underneath "turn-ons" she wrote "spunks" in green biro. She thought about the word "restrictions", then wrote "none". Her "turn-offs" she listed as "nifty, orry, pigs." They were terms she often heard her friend Melinda use.

She had a stainless steel stud inserted in her left nostril as part of the new image. One day she bumped into her sister Cheryl in Macquarie Street.

"You look like a cheap little slut!" yelled Cheryl, wrenching the stud from her sister's nostril and throwing it down. "I thought after all this time, you would get your act together a bit—get yourself a job. Pull your socks up and stop being a bloody little desperate!"

Cheryl, now in her late teens, had a steady job at Oliveri's bus depot as a secretary, and a man to settle down with.

Not so Leanne. If the Las Vegas cafe was empty she and Melinda would wander down to the end of the street and hang around the Commercial Hotel in the concrete beer garden looking for anyone they knew. The Liverpool-based Rebels bikies used to drink there in the afternoons.

Leanne would look for Shifty's bike, the black Harley, painted red, the petrol tank encased in gold pin striping, flames leaping out from the shiny sides. The word "Rebels" proclaimed his club allegiance. If his machine wasn't parked up the long driveway at the side of the pub with the other Harley Davidsons, she would wait and listen for it.

"Give us two bob so I can play the pinnies, Shifty?" Leanne would nab him as soon as he pulled up on the footpath and swung his oversized frame over the side of his black motor cycle.

"What are you doin', Shorty?" Shifty would preface his reply the same way every time. "Here's a dollar. Now go and behave yourself—and keep out of the pub," he'd warn.

"Aw sure, aw yeah," Leanne would call back as she headed up the street to spend her money.

Shifty, the six foot seven inch tall office bearer of the Rebels Motor Cycle Club was the man who had adopted Cheryl Walters, Leanne's elder sister. Cheryl was one of the local kids who used to hang outside his fast food bar in Liverpool, filling in the empty afternoons between school and teatime.

Cheryl was a good kid, but Shifty decided it was time to step in and take control when the child began hanging around with "a pack of yobbos", as he termed them.

"OK m'dear," Shifty said one day when he bailed up Cheryl unexpectedly at the front of his shop. "It's time you got your arse into gear, so listen to me and listen very carefully," he said towering over the girl. "You are to go home, get showered, pack up your belongings, get out your clothes, and get back in here, quick."

"These are my rules and regulations. Do as you're told and you'll be laughing for the rest of your life. Muck up, and I'll flog ya!"

Cheryl started living with Shifty and his wife Eanie, during her early teens, moving in as Shifty's unofficially adopted daughter. Leanne had wanted to move into Shifty's house too, but Shifty already had four kids of his own and enough trouble with them. Instead, he looked on as Leanne grew up, giving her a firm talking to if he felt she deserved one.

Sometimes, he would give in to her whinging and take her for a ride around the block on the back of his Harley. Leanne would clasp on tight to his 20 stone frame, his muscled arms held high and showing "Live to ride, ride to live" and an elaborate design of bones and barbed wire on his upper biceps. The tattoo showing allegiance to the Rebels was also displayed prominently—a Confederate hat on a skull and the Rebels flag with "Outlaws Elite Rebels Motor Cycle Club, Australia". "Mary and "Jane" were tattooed on either hand.

Forty-one years old and into bikes since his teens, he was a formidable sight. His long grey and ginger moustache and his reddish brown hair hanging long over his shoulders and down his back were his trademark. He had dark, hooded eyes, solemn until he smiled. He was used to the stir his physical appearance caused.

His voice gravelly from too many cigarettes, he would talk about his many fights, imagined or otherwise. Like the time he was riding his bike home one night down the country lanes out the back of Liverpool, where he lived, and ran smack bang into a horse. "Had to slit the bloody thing's neck before it crushed me to death," he would tell his audience. "Ended up in

Liverpool hospital for weeks. So you know what I did when I got out? Bloody smashed that fuckin' arsehole's head in, I did, leavin' his fuckin' horse in the middle of the road like that. I told him to pay for the damage to my bike and he said it wasn't his fault—I showed him—drove him out of town.'

5

The war begins

The establishment of the new clubhouse for the western chapter of the depleted Comanchero motor cycle club, in February 1984, brought them to more prestigious premises than those at Granville. 65 Harris Street was a grand old residence, built in the same era as its counterpart in Louisa Road. It was at the western end of Parramatta River, the same river that flowed past Louisa Road. By road the two clubhouses were an hour apart.

Harris Park lacked the grand harbourside views that graced the grounds of the latter. Instead, the views from the upstairs windows were of Harris Street itself, and across to its neighbours—a row of close-packed two-storey cottages. The view out the back was a little better, particularly in spring, when the orange and lemon trees planted by the previous owner blossomed.

The house was reminiscent of a Hansel and Gretel gingerbread cottage, painted cream with neat blue wooden shutters. A Federation-style verandah ran around three sides of the house, supported by thick, round poles capped with a red tiled cover. Below this was a white wrought-iron railing.

Foghorn had found these new headquarters only two kilometres from the old headquarters at Granville. Using his John Carlton alias, he signed a lease, paid a bond of $600 and agreed on rent of $80 a week. He kept a rent book, collected dues from the members, and charged anyone who lived at the clubhouse a full-time share of the rent.

Inside, a narrow wooden staircase led from the hallway up to four bedrooms, each one occupied by an ever-fluctuating number of "permanent" residents. The furniture was scarce. In the living room, the centre-piece was an unusual oval plaque, mounted high on the wall and spotlighted by the glow of a chandelier.

Jock's machete, his most prized possession, was cradled on the wood, supported by three nails, its plaited leather strap dangling freely. Using white paint, Foghorn had written "Bandaid hair parter" on the blade. The new enemy, termed "Bandaids" by the Comancheros, had been declared.

The kitchen was decorated in 1960s Australiana style—pseudo-marble patterned laminex bench tops and imitation wood laminated cupboards. On one of the cupboards the new residents had hung a black and white cardboard skeleton, its joints held together with drawing pins.

The bar, adjoining the kitchen, was the club's inner sanctum. It was built in a room at the rear of the house that opened out to the large back garden. A list of bar prices on white card was taped above the wooden bartop. Cigarettes $1.80 a packet, wine 60c, chips 30c, cans of beer for $1. "No Credit" had been printed boldly at the bottom of the list.

A large pineboard notice board dominated the back wall. Aside from the club rules tacked to the centre, the board was covered with pictures, notes, comics and snippets of club business. The biker's guide to sex was written up as a banana bread recipe and stuck to the board by a drawing pin:

Ingredients:
  two loving eyes
  two loving arms
  two well shaped legs
  two firm milk containers
  one fur mixing bowl
  one large banana
  two large nuts
Method: Look into loving eyes, fold into loving arms, spread well shaped legs, squeeze and massage milk containers very gently until fur lined mixing bowl is well greased. Check frequently with little finger. Add banana, work in and out until well creamed. Cover with nuts and sigh with relief. Bread is well done when banana comes soft. Be sure to wash mixing utensils and don't lick the bowl.
Note: if bread starts to rise, leave town immediately.

A photo board with snapshots of men and their bikes stood against one wall. One of the photographs depicted an aging bikie with thinning long straight hair, muscular upper arms and a face pouched with approaching middle-age.

Underneath someone had written: "Caesar—dickhead, asshole, fuckwit, kill the turkey, gums, son of Jaws. Snodgrass loves Caesar up the ass". An arrow with the word "kill" pointed to the photograph of Caesar Campbell. Then as an afterthought: "Bandaids Honda Clubhouse up the ass". This was the worst sort of insult the Comancheros could levy at their enemy—Hondas were considered despicable motor bikes, not worthy of contemplation.

Another texta colour message stated: "Nail Caesar t-shirts $7.50. All orders for t-shirts must be in by 7/9/84. leave orders with Morts or Sparra.

T-shirts will be $7.50 each (order two). Actual size of picture will be slightly smaller".

The move back to the western suburbs agreed with Jock. He was familiar with the area, his power was unthreatened. When the Comancheros established themselves at the new Harris Park address, Jock had fourteen men. By May 1984, just three months later, his club had tripled in size.

On May 18, Snoddy visited a gunsmith in Merrylands. "That second-hand lever-action rifle that's on the display rack . . .?" the scruffy looking man with long hair addressed the shop assistant.

"Well, it's second-hand—that means there's no warranty on it," the shop assistant answered one of his questions. "It'll cost you $200."

"No warranty . . ." Snodgrass sounded doubtful.

"But, I've got a Rossi Magnum—it's $285 or thereabouts. It's got a warranty of twelve months."

"Yeah, that sounds okay. Can I have a look?" The shop assistant produced the gun. "I was also interested in a shotgun—a cheap one . . .," Snodgrass added after inspecting the Magnum. "Oh, and some ammunition for both guns," he said, having settled on a second-hand Smith and Wesson 12-gauge pump action five shot.

Snodgrass left and then returned shortly afterwards with his shooter's licence. He paid for the guns and ammunition, picked them up and left the store. The salesman was surprised at his reappearance. He had looked like so many of the customers who made enquiries but never returned—window shoppers they were, most of them, he thought.

Until the Comancheros moved to Harris Park, the antagonism between the two clubs amounted to little more than verbal sniping. Then, on Saturday 6 June 1984, the first physical confrontation took place. It was at a swap meet, where spare bike parts are sold, at the Rebels' sprawling Kemps Creek clubhouse, west of Liverpool. Mark "Junior" Shorthall, the baby-faced Bandido nominee who had just turned 21, had ridden to the swap meet with his girlfriend, Kathy, and Val, another nominee.

Junior had won the admiration of his brothers by patiently sketching caricatures of the boys on runs in surreal landscapes, his cartoon figures with club names smoking out of Acme bong kits. In the background of one cartoon he had devised and drawn 'mull-a-matic' machines for mulling up the dope. But he was also treated as the baby of the club. He preferred to wear a helmet and some of the boys jived him because he reportedly slept on a Humphrey Bear pillow case.

Junior had lived most of his life with his parents in the quiet suburb of

Guildford. He had joined the Comancheros in 1981; at age nineteen he was one of the youngest members. One of his enjoyments was looking after children. He seemed to have a way with them, the knack of becoming one of them.

Junior, Kathy and Val stayed longer at the swap meet than the rest of the club. Eventually a fight started between Foghorn and Junior about having some rings made. Another Comanchero, Snow, joined in and Junior decided to leave, at which point Foghorn called Kathy a slut. "What d'yer mean she's a slut?" Junior was quick to defend her.

Foghorn smashed a Harley crank case cover against Junior's helmet.

"We don't want any trouble here," said a member of the Rebels' club. It was an unwritten law that fights were not permitted at swap meets.

Junior mounted his bike and left. He heard the bikes approach him from behind when he was about 300 metres down the road. Foghorn, Snow and Pee Wee forced him to pull off the road.

Junior got off his bike, his mouth dry. Snow and Foghorn laid into him with their fists, then Foghorn pulled out a knife and cut Junior's helmet strap. While Snow held Junior down, Foghorn attacked him with a fork leg and broke his jaw. ·

They left him bloodied and battered on the side of the road. Kathy stood by his fallen bike, sobbing.

Big Tony visited Junior in Liverpool hospital the following day. Junior's jaw had been wired and there were dark stitches around his right eye and across his chin. "I just want it forgotten," Junior mumbled through his puffed up mouth. "I don't want any more trouble for the club from those bastards."

When word of Junior's bashing spread around the Bandido camp, the rift between the two clubs deepened considerably. It called for action on the Bandidos' part. Jock decreed that it was Foggy's blue and shrugged when he heard the tale.

Junior was hospitalised for two weeks.

July 1984 was a month Raymond Kucler, or Sunshine as he was now known, would always remember. The 27-year-old Yugoslav, an estranged father of two, had already received his strip, a heavy black strip of material with "Comancheros" written in gold, and now was to receive his full colours.

It was Sunshine's official sign of acceptance into Jock's exclusive brotherhood which usually required a minimum of nine months before a man became a full member. This was divided into a minimum of three months with a strip, a further three months with the yellow embroidered horseshoe. To complete the Comanchero colours, providing the probationary member made the grade, he received a patch, a grey and white condor with a yellow crest. It sat inside the horseshoe.

It was a cold Saturday night in July in the backyard of the Harris Park clubhouse. Sunshine stood with his hands on his hips, his leather cut-offs displaying his newly acquired status. He was a new breed of Comanchero, a ruthless man who was prepared to be loyal.

In front of him Jock, his leader, in black leather jacket with full colours, led Sunshine in the Comanchero oath, his Scottish accent rolling over the "rs" while his voice remained deep and harsh, fitting the solemn occasion. Curling his upper lip, he delivered the words with a snarl: "Membership of the Comanchero brotherhood requires you to swear an oath. Repeat after me: I swear allegiance to the Supreme Commander of the Comancheros—Jock Ross."

Jock's steel-framed glasses glinted in the light from a flash bulb as one of the Comancheros recorded the event with an instamatic camera. Other full members, whose ranks Sunshine would soon join, stood watching the ceremony with undivided attention.

Jock read out the Comanchero rules, pausing between each one to gain dramatic effect. But there had been some changes. Jock was replenishing his forces by relaxing his rules. No longer did a man have to wait a minimum of nine months before he became a full member. Now he rushed through memberships, shortening the normally stringent three month nominee and probationary periods. He needed to build up his strength and quickly. These days, men received their patches in a matter of months.

Jock continued to force his men to contribute to a war fund. It was rumoured he spent the money on himself. At parties or social occasions, he clung to the image of his old self, singing dirty ditties as the whisky warmed him in true army-style. To Jock, a fighting man was worth his salt and now he needed fighters more than ever before. Sunshine had the makings of such a man, he was tough.

Sunshine had had his first brush with the law in 1975 at the age of nineteen. He was fined $250 for receiving a stolen motor cycle. Later that year he was charged with possessing Indian hemp and resisting arrest. Three years after that he bashed a police officer and received a two year good behaviour bond.

When Sunshine swore his oath that night, he became an important addition to the new identity of Jock's army, the new order of Comancheros.

But Jock had introduced a new rule to protect himself—any member found guilty of breeding dissension in the club, and that meant running down the president or club policies, would be thrown out. "Bad shit rumours" as Jock called any threat to his leadership were out.

When the ceremony was over, the boys trooped through the kitchen to the bar to celebrate. Tonka and Morts opened the bar. Sunshine had been given $50 credit to buy drinks for everyone, as was normal procedure for all fledgling Comancheros.

Jock was in a benevolent mood. He wanted to celebrate. He moved among the crowd of men, the beer and bourbon heightening his sense of pride.

Walking up behind Kraut (Kevork Tomasian), he placed his hand firmly on his right shoulder. Kraut swung around and faced him.

"Do you know who I am then, Kraut?" Jock said, his eyes slightly glazed, his thick Scottish voice slurred by alcohol.

Kraut's plump face spread into a smile. "The Supreme Commander," came his reply.

Both men laughed and Kraut hugged his mentor. "Give me another beer, you old bastard!" Jock shouted to Morts.

About ten o'clock on the night of July 26, the Bandidos Lout and Lard, on their way home from a meeting at the Louisa Road clubhouse, called into the Royal Oak Hotel in Church Street, Parramatta.

The Royal Oak had been claimed as a Bandido Hotel. It was an old fashioned pub with murals of battleships, ocean liners and old sailing ships decorating the walls of the saloon bar. Space invader and pinball machines were incongruous in this setting, with its cream painted brick walls and dark timber doorways. A video screen had been placed in the public bar. Outside, there was a concrete beer garden with Tooheys Draught umbrellas and brown slatted tables and benches. Bob Woods, the publican had not concerned himself with the decor; he had enough local customers not to warrant the expense.

Lard's brother, Peter Melville, worked there as a barman three nights a week, and Lard coached the Royal Oak football team which played in the western districts competition. Roo was one of the team's star players. Bob Woods had known Lard's family for years and was fond of Lard and his biker mates. He would unlock the back gate so the Bandidos could park their Harleys off the street because parking on Church Street, a main road through the Parramatta central business district, was limited.

Woods knew about the trouble with the Comancheros and he told the boys he didn't want both clubs drinking in the hotel at the same time. So when Lout and Lard pulled up that night, they bristled at seeing a Comanchero called Noddy, in his colours and with three other Comanchero noms, heading into the public bar. "This is a Bandits' pub, Noddy, you and your friends aren't welcome here," Lard said.

Noddy turned and left peacefully enough; there was no trouble. But the following night, when Lard was sitting near the bar, Jock, Leroy and a Comanchero nominee he didn't recognise, burst through the public bar door.

Jock went straight up to the bar. "Three beers, mate!" he yelled at the young barman, Graham Marshall.

"Sorry, mate, but the boss says no drinks."

"Whaddya mean, no fuckin' drinks!" Jock slammed his fist down and the barman jumped. "You serve those fuckin' arseholes over there," he pointed at Lard. "I want to know why my men were refused service last night. Who says this is a fuckin' Bandaids' pub? How many pubs do they want?"

"I'm sorry mate, but I have my orders, the boss . . ." Graham never finished his sentence. Leroy lurched forward suddenly and took a swing at him, missing by inches as the smaller man ducked under the wooden bartop.

Jock picked up a stool and threw it across the bar. It flew over Marshall's head, smashing several glasses. "No-one tells me where my men can drink!"

Jock glared across at Lard with hatred in his eyes. "Fuckin' Bandaid . . ." he muttered as he turned and left, Leroy and the young nominee following close behind.

Three days later, after lunch, the blonde barmaid looked up as two Comancheros, Sparrow and Morts, approached. Lard was sitting alone at the end of the bar, sipping a middie of light.

Sparrow and Morts leaned over the bar. They were refused service. "Well, I want to hear it from the publican then," Sparrow insisted in a loud voice.

The barmaid rang upstairs and Woods appeared a few minutes later. "Listen, mate, I don't care what you have to say, you're not welcome here, I'm not going to serve you and it would be better if you left just the way you came in . . ."

Woods turned and walked through the doorway into the back bar. Sparrow followed him. As Lard stood up he heard the whack. He raced through and found Sparrow standing over Woods who was sprawled face down on the floor.

"You fuckin' idiot!" Lard grabbed Sparrow and tried to wrench him from Woods before he landed a second blow. Morts came up from behind, a bar stool held threateningly over Lard's head, when the barman came from nowhere and knocked him off balance. Morts dropped the stool and the barman restrained him.

"Listen, Sparrow, just fuck off out of here—now!" Lard shouted.

Sparrow pulled himself free, and Lard attended to Bob, who was semi-conscious on the floor. "We'll be back," Sparrow grunted as he and Morts left the hotel.

The following day, Bob Woods reported his assault to the Parramatta police and said he would like to press charges against Ivan John "Sparrow" Romcek.

He arranged for the local police to patrol his hotel regularly.

Snoddy sent his message to Jock on the last day of July. It was delivered by Glen Eaves, a clean cut soldier, a tank gunner with the Australian Army, who recently had become a full member of the Comancheros.

Eaves was Vanessa Ross's kid brother. He was nineteen when he met Jock, the same year he joined the army from the Army Reserve. Jock found in his young brother-in-law the same doting loyalty Snoddy had once shown him. Eaves admired Jock, a powerful, strong man who liked him and protected him, unlike his own father who had started mistreating the boy when he was only a few years old.

Glen Eaves's father was an alcoholic, his mother a sickly devout Catholic woman unable to control her husband's frequent rages. In comparison, Jock seemed strong but compassionate. Jock became Eaves' protector.

Eaves was near his Westmead home at 6pm when he saw Snoddy astride his bike, waiting for him in a side street in the fading light. As the rider approached, Snoddy pulled up beside him and signalled him to stop.

"Tell that fuckin' crazy President of yours that he and his club had better stay out of Parramatta." Snoddy was still smouldering from the battering Junior received, but he had respected Junior's request not to retaliate. The incident at the Royal Oak had given him the chance he wanted. "If he doesn't stay out, you can tell him from me that he's a dead man."

Billy "Davo" Littlewood, the smiling ginger-haired Bandido with wrap-around sunglasses, who dressed up as Santa at Christmas parties, rode down to the Comanchero clubhouse at Harris Park shortly after the trouble at the Royal Oak, an unofficial emissary in search of peace. Leroy and Noddy met him on the front verandah.

Davo's reception was cold. He was hurt because he considered Leroy a friend. Why, only a couple of months ago, he'd given Leroy a front end for his Sportster, and Charlie had helped put it on for him. "Look, mate, I don't want no hassles, I just want to know why you guys are coming and hassling our men at the Oak? I mean, I don't understand it, you guys have got your own pub at Auburn."

"Hey, I don't want no trouble either, Davo," Leroy replied. "If you want the truth, it's Jock and Sparra. I'm just following orders. He's just stirrin' up trouble."

"Well, it's not cool, man. Come on now, we're all bros, you know that. I mean what the fuck does he think he's doin'?"

Leroy said he would talk to Jock and try and sort things out.

"Okay, thanks, mate." The two men shook hands.

"How's the Sportster going?" asked Davo.

"Purrin' like a happy pussy!" Leroy smiled.

"Good to hear. Be seeing youse!" And with that, Davo was gone.

"Bye darls—won't be late."

Jock heard Holly crying as he slammed the front door and walked around to the side of the house, where his blue 81 Electraglide Harley stood at the bottom of the steep concrete driveway. It was a cold night in winter, Saturday August 4, and just dark. Jock put on his gloves and helmet and kick-started the bike.

He knew he was nearly out of petrol. He glanced at his watch, it was just on 7pm. He would be at the Melton Hotel at Auburn in 15 minutes. All the boys should be there.

Jock switched on the headlight, rode up the drive and turned into the traffic on Pennant Hills road. He putted along for a kilometre before he turned into his regular Esso Service station on the corner of Mahers Road.

Nodding to the middle-aged man who sat behind the cash register in the heated service station, Jock filled his petrol tank and then paid for the fuel, exchanging pleasantries about the coldness of the night. Continuing along his usual Saturday night route, he turned left into Marsden Road, heading towards Ermington.

He had almost reached the Kissing Point Road junction when he noticed the white Holden one-tonner pull in close to his right-hand side. Jock shifted his right leg which sat firmly on the rubber mounted running board, skirting both sides of the bike. He glanced across, but could not see the driver.

Suddenly the van lurched forward and skidded across to the bike. Jock swerved up and out, and under full throttle pulled ahead of the van. His bike, being a "full dresser", was sluggish. He leant over, his body almost horizontal on the bike. He felt its heavy frame flex under the pressure.

Jock's powerful arms strained to hold the machine which was already bent 45 degrees to the road. In his rear view mirror he saw the lights of the Holden bearing down on him. It dropped a gear and rammed into the back of the bike, smashing the tail light and cracking the pannier.

The bike bucked and skidded. Jock began to panic. He knew if he lost it and the bike fell, his right leg would be ripped to shreds.

He struggled to right the machine. Sparks flew as the right running board hit the road and bounced back up. He lost control, kicking the bike as he fell in an effort to fall clear of it. The machine careered along the roadway for 70 metres before it somersaulted and finally stopped.

Jock had been travelling at about 70 kilometres when the bike fell. The momentum forced him upward before he landed heavily on a patch of grass in the middle of a paved concrete driveway.

He rolled over and watched the van stop. He strained and saw two men alighting. He tried to stand, and as soon as he moved, they jumped back into the van and sped off out of sight. He felt pain and the warmth of his own blood as it began to seep through his clothes, adhering their tattered remains to his broken skin. The right leg of his riding leathers was shredded and bloodsoaked.

Vanessa was ironing a dress when the telephone rang fifteen minutes after her husband had left the house.

"Vanessa, get down here, quick."

"What's happened? Are you all right?" she heard the shakiness in his voice, which took on an even thicker Scottish accent under stress.

"Those cunts have done it this time. They've run me off the road."

A trail of broken bike debris along Marsden Road led Vanessa to her husband.

"I had a full petrol tank. The fucking thing could have exploded." He was standing beside his battered bike when she arrived. She walked back up the road, salvaging what broken parts she could. She collected the arm of the rear view mirror, a battered side pannier and crash bar, and bits of chrome trim from the windscreen, panniers and running boards.

"Those fucking Bandaid arseholes. I could have fucking died," he kept saying. "They meant to kill me."

While Jock rang the police, Vanessa rang the Melton where Foggy and the others awaited their leader's arrival. Foggy came to the phone.

"You've got to to put a stop to this, Robbie," she said. "It's just got to end," Vanessa spoke quickly, she was shaken. She could not remember seeing her husband so upset. "The petrol tank was full you know, the bike could have exploded. He's rung the cops, they're with him now. They're gonna take the bike away. Jock says there's easy five thousand bucks worth of damage. Christ, he's so angry, Robbie, you have to do something to stop it, it's just crazy."

Jock meanwhile was remembering Snoddy's threat to Eaves, less than a week previously.

Kevork Tomasian—George to his work mates, Kraut to his club mates—felt increasingly uneasy about the way things were evolving. He turned things over in his mind as he sat at his desk in the Crown of Lands office in Bridge Street, Circular Quay. He had worked there as a clerk since 1969.

Kraut was a solidly built Romanian, 38 years old, with strong Slavic features and a full wiry beard. He was an only child, a gifted violinist and pianist, who at twelve years old won a place at the Bucharest conservatorium.

With no understanding of the English langauge, Kraut and his parents arrived in Australia in 1960 and lived in a Sydney migrant centre. Kraut's father worked in a factory and his mother was employed as a domestic servant.

When the Tomasians moved to a small one-bedroom flat in Newtown, Kevork enrolled at Enmore High School, but the language barrier foiled his studies, and his nationality caused social problems.

Assault, robbery and malicious wounding charges saw him committed to Mount Penang detention centre at Parramatta in 1963. From there he studied by correspondence and when released two years later he enrolled at Sydney Technical college and obtained his leaving certificate.

He began playing piano in a nightclub and in 1968 went back to Tech full time. He left this time with his Higher School Certificate and matriculation to the University of New South Wales.

A clerical job offer at the Crown Lands Office lured him from his university studies. He took the job and continued studying public and personnel administration. They were part-time courses, studied on those nights he was not playing piano.

In 1975 Kevork joined the Army Reserve and remained in it until he resigned in 1981. Also in 1975, he married. He and his wife Jenny bought their first home at Oatley, a southern Sydney suburb in 1983.

Kevork was a recent recruit to the Comancheros. When the news of Jock's accident reached him, he decided to act on the feeling which had been gnawing at his stomach.

He told his boss, Kevin Tate, he had something he wanted to talk about. Tate liked "George", whom he had found keen and reliable during the three years he had worked for him. "What can I do for you?"

Kevork sat on the proffered seat and stared ahead of the large teak desk before he answered. "What would be the position with me if I got into serious trouble?" he said, shifting uneasily in the leather chair.

"What are you talking about, George?"

"If I got into serious trouble involving imprisonment, what would be the position in regard to my job?" he continued.

"Why?"

"I just want to know what the position would be."

Tate was puzzled by this behaviour. He tried to hazard a guess at the reasons why. He had heard the rumours spread by office gossips about George's affiliation with the Comanchero bike club. For Kevork made no secret of the fact he was a Comanchero. He would often speak about his bike, where he would go for weekend runs and the group's general activities, while he was in the large open tea room at morning tea break.

Tate pulled out a copy of the Public Service Board regulations and studied them.

"If you commit an offence that involves imprisonment for longer than twelve months, it is a matter for the Public Service Board. If it's less than twelve months, it's a matter for the Department," Tate read from the large book. "I can tell you no more than is in the regulations, the rest would depend on other circumstances."

Tate thought little more of his conversation, until the events of more than a month later. Then, he wished he had probed a little more.

On that Wednesday just before the two men broke for lunch, the conversation turned to a more pleasant subject—Bach's violin concertos—an interest they both shared.

But as Kraut had rightly suspected, the events of recent weeks did not stop there. Three days after the discussion in his boss's office, the Bandidos and the Comancheros clashed violently once again.

This time it was at the Bull and Bush Hotel, a sprawling building in mock-Tudor style on the corner of Windsor Road at Baulkham Hills. Bands played there on Thursday nights, when the Bandidos would arrive around 10.30pm. They drank until midnight, often with their old ladies in tow.

Nicholas Kennedy, the 31-year-old publican, had been at the hotel since April. It was a new challenge for him, a brown-haired blue-eyed surfer, who had previously managed oceanside hotels in Sydney and on the New South Wales central coast.

Kennedy earned Snoddy's respect, and the Bandidos had agreed not to wear their colours or fight in the hotel. While he was inside the hotel, Snoddy would also surrender into Kennedy's care the long-bladed knife he wore in a sheath.

It was a tough, suburban pub, reputedly then the biggest drug supermarket in the western suburbs. Kennedy and his staff would often find needles and other remains of illegal drugs discarded in the large carpark and under the hotel building every Friday morning. Thursday nights were busiest, particularly since Kennedy had organised weekly live music.

He knew the Bandidos and Comancheros were feuding. Snoddy had assured him there would be no trouble at the hotel, but just the same, he could never relax on a Thursday night.

On August 9, as he looked out of the window towards the sound of Harleys pulling into the carpark, Kennedy could smell trouble. A marked police car followed the Bandidos into the carpark.

Three Comancheros were drinking in the Tudor bar. Dog (Tony) McCoy was just getting up for another round of beers when he heard approaching bikes. Wearing his Comanchero colours, Dog glanced across to his mates, Pee Wee and Noddy, both in black t-shirts and jeans, and sat down again.

Kennedy who had been eating his dinner with his wife and two daughters, upstairs in the publican's living quarters, left his meal and ran down to the Tudor Room. As he lifted up the bar gate at the end of the room he saw six Bandidos walk through the front door. He recognised Snoddy straight away. They all strode to the table where the three Comancheros sat.

"Hey, what's going to happen in here, mate?" Kennedy approached Chopper, who was standing nearest the bar.

Chopper, dressed in his full Bandido colours, turned and said, "No problems."

Kennedy was not convinced. The six men surrounded the small wooden beer table like pugs around their quarry.

Snoddy spoke first. "What exactly are youse playing at? You bash Junior and start fucking hassling his ole' lady." Snoddy's gingery beard jutted out slightly as he faced Dog front on. "And then you start on his kid and his father-in-law—you fucking cowards."

"I don't know what you're talking about." Dog showed no sign of fear.

"You certainly fuckin' do, Dog. And you certainly fuckin' will when we've finished with you. You know full well Foggy beat the shit out of Junior at the Liverpool swap meet two months back. Junior wanted to sort it out on his own but I'm telling you, you've started hassling his family and you've got the Bandidos to deal with. You can tell your so called leader that, shithead."

"Aw, fuck off man. It's got nothing to do with me." Dog turned away.

At a nod from Snoddy, his men moved in. Snake, Chopper, Roo and Shadow. Kennedy heard a dull thump as fist met flesh. The table was upturned, beer spraying the wall. A chair was hurled above his head and smashed into a dirty wooden wall plaque, engraved with the words of Henry Lawson's, The Lights of Cobb & Co. As the three victims fell to the floor, the boots went in, vicious kicks aimed at kidneys.

"Hey, break it up, you guys!" Kennedy grabbed the jacket of one on the edge of the fracas, but was pushed back towards the wooden bar.

He ran to the door and yelled to the police. Outside, two police officers, notebooks out, were questioning two remaining Bandidos about their helmet exemptions. "Quick there's a fight! Get in here before they kill each other!"

Inside, the three Comancheros lay doubled up on the old carpet, now wet with blood and spilt beer, and crunchy underfoot from broken glass. The assailants were still kicking, jabbing the men with the toes of their hardened leather riding boots.

The police and the publican managed to contain the bashing, and the rest of the Bandidos pulled back their mates. "Okay, let's move it outside, come on, everybody out." The two police officers and Kennedy moved the Bandidos out to their bikes and Kennedy ordered them to leave the hotel. When the last Bandido bike had turned left on to Windsor Road, the three Comancheros hobbled out.

As Kennedy cleaned up, he discovered three socks, each stuffed with billiard balls, lying on the floor.

The following evening, Kennedy was sitting in his office preparing the bar floats for the next day, when he heard the shouting.

"Has anyone seen those fuckin' Bandaid pricks?"

He jumped up, threw the money in the safe, turning the lock before he ran out to the saloon. He saw the group of fourteen men standing at the door. They had marched through each of the hotel's four bars, looking for the Bandidos. Kennedy recognised Dog as one of the three who was bashed the night before. That familiar anxiety began to rise.

Dog was a small man, about five eight, with ratty-brown shoulder length hair. His face was puffed and bruised and his right cheek bone swollen. The right eye was a purple half-closed slit. He had a fresh blood-red scar on the corner of his lip and when he opened his mouth to speak, the publican noticed several front teeth were missing. He was wearing leather studded gloves and wrist bands. The men with him were in duffle coats. Kennedy could not see any weapons.

"Now come on, mate, let's not have any more trouble." Kennedy cornered him at the back door of the bar. "They haven't been in here all night, I haven't laid eyes on them."

The Comancheros left without a word.

Jock later referred to the Bull and Bush incident as the start of the war. He was shocked at Dog's injuries. The two men knew each other well. Dog worked on the truck Jock used for his fencing business, six days a week.

"What a bloody mess," he had remarked, looking at Dog's face.

Hours after the bashing, the Bandido clubhouse was shot at.

Two days later, the night of August 11, Snoddy called a general meeting. Bikes and cars choked the turning circle and spilt over into Mrs Proudman's neat driveway. It was this meeting Reverend Connolly observed.

A party was planned and the downstairs kitchen was already geared for it: rolls and sausages, steaks and salad with signs up—$1.20 hot dog, steak and salad $3.50.

But before the party started, Snoddy called his full members into the pool room. "I've just been on the phone to Jock and he's told me we're at war."

"That's bullshit! He's not forcing war on us. What's he talking about?" Lance Wellington, fair-haired, clean-shaven, recognised mechanic for the Bandidos, jumped to his feet.

"Well, that's what he said, and he said it's guerilla warfare and it starts at midnight."

"Well, it's not on," the protests increased.

Snoddy shouted over the din.

"Let's vote against war," Lance yelled.

"What else did Jock say?" Whack Campbell spoke up.

"He said, 'You bashed some of my blokes at the Bull and Bush. Now it's on, it's going to be a long one'," Snoddy answered. "I said, 'What's that mean, are you going to shoot us, run us off the road or fight it out?' He kept saying something about it's going to be a long one. I told him he should meet us on a football field and fight it out. He said, 'No, it's going to be guerilla war', and he hung up."

"The only thing he's at war with is himself," Lard, the club's resident comedian, said.

"All right, we'll vote," Snoddy said. They decided against war, by two votes.

"That's it then, you'll have to get on to Jock and sort this all out," Lance said. "There'll be no war."

Snoddy looked around the room at his men. He knew that as President he had vowed not to go the way of Jock, but he was to find himself swept along. Jock meant what he said, whether the Bandidos wanted it or not. They would have to protect themselves. There was no turning back. That night their clubhouse was shot at for the second time.

After the shootings, the Bandidos agreed to cooperate with the police. Statements were taken. Snoddy agreed to report any other incidents to the law.

He had paid $400 to Chris Murphy, a solicitor in the city, as a retainer. He called the prospects to a meeting.

"I've been to see a solicitor. Any other incidents like this and they are to be reported to the police," he told them. "I want you all to work out a roster so that the clubhouse is occupied at all times. Understand?"

Ray Denholm, Snoddy's de-facto brother-in-law was assigned daytime watches. He and the other prospects would stand outside Mrs Proudman's house on guard.

Any observor could see events were moving towards a showdown. The battlefield was not yet chosen, but death on either side had moved from the realms of possibility to certainty.

One week after the shooting at the Bandido clubhouse, the Harris Park clubhouse was attacked. This was a lesson to Jock, occurring as it did early one morning while his men were lost in deep, drunken sleep. They had been partying the night before, a Friday, and alcohol had flowed generously from the club bar. It soaked up all the caution displayed in previous weeks, ever since Jock had been forced off the road. There were no guards on duty.

One shot ricocheted off a car parked outside and hit the gate. Several others spattered the garage door and some hit the side of the house and the roof. But what really angered the Supreme Commander was that his men slept through the entire episode.

Jock took the hit seriously, and the grand old house at the end of the street bedded down for a siege. Gun barricades made of double thickness hardwood lined the fence and boarded the windows and blue double doors fronting the house.

"Fortification is essential," Jock repeatedly hammered into his men. They would not be caught napping ever again.

The men worked solidly fortifying their headquarters. A wooden defence barricade was to be erected on a trailer. This would act as a portable barrier, designed to be wheeled in and out at need. "Shocking workmanship," Jock berated his men after their first attempt to barricade the windows. "That wouldn't stop a bloody thing! It has to be built at an angle so it's deflective for shotgun fire. Can't you see that? For Chrissakes, pull it down and start again."

Inside the clubhouse, a weapons board was erected to the left of the stairs and adorned with baseball bats, shotguns and pieces of metal piping.

On August 20, it was the Comancheros' turn to strike back. Roo and Peter Melville, Lard's brother, had arranged to meet for a drink at the Royal Oak when Roo finished footy training at 7pm. They went on to a second pub and drank until just before midnight, when they left for a friend's place.

Roo leaned back in the passenger seat of Melville's new Toyota Tarago van as it headed down Church Street in Paramatta. Roo, his glossy black hair cropped short on top and long at the back, had a reputation with the ladies. Once he was photgraphed for the cover of the New Zealand *Women's Weekly* magazine, holding his pop star lover. "Drove a Daimler when I was in Saudi Arabia with the army," he would tell his club mates. "Just missed out on being in the SAS."

He lit a cigarette, enjoying the easy alcoholic euphoria, tapping away at the late night music from the car radio.

Then Melville noticed the black funereal vehicle up front, also travelling north along Church Street. "Hey mate, isn't that Foghorn's ute in front, and that looks like Dog beside him," Melville nudged Roo.

"Yeah, it's Foghorn all right. Wonder what that prick's doing around here. I think we should let Snoddy know he's cruisin' around a Bandits' pub." Roo became self-righteous under the influence of Jack Daniels.

Melville drove the van up Church Street and through north Parramatta. As he passed the Tollgate Hotel, the road widened into three lanes. He crossed to the far lane and Foggy pulled up beside him.

He slowed the van as he approached Briens Road, where he wanted to turn left, but as he slowed, the black ute slowed too. Melville was breathing heavily. "Fucking arsehole," Roo said, "don't worry, just keep going."

Melville continued down Church Street to Windsor Road. The lights ahead at the intersection of James Ruse Drive turned red and both vehicles slowed to a stop.

As they approached the lights, Melville glanced across and saw Dog reach down and pull up a single-barrelled full length 12-guage shotgun. He raised the gun and pointed it towards the van.

"Fuck, look at that, those guys are fuckin' crazy!" Melville began to panic. Then he saw the pistol in Foggy's right hand. He seemed to be smiling. "Christ, Foggy's got a fuckin' handgun. We'd better get out of here!"

Melville stood on the brakes and came to a near halt. The traffic lights turned green and Foggy's ute pulled forward ahead of the van. Melville followed for a short distance, then darted left and turned down a side street.

"We'd better get up to the main road and into the traffic. They wouldn't dare try anything there. Turn left at the end and head back up to James Ruse Drive." Melville followed Roo's directions and when he reached the intersection the lights were red.

As he waited, he saw car lights approaching from behind. "Fuck, they're on our tail again. Fuck the lights, Pete, just get out of here."

Peter glanced left and screamed through the red lights, Foggy's ute close behind.

As the van skidded round the corner, Melville felt it rock and jolt suddenly as the blast of shotgun fire sounded through the night. "Fuck they've hit us—keep low!" Roo shouted above the two blasts.

The black shape moved away from them, turning left and driving off. Melville continued right up James Ruse Drive.

"You okay, mate?" Roo asked him. Melville's heart was pounding in his throat. "Yeah, fuck that was close, those bastards, they had me worried for a while there. D'you think they'll come back?"

"Nup, that's it. Snoddy should know about this and now. We'd better head up to Wentworthville," Roo said.

Melville surveyed the damage to his car while Roo stood on the porch of the small fibro house and relayed the night's events to Snoddy. He noticed the model badge and number plate surround was missing from the back panel of the van. He ran his hand over the bronze metal and shuddered as he felt the shotgun pellet dents spattered over the back. A pellet had shattered the plastic lens of the left tail light.

"Fuck, my new car!" Still, they were lucky they hadn't been killed, Melville thought to himself.

When he made a second statement about the incident more than a month later, he told the police he gave a false name and address when he reported the incident from Snoddy's that night, because he feared for his life. He was pretty vulnerable working as a barman at the Royal Oak; the Comancheros knew who he was and where he worked, he had explained to detectives.

At the Bandido's next meeting on August 23, Snoddy announced that it was compulsory to attend the swap meet at the Viking Tavern on Fathers Day, 2 September. "If the Comancheros are there, we'll bash 'em and take their colours," Snoddy told his men. "You've all heard what happened to Bongo Snake. This has got to stop."

Bongo Snake, a Bandido member, had been stopped on his bike at traffic lights on Parramatta Road two nights previously. He was attacked from behind by five Comancheros led by Leroy. He was forced off his bike, clubbed with baseball bats and kicked. Then his 600 pound Harley Davidson motor cycle had been dumped on top of him. He was left lying in the gutter.

A few of the men muttered agreement. "Where is it?" Lout said.

"At Milperra somewhere, in two weeks time."

Discussion turned to the shooting three days previously, at Roo and Peter Melville.

After the toast to lost brothers and their emblem, the meeting broke up and members began to drift outside into the pool room.

Three days after the shooting at Roo and Melville, and the Bongo Snake incident, another shooting took place. The casualty was a plate glass window at the front of a real estate agent's office facing Wentworth Avenue in Wentworthville, next door to Shadow Campbell's house. The bullet left a hole one-and-a-half centimetres in diameter.

Detective Sergeant Merv Masterson visited the scene with policewoman Constable Moran to assist. It was one of the policewoman's first jobs.

Masterson questioned Shadow Campbell, who was still at the scene.

"Do you fellows know anything about this?"

"Yes, it was the Comancheros, they were shooting at us," Shadow answered.

"What for?"

"It's just a dispute over territory."

"What's your name?"

"Robert Alan Richardson," Shadow supplied the alias without hesitation.

"Could you come up to the Wentworthville Police Station with me now? I'd like to get a statement from you both about this," Masterson nodded towards the other man, who had identified himself as John Francis Campbell (Whack).

Shadow had long been disenchanted with the Bandidos, feeling the continual rivalry with the Comancheros was getting out of hand. It was destroying his family life. In many ways, it was a relief that the police had become involved. He told the police about the incident, for the sake of some help from the law.

John Campbell and his wife had been driving past Bridge Street, he told police. They were driving around the corner from Shadow's own house when they had noticed a group of men standing just across the railway bridge. One of them had a gun. John Campbell turned his car back across the bridge and headed back to tell Shadow, his elder brother. Shadow neglected to say that John was his younger brother, having given the police an alias.

Armed with a baseball bat, Shadow's rifle and Rex, his Great Dane, Shadow and John Campbell drove to Bridge Road. As they crossed the railway bridge one of the men from the group moved on to the road in front of their car and spat at it. Shadow saw one was armed. The Campbell brothers decided it was time to leave. They drove back towards Shadow's house on Wentworth Avenue. As they turned into his street, they saw the two cars that had been parked near the group of men on the bridge coming towards them. Shadow saw the long-barrelled gun pointing in his direction from the front of the white van. Then he heard the loud bang resonating around the quiet suburban street.

Shadow fumbled in the back seat of his car, picked up his rifle, loaded it and fired two shots in the air.

During the exchange of gunfire, the window was damaged.

"We have offered to meet with them and settle it properly but their President is a militant type and he wants to run the only motor bike club in Australia," Shadow told Detective Masterson. "He is supposed to be an ex-army SAS man," he added, "and he even gives his men battle drill.

"It has come to the point now that I can't even take my wife and kids out without having some of my brothers with me. All this hassling is going to lead to an open war and I dont wanna see that. We are prepared to settle it among ourselves, but he, 'Wally Ross', wants otherwise.

"The gun I had with me that day wasn't loaded, but it was there for my protection. I had to load it and everything before I fired a shot. I know I'm puttin' meself in but this only brings out what's been going on."

Shadow did not sign the statement.

Meanwhile, Jock Ross was being told a different story. Glen Eaves told him what had happened. "I was out the front loading the car. We were off to Windsor for that barbeque when those fuckin' Campbell dogs pulled up on the other side of the lights—you know, near the real estate agents there—and they fired at us."

"They've broken their own rules. They're hitting our houses, the bastards," Jock replied.

The police were attempting to find out who was responsible for the shooting.

Detective Steve Grandidge and young Constable Moran went around to Shadow's place to pick up the gun.

Joanne, Shadow's de facto wife answered the door. A long hallway led into the loungeroom with doors leading off both sides. In the loungeroom, Grandidge's practised eye took in the scene. It was a typical bikie's home, he thought.

On the mantlepiece was a mug. Shadow handed it to him for a better look. "To Shadow a real one-percenter," the inscription read. He seemed proud of it. The police officer felt embarrassed by this show of loyalty.

Other bikie memorabilia filled the room. Harley Davidson posters and one depicting a bare-breasted woman, a large copper clock in the shape of an eagle and *Ozbike* magazines on the floor.

Then Grandidge saw the large square glass tank sitting against the right-hand wall. Coiled in the bottom like a thick, sinewed rope was a tiger snake.

Shadow was taken to the police station and charged. Davo Littlewood, who had also been at Shadow's house, came with him to pay his bail.

Outside the police station, while Shadow was inside with Moran and Detective Masterson, Grandidge confronted Davo.

"Do you want to tell us what you think is going on?"

Davo decided to talk.

"It's all over the split up. You see, Jock is a militant. You know who I'm talking about, don't you," Davo's ginger eyebrows were raised.

"You're talking about the boss of the Comancheros?" Masterson joined Grandidge.

"Yeah," Davo paused. Masterson was surprised to see his lower lip shake a little. "He's mad, you know, his idea is to take over all the bikie groups in Australia. He has even given his men drill and lessons in self defence."

"Has anyone tried to reason with him?"

"We've tried to talk to him, but he's mad—you can't reason with him. We've offered to talk it out but if he wants a fight we'll even meet him man to man. He's the one who started all the shooting. The Bandidos as a motor cycle club is a democracy. He's got his followers doing all this and he would only have to say the word and they would do anything. He's too smart to get himself involved, you won't get anything on him."

"Well who are the main men?"

"Foggy Lane's his name, Robert Lane, and there is Phil—Leroy that is—he's on the run from Queensland for robbery. He's always packing a gun, so's Foggy. Neither of them have got any brains, they'll do anything."

Masterson decided to act. The following day he, Grandidge, Moran and another Constable went to JJ's house, to the address supplied by Shadow. JJ answered the door. He looked the four police up and down with his customary cat-like stare. "It was none of us. When it started we fucked off—sorry lady, I didn't mean to swear in front of you," he said to Constable Moran.

Kristine Duffy stood silently next to her partner, holding a six-month-old baby boy.

Masterson tried another tack. "Well, we know that it is a dispute between the Comancheros and the Bandidos and you're a Comanchero aren't you?"

"Yes, we both are." ?

"Well, where are we likely to find your leader Jock?"

"You won't get him at home, he's away fencing."

"When's he likely to be home?"

"I don't know, who knows?" JJ shrugged nonchalantly.

"Will you get this message to him? I want to see him and pretty quick. I am going to put a stop to this and I want the man who used the shotgun. Is that clear?" Masterson was losing patience.

"Here's a card with our names on it. Get Jock to ring me and I want to see him before Wednesday. Now while we are here, do you have any firearms in the house?"

Kristine spoke for the first time. "Yeah." She took Grandidge to another room. They came back with Grandidge holding a Bentley long-barrelled pump-action 12-gauge shotgun. There was dust around the stock and the firing mechanism and the inside barrel was corroded. It didn't appear to Masterson it had been recently fired or cleaned.

"Have you any ammunition for this weapon?"

"Yes." She fetched two shotgun rounds. "I've got a shooter's licence, but not on me," she said.

Masterson received this information in silence. Later, he dropped in on Shadow who told him about the Tarago van being shot up. "Also there's a cop called Scotty who works at Kings Cross, he is riding with the Comancheros."

Masterson told him to keep in touch.

Throughout this incident the rest of the Bandidos had been down in Griffith, where they were starting up a new chapter. Eight members of the club had gone on bikes. Snoddy had taken his car. He and Podgorski had taken some guns, planning to do some shooting at a property near Griffith.

Robert Lissner the sales asistant took the gun down and handed it to her. He watched as she inspected the weapon closely. He attempted to show her how to operate it, but it was unneccessary, she already knew.

"We already have a long-barrelled shotgun, but it's too heavy," she explained. "We want to do some clay bird shooting, you see."

The woman looked straight at the man across the counter with cold, piercing brown eyes. She was about 160 centimetres tall, wearing blue denim jeans and a black t-shirt with a white Harley Davidson emblem across her breast.

"How much?"

"That'll cost you $200," Lissner told her.

"Could I lay-by it and leave a $10 deposit?"

She produced a shooter's licence and Lissner transferred the details to the lay-by slip. August 27, Kristine Robyn Duffy, 6 Warialda St, Merrylands.

She took a crumpled $10 bill from the right hip pocket of her jeans and placed it on the counter. Another man, a friend of the woman, came into the shop. He was still carrying the box of shotgun ammunition that he had bought earlier that morning.

He was taller than her, about a head taller, his long blond scraggly hair in a crooked parting. He wore a dark brown leather jacket, with a pale coloured shirt and a green t-shirt underneath. He had eyes like a cat.

The shop assistant heard Kristine Duffy call the man JJ. Lissner handed them the yellow copy of the docket. "Thanks, mate," JJ said. They turned and left the store.

Saturday September 1 was declared a day of rest for the Bandidos. Charlie spent the morning cleaning his bike. He carefully rode it into Davo's garage when it started to rain.

Most of the members had hangovers. The previous night Gloves had won his first professional fight in two years.

The Bandidos had arrived early at the Marrickville RSL, where Gloves had tackled his opponent, Tony Campbell, the Junior Middleweight title holder. Gloves won on points after eight rounds. The party had gone on all night—until 9am the following morning for Big Tony.

Gloves had been training seven days a week for the big event. In the mornings he spent time on the footy field. At lunch-times he would go to the pool and do a work out that his brother and trainer, Knuckles, devised for him. At night he went to the gym. He was in peak condition. After Bongo Snake was attacked, he started carrying an axe-handle strapped to the side of his bike.

Gloves had been nervous. He was supposed to be fighting an unrated fighter, but he had pulled out at the last minute. Campbell was a much more formidable opponent.

Like Knuckles, Gloves had been brought up as a boxer. He always joked that when Knuckles had been training seriously, he had been looking down a bottle of bourbon. He was an amateur boxer until he was 22. He had won Golden Gloves and New South Wales titles.

The club had been behind him in his decision to turn professional again. Kid Rotten was his conditioner and manager. Davo cooked him dinner and made sure he was eating well.

On the night before Father's Day Snoddy went with Lee and her brother Ray, a Bandido nominee, to a Denholm family engagement party. "There's a swap meet on tomorrow," Ray told Tom Denholm, his older brother, a former Comanchero who had left bike clubs some years before. "You should come."

On Saturday night, Davo spent three hours polishing his trike in the hope there would be a competition at the swap meet the following day.

Gloves too had spent Saturday morning polishing his bike. It was the first morning for months that he had not spent training.

6

Presents for Father's Day

In 1984, Father's Day fell on Sunday September 2, heralded by the usual fanfare of consumer advertisements: gaudy brochures stuffed through letterboxes advertising lawn-mowers, shaving cream and golf balls.

Leanne Walters had chosen her Father's Day present from the Avon lady.

It was three chunky letters, made of opaque glass, spelling the word DAD. Under the letters, she carefully taped three instamatic colour photographs of herself dressed in a white top and red jeans, standing in Mrs Johns' backyard against a dilapidated wooden fence. Sheets and towels hung drying in the background. She backed the photos with a white card.

117 Elizabeth Drive was Leanne's new home. The house was on a four-lane arterial road which ran through Liverpool. Pamela Walters had moved to The Entrance on the New South Wales Central Coast. Leanne had chosen to board with Mrs Colleen Johns, Melinda's aunt.

The Johns' house was painted pale turquoise. It had a neat lawn devoid of flowers, a concreted back yard and a blue and white wrought iron railing around the front verandah.

Here Leanne was close to her job at Smith's Furnishings, a curtain factory in nearby Hoxton Park Road. She could walk to work in fifteen minutes. It was her first job.

By May, Leanne and Melinda had tired of not having any money, and they both applied for jobs through the Commonwealth Employment Service— from which they had formerly drawn the dole.

At the huge, barn-like curtain factory, Leanne adopted another friend to take care of her, Mary Larkin, a woman in her late fifties. Leanne christened her Gran.

Gran was a small bird-like woman with dyed black eyebrows and hair the colour of ash. She had bright blue eyes and a sympathetic manner. She was Leanne's boss at the folding table.

Gran and Leanne would start at 6am, standing on the cold cement floor at the big table, folding hundreds of curtains by morning tea time—cafe

77

curtains, heavy cotton curtains with pinch pleats, lined drops, rod pockets and lace curtains. Each set would be folded, placed in a plastic packet and sealed—all in the space of two or three minutes. Melinda worked on the friller when she turned sixteen, she was then considered old enough for the job of overlocking the curtains.

Each day at 9 o'clock, Leanne would make the morning tea for twenty workers and then buy herself a can of Coca-cola.

"I've got a toothache, Gran," she complained one day.

"Well, that's because you don't clean your teeth properly," Gran replied.

"But I don't have a toothbrush."

The following day Gran presented her with a new red toothbrush.

"Hey, thanks, Gran," Leanne said. "Nobody ever buys me anything, this is great, thanks."

Leanne would chatter constantly as they folded the curtains each day, above the sound of the machines. Sometimes Mary would tell her to hush up.

"I'm going to get a legacy when I turn eighteen and I'm gonna buy a car," she said one morning.

"What legacy?"

"Oh, just some money me grandad said he'd leave me."

Mary Larkin had grand-daughters of her own. She felt sorry for this fifteen-year-old child. "A hard worker if ever I've seen one, maybe rough, but a hard worker, not like most kids her age," she would tell her husband at night in their neat suburban home.

At 5.45 each morning, when Mary arrived at the factory, Leanne would be there without fail, sweeping the floor.

In August, on Mary's birthday, Leanne gave her a card and a disposable cigarette lighter.

"Another birthday and we've finally reached that interesting age" the gaudy card read, and inside: "Somewhere between on the pill and over the hill. Love from Lynie and Leanne. Happy Birthday."

The present was in much the same vein, a little risque for Mary who laughed just the same, thinking it was not the sort of gift she would receive from her own grand-daughters.

"I am a virgin," the lighter read. And on the other side, "This is a very old lighter."

"Why did you have those silly tattoos done?" Gran asked her one day.

"I dunno, I just wanted them I s'pose. I know it was dumb, they'll look shithouse in summer," Leanne replied.

Leanne showed no ambition to move to the machines with Melinda, nor did she ever talk much about the future. At lunchtimes, Melinda and Leanne would go to the sandwich shop opposite, buy pies and chips and sit in the sun to eat.

On the Friday before Father's Day, 31 August, after work, Gran offered Leanne a lift into the main shopping centre in Liverpool.

"Now, you make sure you buy those shoes like you said you would," Gran turned around as Leanne got out of the back seat. "Your toes are fair showing through your other ones."

"Aw sure, Gran. You just behave yourself on the weekend, okay?"

"Never mind about me, you're the one who should be behaving yourself," Gran chuckled at her impudence. "Now get going, I'll see you on Monday."

Leanne left Melinda at the shopping centre and started the long walk home. It was a warm day for August, the sort of day which hints at summer, cloudless blue skies with a faint chill in the breeze. She decided to stop at McDonalds for some hot chips. Walking past a small takeaway shop in Elizabeth Drive she heard someone call.

"Leanne, hi! What are you doing here?"

It was her father, Rex.

"Hi, dad, what are you doin' round here?"

"Just getting some fish and chips. Have you knocked off for the day love?"

"Yeah, we get half day on Fridays. I live just over the hill, number 117."

"Who lives there?"

"You know, Melinda's auntie and her mother . . ."

"Oh, right. So how have you been, love?"

"Much better. Look how much weight I've put on," she stood back for his surveillance.

"D'you like my hair dad? I've just had it done. You know, I've been workin' for nearly five months now, and earnin' money."

Rex Walters smiled his old familiar smile.

"That's my girl."

"I've got something for you for Father's Day."

"Oh that's right, it's Sunday isn't it? Well listen, love, how about you come around on Monday or Tuesday night—give me a ring first. I'll tell you why, I won't be home on Sunday, I think I'll be down the snow—you know it's our busy season, August. It's the busiest time of the year. But I'll be back after the weekend," he added quickly, seeing her face darken.

"You know Lorraine and I have moved now. Here," he took his bus driver's pad and scribbled down his address and phone number and handed it to her.

"I might come down the snow with you one weekend," she said, brightening.

"Sure, Calabros wouldn't mind—you being my daughter and all. We'll fix something up." Rex collected his fish and chips and said, "Listen, I've got my car here, just round the corner. D'you want a lift?"

"No, I'll walk. I wanna go to McDonalds and get some lunch. See ya."

"Yeah, see you Monday or Tuesday. Look after yourself."

He watched her walk up the hill, a lone figure, but almost back to how he remembered her. She had filled out again into a young woman.

Jock woke on Father's Day restless after dozing fitfully into the early hours. He had planned to spend the day at home, but now in the grey light of dawn, he felt like getting out of the house.

"I don't feel like digging in the yard today, darls," he said to Vanessa after a breakfast. "How about we do something?"

Vanessa had a fleeting vision of them driving along in the country, just the family on a leisurely weekend drive, off to a quaint country pub for lunch.

Holly started crying again. She was just over the measles. "What sort of thing were you thinking of?"

"Well, it's 11 o'clock. How about I ring the clubhouse and we'll have a barbie. The boys'll still be there from last night—hungover but ready for a feed."

"But we don't have any meat, darls," Vanessa looked in the freezer.

"Snow'll have meat. Snow's always got meat. We'll have a barbie."

Vanessa knew it was no use arguing.

Jock phoned the club, Leroy answered.

"Listen mate, how many boys are down there today?"

"Aw, half a dozen. Why?"

"Well, why don't you all come over here for a barbie—to my place for a bit of a feed."

"I think most of the blokes are still going to that swap meet, I know Foggy is, and I was thinking of going too—you know, have a look around, few beers . . ."

"Where's it on again?"

"Liverpool I think, somewhere in Liverpool. We haven't got organised yet."

"Hang on a minute." Jock covered the mouthpiece. "Vanessa, d'you want to go to a swap meet at Liverpool with the kids?"

Vanessa could see the plans of a day with the family fading. She hesitated.

"I don't know Jock. Holly's started whinging again. I don't like taking her out."

"What time's it on?" Jock spoke back into the mouthpiece.

"Starts at midday. I thought I might head off to Mittagong after it's over," Leroy answered.

"I'll ring you back." He was torn between staying at home for Father's Day and going down to the clubhouse.

Just twenty minutes after he spoke to Leroy, Jock's dilemma was solved for him. The phone rang. It was Glen Eaves. He was due for manoeuvres in Victoria the following day. Today was his last day of leave.

Jock could tell immediately that he was excited. He could barely string his words together. "Fuckin' Bandaids just rode past my house."

"When?" Jock felt his anger rise. It was a deliberate taunt.

"About ten minutes ago."

"What, on bikes . . ."

"Bikes and Bull's car. The car was full, Roach was driving, and I saw Snake on a bike, but I couldn't make out the others. Looked like three Campbells, though. I bet they're going to the swap meet."

"I'll meet you at the clubhouse in twenty."

Glen said he would get Andy, a nominee, to drop off his wife Lisa and their baby at Jock's place.

"Yep, okay," replied Jock. "Then Andy can take me down to the clubhouse." He hung up. "I'm going to the clubhouse, Vanessa."

He phoned Andy and told him to pick up Glen's wife and the baby, Jessica, bring them to Pennant Hills, then take him down to Harris Park.

Jock rang Foghorn and Snow and gave them instructions to muster the men at the clubhouse for an urgent meeting. "The Bandaids could be going to this swap meet. A few of our boys plan to go, so I reckon we should all go—as many that can. There could be trouble."

Foggy rang Littlejohn.

"Is Sparra there with you?"

"Yeah."

"What are you doing?"

"Nothing, why?"

"Come down to the clubhouse, Jock wants you there now."

"Why?"

"You'll find out when you get there. Just hurry."

Littlejohn knew better than to argue with Foggy or Jock. He went outside to tell Sparrow the news.

Vanessa was on the phone to a girlfriend when Jock was ready to leave.

She picked up her thong and threw it at him. He ducked behind the door, calling back, "Okay. Be back in an hour."

The clubhouse backyard was packed with Jock's men. Glen, JJ, Dog, Flash (Andrew Thomas), Peewee, Morts, Foggie, Kraut, Leroy, Snow, Tonka, Blowave (John Bodt), Terry (Terrence Parker) and Sunshine stood around awaiting their instructions. Rick Lorenz, a new recruit whose club name was Chewy, was one of the last men to arrive.

He stood six foot six, with long, fair hair and a Fu-Manchu style moustache which drooped half way down his chest.

He had become involved with the Comancheros after leaving his wife and their baby a year earlier. He abandoned the responsibilities of a family and two jobs and fell into a life of partying and drinking with the mates he had met working at Landmark Autos at Bankstown.

Chewy was super fit and one of the strongest workers his employer had seen. He would often amaze his workmates by lifting car motors off trucks single-handed.

He had been awarded his Comanchero strip the previous night, in a solemn ceremony before the party started. The women had been invited to the party, but the ceremony had been out of bounds to them.

Just before the party had started, Jock made an announcement. "If anyone is going to the swap meet tomorrow, I want you to go in a group of at least four men and to watch your bikes. If anyone doesn't want to go, don't worry, 'cause I'm not going 'cause I know it's Father's Day and I'll be at home with Vanessa and the kids."

Joanne Warner, Sparrow's twenty-year-old girlfriend, had left the club-house just after midnight with Sparrow, John "Littlejohn" Hennessey, and his blonde-haired wife Lucy. It was a relatively early night for the four; parties at the clubhouse usually extended into daylight hours. Joanne and Sparrow decided to stay overnight at the Hennessey's place in Heckenberg because Sparrow's car had a flat tyre.

The four had slept in until quite late and had a leisurely morning drinking coffee. Just before midday the phone rang and the two men disappeared inside.

Joanne and Lucy had been chatting in the backyard when Littlejohn came outside to tell Lucy he and Sparrow were going to the clubhouse.

"What for? I thought we were having a day here." Joanne was annoyed at the change in plans. She went in to talk to Sparrow. "Are we going too?"

Sparrow looked at her blankly. "Who?"

"Me and Lucy."

"No, you two can stay here."

"Well, I'm still going to see mum and dad." Joanne had already rung her parents and arranged to meet them with Sparrow that afternoon for a few drinks at the Parramatta Golf Club.

"You can give me and Littlejohn a lift to the clubhouse. We're just gonna change the tyre. You ready to go?" Sparrow replied.

Bloody club, she thought, as she watched her boyfriend of two years place the pump-action shotgun he had bought the week before in her car.

Sparrow, she decided, was acting strangely. He was anxious about something. She decided not to argue over the change in plans.

Neither woman spoke as the four drove to the clubhouse. When the familiar cream building came into view, Littlejohn turned and looked at Sparrow. "Well, this is it then, mate."

"Yeah, I s'pose it is," Sparrow replied, looking at the road.

At the clubhouse, Joanne joined Sparrow in the backyard. She nodded to some of the men gathered around Jock. "Get the bullets out of the console, hun," Sparrow said to Joanne.

Obediently, she walked back to where the Holden was parked on the grass outside. She reached into the console and found the plastic bag full of big, fat bullets, with little grooves along them. When she returned with the ammunition, Sparrow was sitting on an upturned box sharpening a knife. She glanced across to Kristine Duffy who was sitting on a crate, bouncing a baseball bat on the concrete between her legs.

Joanne kissed Sparrow goodbye, and he grunted.

Donna Campbell was in the kitchen on Sunday morning buttering slices of bread for her son Daniel's third birthday party. There was to be a combined celebration on Father's Day, with a barbeque later on in the day for the adults. Caesar would probably do the cooking. He often cooked at barbies. Invitations had been sent out six weeks in advance.

The chocolate cake covered with coconut icing stood proudly in the centre of the table in the kitchen along with fairy bread, sausage rolls and tiny cocktail frankfurts.

Donna was Caesar Campbell's old lady, his second wife, who had borne him two children. Irene—Caesar's real old lady, his first missus—lived in the same suburb as Donna at Ashfield. Both women got along well enough. Irene had borne four of Caesar's children, all older than Donna's pair. A tall leggy blonde, once attractive, Irene was in her late 30s. Donna was in her prime at 25.

Irene would be along a little later, as would most of the Bandido women. It was a party for women and kids, the men would join in later.

Davo and Dukes (Greg McElwaine) had left their wives at Donna's to help her prepare for the party.

Christine Campbell, Bull's wife, arrived with a jigsaw puzzle for Daniel. Christine was tiny—just on five feet tall—but she was strong and happy with five children and her big, bear-like husband, who was the third son of fourteen Campbell children.

Donna's house was a run-down wooden building with a toilet out the back. The kitchen and dining room, where the women congregated, was combined.

Donna locked her two dogs in the toilet so the kids could play safely outside. Like many of the bikers, they had a bull terrier, and also a mongrel whose height showed one of his parents was related to the Great Dane breed. The women kept a watchful eye on the kids from the kitchen, where a few of them sipped wine from an opened flagon. The sky grew ominous, hanging heavily over the small party, threatening rain. Christine Campbell thought of the two missing side windows in her two-door Holden Torana.

For the past few weeks, Bull had been taping up the doors of his wife's car. Each morning, before she drove the girls to school, he would check the doors, in case the Comancheros had planted a bomb. Every night, they would put the couch in the lounge up against the wooden front door of their Merrylands house.

Christine knew there was trouble looming and she saw her husband was seriously worried. When he had been told about the shots fired at Shadow's place and the next door real estate agent, Bull had begun to fear for his life and his family.

He had sat down with Christine and told her just how frightened he was. Together they decided Bull should leave the club. Christine, too, was frightened because she realised the enormity of her husband's decision. She worried he would not cope away from the brothers he loved so much.

But Bull had gathered up his colours, and had gone with Christine and the children to Snoddy's house. "I'm leaving, Snoddy. I'm not taking any more chances with Chris and the kids. They're fuckin' mad and I'm not going to risk my wife and kids gettin' hurt." He had looked away as Snoddy tried to make him change his mind. He shoved the colours in his President's hands. "It's no good, mate, I'm leaving."

He was visibly upset, and not even the kids spoke as they drove home.

Christine had not been surprised when Snoddy arrived on their doorstep two days later holding Bull's colours.

She was out the back with the kids when Bull came outside and told her Snoddy said he'd been to the police and they had promised to go and talk to Jock, and there would definitely be no more trouble. "He wants me to take the colours back and think about it for a couple of weeks. What do you think, Chrissie?"

"I don't know," she said. "It's up to you."

Bull had taken back the colours, but warned Snoddy if there was any more trouble, he'd be leaving straight away.

Now, on Father's Day morning, Chopper, the adopted Campbell who lived with Christine and Bull, had come home from a night out and told Bull, "All the boys are going to a swap meet at Milperra. Then we'll go to the party at Caesar's. You coming?"

At first Bull said no, but Chop said he needed a lift. "Chris, do you mind if I go and have a drink with the fellows for a while?" Bull pleaded.

"You're lucky it's Father's Day," she said.

"See you down at Caesar's in a coupla hours," Bull assured her.

Never a day went by when the Campbell brothers did not see each other, Christine thought as she washed up. They were the closest family she had ever known and it took her some time to be accepted. Now, at 34, after five children—four to Bull—she felt she had earned her place in the Campbell household. Still, she and Bull had never officially married and she retained her maiden name of Howlett which she used from time to time.

Shadow's house in Wentworth Avenue was in much the same state as Bull's. For the last few weeks his children had been sleeping on the floor on mattresses.

Shadow was one of the most popular men in the Bandido Motor Cycle Club. His commitment to the club was deep. But he did not regret giving a statement to the police about the shooting at the real estate agent's window. Snoddy had been against this. He was wary of the law.

For the past week, Shadow had sat up through the nights with a gun by his side, guarding his house. He slept during the day.

When Bull and Chopper arrived at Shadow's on Father's Day morning, Pig and Opey were in the loungeroom. Shadow was still in bed. Bull left for the Highway Hotel up the road to get a carton of beer and when he came back Snake, Whack and Roach had arrived.

Just before 11 am, they left for Lance Wellington's place at Condell Park, Bull asked Roach to drive because he was drinking. Shadow, Chopper and Whack sat in the back, Pig, Opey and Snake started their bikes and the party moved off. The bikes led, up Wentworth Avenue and into Bridge Street where Glen Eaves lived.

As they approached number 102, Bull saw Glen sitting in the driver's seat of his Cortina. He was reversing into the street. Then he jumped out of his car and ran into the house.

"Fuckin' fool . . .I wonder what he's up to . . ." Shadow mumbled from the back seat. "D'yer think they'll be at Milperra?" The question hung in the air unanswered. " . . .Yeah. Bull, like I was sayin'," Shadow continued talking to his brother, the conversation turning to one of their favourite topics. "I'm thinking of getting a new dog, how 'bout we go shoot some pigs on the October long weekend, it's only a couple of weeks away . . ."

Shifty changed down a gear and slowed to a dawdle for the Sunday morning strollers wheeling across the pedestrian crossings, church-goers and families out for the day, children licking pink ice creams.

They reacted predictably to the tall, bearded biker, greying hair blowing in the breeze, long legs almost as high as the handle bars, strong arms outstretched. From the rear, he was an impressive sight—black leather cut-offs bearing the stamp of the Rebels. Shifty was out on business.

Behind him, wedged into a brown milk crate, strapped on to the back, was a bull terrier pup, the club's new mascot. "He'll get used to the bike sooner or later," Shifty had told his Pres.

In the inside pocket of his cut-offs, Shifty carried two sterling silver rings bearing skulls, the sign of the Rebels. He was heading to Bankstown markets to have three more made up.

Halfway down Scott Street, he recognised instantly the slight figure of the girl walking towards him. She looked like any other Liverpool teenager dressed in jeans, a t-shirt and mohair jumper and thongs. A lanky, long-haired boy walked beside her. Shifty knew her smile.

It was Shorty. With that good for nothing scumbag arsehole she called a boyfriend. She waved, expectant as ever that he might have something for her.

Shifty hadn't seen much of Leanne since she had been discharged from hospital. When he had visited her in B Wing at Liverpool, he had been shocked by how thin she had become. "Blew me right out it did," he'd told Cheryl later.

He slowed his bike and pulled up alongside the couple, resting his huge feet on the roadway.

"G'day, Shifty, where ya goin'?"

Shifty looked at Leanne, ignoring the boy. "I'm going to the markets, and then I'm goin to a swap meet at Milperra."

"Aw, can I come too, huh, can I . . .?"

Shifty remained stern.

"Aw fuck, come on, Shifty, I'm bored. Don't be an arsehole, go on . . ."

"Listen here, Shorty, I told you to quit that swearin' or I'll be off this bike as soon as look at ya and slap y'r arse in front of all these people . . ."

The boy she was with was a junkie. Shifty glanced over his waif-like frame, acned face and glazed eyes. He was just the type of company Shorty could do without. He knew she was already dabbling in drugs and he was determined to keep her off the hard stuff.

"I'll tell ya what I'll do, Shorty. You can come with me to Milperra, right? But first I'm going to the markets. You stay with the bike while I'm at the markets. Don't leave it for one minute, don't let nobody touch it, y'hear? And if you pull the contract off, then I'll take you to the swap meet." Leanne smiled, the boyfriend forgotten.

At the markets, Shifty was swallowed into the crowds. People clustered like ants between the stalls of pot plants, racks of cheap gaudy clothes and rows of cut-price make-up.

He returned more than an hour later, after catching up with a few acquaintances, and time spent discussing prices with the jeweller. He found Leanne standing beside the Harley, a stick in her right hand, brandished threateningly towards a small crowd of children who had gathered to admire the bike.

"Don't you come near it . . .fingers off, shithead!" she yelled at one freckle-faced kid.

Shifty laughed out loud.

"Okay, Shorty. Come on then, you've earned a ride. Hop on."

Shifty started up the bike. Leanne sneered at the children as she mounted.

"I've never been to a swap meet before," she said as she clasped her arms around Shifty's waist.

"Where is it again, Shifty?"

"The Viking—a pub at Milperra."

7

The Viking

The Viking Tavern stands 200 metres back from Beaconsfield Street, a sprawling barn-like building reminiscent of a child's Lego construction, nestled comfortably at a slightly lower level than the wide, curbed roadway of suburban Milperra. Entrance to the carpark is via a wide driveway at the eastern end of the hotel grounds. Faded, white parking bays form a border at the top of the carpark parallel to the street. From here, the quiet industrial buzz of Beaconsfield Street is obscured by a graduated, landscaped rockery which leads up to a thin strip of green lawn and a footpath next to the roadway.

In September, rich pink azalia bushes blossom among native grasses and young gums. The carpark is otherwise dull, the monotonous bitumen broken by intermittent clumps of trees planted on raised islands to mark the ends of designated parking bays.

A previous publican settled on the Viking flavour to lure his customers in for a beer. Apart from the neon sign, which towers above the entrance, the two main bars are the Norseman Public Bar and the Scandia Valhalla lounge bar.

Three tired, incongruous palm trees line the terracotta coloured hotel wall at the entrance to the bars. A drive-through bottle department, built later than the hotel proper, juts out toward the roadway at the western end of the carpark, making the building L shaped.

Opposite the Tavern, an Esso service station advertises cheap diesel fuel. On weekends, the Beaconsfield Street factories—Quality Kitchens, Bankstown Blinds, Liquid Air—are closed and quiet.

Further east along the street, the factories and workshops disappear and the buildings become residential, mostly single-level middle-class dwellings on the fringe of a light industrial area.

At the southern end of the Tavern is a green reserve, council-owned land where local children on pushbikes play on weekends and after school.

The Viking Tavern Swap Meet had been well advertised. Black and white posters had been put up around Milperra, Bankstown and Liverpool. Pamphlets had been handed out and signs displayed in motor cycle shops, pubs, petrol stations and shopping centres.

SWAP MEETING

Viking Hotel
Beaconsfield Street, Revesby
Sunday 2nd September, 1984.
Stalls—$5 each—to be ready by 11.00 am.
Hotel opens at 12.00pm.

Live Band   Snack Bar.
Wet t-shirt competition.
All Welcome. (British, Japanese, European, American).

Organised by the British Motor Cycle Club.

It was the BMC's first swap meet. Al Smith, the club president and Geoff Coasby, or Jethro to his mates, had done most of the organising. It was a day for buying and selling motor cycle parts and biker paraphernalia, and the club hoped to raise a bit of money from the raffles and the lamb they planned to roast on a spit. Joanne Caestro, Al's girlfriend, had been given the job of distributing the pamphlets.

Unlike the outlaw bike clubs, the BMC had no clubhouse. Their regular meetings were held at the High Flyer Hotel in Bankstown. When Jethro began working at the Viking Tavern at Milperra his new boss, Mike Langley, met some of the members, and agreed to let them change their meeting venue to the Viking. It would help business.

The response that morning was pleasing. Bikers began drifting in long before midday, guided by the neon-lit Viking, high on a signpost. The crowds came in station wagons and utilities, lowering their back doors, spreading spare parts inside the cars or over the ground near their vehicles on tarpaulins, blankets or sheets. Stall holders paid their $5 to the BMC then staked their claims in the large bitumen carpark.

"We'll go for an hour. You can have your show and leave. If they're there it'll be on for sure." Jock glanced around at the circle of men. "Those on the bikes will go in colours and the others in cars will support those on the bikes. Guns aren't to be loaded when you've got them in the cars. Use them as a last resort.

"Foggy's organised the order for the bikes. He'll lead in the ute. I'll be in Eaves' Cortina, bringing up the rear. "Now remember, stick together and stay in contact. If you have to shoot, shoot at the legs."

Jock knew he could be outnumbered, so tactics were important. "Okay men, let's move it out!"

At Jock's command the men moved silently to their bikes, and started up their engines. They doubled up on bikes: John Bodt (Blowave) jumped on behind Scott Dive (Bones), Leroy behind Terry, Kraut with Peewee, Kristine Duffy straddled the bike her de facto husband, JJ, was riding, Sunshine and Chewy rode Tatts' bike, and Dog, carrying his baseball bat, went on the back of Andrew (Andy) Thomas' Harley. The noise reverberated through the neighbourhood.

Foggy backed his black ute out of the driveway. Littlejohn was sitting in the front seat, Tonka and Snow in the back. Jock sat in the passenger seat of Glen Eaves' car. Morts and Sparrow were in the back, Glen behind the wheel. The cavalcade, led by the black funereal utility, moved out into the quiet street, weaving its way through the slight traffic down to the used car yards on Woodville Road.

A Department of Main Roads sign at the Church Street junction signalled Milperra was fourteen kilometres away.

Jock was silent as the Comancheros travelled abreast in three lanes of traffic through Merrylands and South Granville. Occasionally he glanced across to Foggy's ute. He was reassured by the sound of his men on their bikes.

They passed through Villawood. Six kilometres to go. Foggy looked at the cortege behind him. Like Jock, he was proud.

Sunday drivers looked on in awe at the bikies, stopped in the 12-lane traffic at the major Milperra Road, Henry Lawson Drive intersection. From here, Foggy led his men left, through rich, green national parkland, the muddy Georges River swollen on their right.

The bikes leaned easily into the gently curved road, and despite their riders' bulk, the bikes looked strangely poetic; the Cortina and the utility, clumsy four-wheeled vehicles, broke the spell.

Still, the cars were essential. They carried most of the weapons. Foggy and Snow would remain in contact via handheld walkie-talkies they would carry around the carpark. It was a fitting choice for Jock to make: the two men had gone to school with each other at Miami High in Queensland. They had reunited in Sydney ten years later.

By midday, Joanne Caestro was well and truly pissed. She and Al Smith arrived at 8am and they started drinking as soon as they had filled the 44–gallon drum with cans of beer and covered them with ice.

Joanne was surprised to see so many stallholders at the pub so early. By 9 o'clock, most stalls had been set up. Long-haired leatherwork artists crafting belts and beer can holders bearing individual bike trademarks were scattered among the bike parts vendors. Two women chatted over a shaky wooden table covered with red and green toffee apples and lollipops.

Jethro's bike bits were on display from the back of his car, which was parked near the rear fence. The carcass of a lamb turned on a spit and the smell of roasting meat hung heavily in the air.

Jethro was busy in the bar, so Joanne was minding his stall. She found a seat in the sun and dozed while Al was off organising the band. It had turned into a beautiful, warm spring day.The gentle morning rays, combined with the beer, were intoxicating.

Joanne's brother-in-law and his mates had been hassling her since she got there, urging her to enter the wet t-shirt competition at 4 o'clock. "Piss off," she laughed, "I'm not drunk enough for that." So they bought her another beer, and another and another. She had three lined up and the guys kept telling her to drink faster. She was gone and she knew it, so she just laughed and kept on drinking.

She saw Al just before noon. He came over with Jethro, looking for more raffle tickets. The club was raffling a bottle of scotch and a bottle of bourbon at a dollar a ticket. They'd already made a couple of hundred bucks. "The bar's doing really well," Jethro said to Al, "Mike's really pleased. Looks like its going to be a great afternoon. We'll have to make it a regular thing."

Linda Motton and her boyfriend David Irving chose to set up their stall down at the back fence, not far from the roasting lamb. More chance of customers that way. They arrived at the Tavern at 10 o'clock in a white Fairlane. David was a passionate biker who rebuilt motor bikes in the spare bedroom of their home in seaside Maroubra. For the swap meet he had borrowed his flatmate's white Fairlane and trailer, which was full of bits and pieces of the many bikes David had tinkered with over the years.

Driving through Redfern, an inner city suburb en route to Milperra, the van had overheated. "I don't know, Dave," Linda had said. "I've got a funny feeling about today. Something's going to happen. I can just feel it."

David, ever practical and sceptical of Linda's refined sixth sense, did not even look up from the radiator. But Linda, a 22-year-old barmaid, shuddered at the similarity of this feeling to the one she experienced just before her last bike accident. She felt uneasy and worried about the possibility of an accident during the remaining 22 kilometres of their trip to Milperra.

But they had arrived at the Tavern intact. David set his wares out on the trailer and blended quickly with the fast growing crowd in his black t-shirt, leather cut-off vest and blue jeans—standard dress for a biker who rode alone. He wandered off to chat with someone he knew, a former member of the Hells Angels. Linda, bored but resigned, settled into the front seat of the

Fairlane with her Agatha Christie book, and was soon engrossed in it.

The Comancheros had first gone to the High Flyer Hotel at Condell Park by mistake, looking for the swap meet. At about 1.15 pm, the cavalcade pulled up at the entrance of the Viking Tavern car park.

Janelle Bushell, whose husband Bill was a member of the BMC, was collecting money at the car park entrance when the black ute approached. She held her arm out and signalled Foggy to stop.

As the car slowed, Janelle moved over and put her head through the driver's side window. "Hi there. Are you guys here to set up a stall today, or are you just looking for parts?"

Foggy did not look up at the woman, nor did he reply. He turned to JJ and said something which Janelle couldn't hear. She began to feel uneasy.

The two men burst into sudden laughter. Foggy turned to her and said: "No, we're just looking for parts." He laughed in her face.

As Janelle stepped back to let them drive through, she noticed the lumpy black canvas in the middle of the back seat, under which Foggy's M1 carbine lay.

Joanne heard the throb of bikes approaching. She counted six bikes and two cars. Foggy's black utility led the way, crawling into the car park. The ute circled the two rows of aisles to the left of the driveway, finally parking close to the exit, away from the centre area. The bikes moved into the centre, near a small clump of trees that separated them from the main entrance to the hotel. Glen Eaves followed the bikes and parked the Cortina to the right of them, his car facing the back fence.

Joanne realised they were Comancheros. She recognised Jock as he stepped out of Glen's car and she saw Rick Lorenz, known to the Comancheros as Chewy, getting off the back of one of the bikes. Heads turned as they drove in. Several people noticed the leather scabbard strapped to the front of one bike. Several riders had baseball bats in their hands when they dismounted.

Joanne thought nothing more of it until Debbie, who had been selling raffle tickets, came running over twenty minutes later and grabbed her by the arm. "Where's Al? The Commos have just come in and they've got guns on their bikes!" she panted. "We've got to tell Al . . ."

"I dunno," Joanne replied dismissively. So what, she thought, they always carried guns. Debbie was over-reacting as usual. The beer had made Joanne mellow. She opened another can.

Debbie couldn't find Al, so she told Eddie, another club member, who went straight into the lounge and found Jethro.

"The Comancheros are here, mate," Eddie said.

Jethro looked up. "I know," he said. "So what?"

"They've got baseball bats and one of them's got a machete and it looks like they're here for trouble."

Jethro was not unduly worried. He'd seen them arrive. Rick Lorenz had said hello to him. He hadn't noticed anything strange. But he decided to check it out anyway. He walked outside towards the Comanchero bikes. He saw Mike Langley and waved. The two men walked over together. As they approached the bikes, Jethro saw a Comanchero he didn't recognise, holding a baseball bat.

Jethro noticed his dirty black hair and unshaven face. Dog wore a black vest with Comanchero colours and over the missing backside of his blue jeans he wore black leather overpants. Close up, Jethro saw he was missing several front teeth.

"What are you planning to do with the baseball bat?" Mike Langley said.

"Who are you?" Dog said.

"I run this show, mate, and. . ."

"Well, just fuck off."

A second Comanchero appeared. "What's the trouble?" he said. "I'm Kraut, the Sergeant-at-Arms," he lied, hoping a title of office might allay the publican's fear.

Jethro looked at him as he shook the outstretched hand. He was bigger than the first bloke, thick set, German looking, and he guessed at least thirty-eight.

"I'm Mike Langley the publican and this is Jethro, the Sunday manager. Look, this is a nice quiet family day and I don't want any trouble. What's this bloke doing with a baseball bat? I don't want any disturbances or I'll call the police. There's no need for bats and knives here."

"It's my son's baseball bat, I carry it to protect myself," Dog said. "I wouldn't give it to nobody . . ."

Kraut interrupted Dog with a whack on the back of his head. "There won't be any trouble," Kraut said.

"Who's this bloke wandering around with a machete that we've been told about?" Mike asked.

"That's the President. He can do what he wants," Dog said.

The first thing Jethro noticed about the grey-haired man who at that moment approached was the machete strapped to his hip. Then the dirty, dark grey woollen jumper under the leather jacket. All eyes turned to him.

"My name is Jock Ross," he said, his accent distinct. "What's the problem?" He stared straight at Langley, eyes masked by square tinted glasses.

"I'm the publican and this is a peaceful day. I don't want any trouble—I want the weapons put away."

"There won't be any trouble unless the Bandaids turn up," Jock said.

"Look here, mate. I want no trouble, period," Langley replied, his voice rising. "Now, put the weapons away."

Jock said nothing. The three men turned and walked back to the black utility truck where three other Comancheros stood. Mike and Jethro headed back to the hotel, both men felt uneasy.

"What'd you make of that?" Jethro said.

"Dunno. I just hope there's no trouble. Better keep a close eye on them."

"Christ, that one's got a walkie talkie, look." Jethro pointed to Foggy, who was standing by the driver's door of the black ute speaking into the small oblong box he held up to his face.

By the time the five Bandidos reached Lance Wellington's house in Condell Park, Opey knew he would have to do some work on his brakes.

Lance's house in Pringle Avenue was a white fibro place with dirty-pink paint slapped carelessly around the windows. A bright blue letter box stood at the head of a concrete driveway leading up to a back fence.

Lance, a 33-year-old divorcee, lived with his twelve-year-old daughter. He had recently become manager of his father's sheet metal business. For years he had collected motor cycle parts and rebuilt Triumphs and Harley Davidsons. His favourite bikes were Harleys, models built from 1939 to 1965. Among the Bandidos he was known as Mr Fix-it.

The barbeque in the backyard was makeshift, consisting of a pile of bricks. Clumps of grass sprouted up the driveway and a rusty wheelbarrow stood down by the back fence. A single blue towel and a pair of faded blue jeans hung on the washing line.

The first of the Bandidos had already arrived when Lance drove in in his Chevy truck just after noon. He had just picked up his daughter from her friend's house.

Graeme Wilkinson, the 1.91 metre Bandido known as Tiny, sat on the fence with his legs dangling.

Roach had driven Bull Campbell's stationwagon with four Campbell brothers—Bull, Shadow, Whack and Chopper—in the car. Snake, Pig and Opey had followed on bikes.

Snoddy arrived next. Then Caesar Campbell on his bike, and Davo resplendent with his trike. Knuckles' bike had broken down en route. They had had to abandon it at Caesar's local garage.

The weapons were in the cars. They were prepared for the worst. Chopper had a small hessian bag with two cue balls sitting in the bottom, Snoddy had his long machete-style knife. Big Tony, Sparksy and Caesar had baseball bats, Roach a pick handle. Bull had an iron bar. And there were the guns.

Bernie Podgorski was running late. He was sure he would have missed the boys by the time he arrived at Lance's. He had had an early Father's Day lunch with his wife and three-month-old daughter at his folks' home at Normanhurst.

Traffic banked up at Thornleigh and Podgorski found himself stuck in a stationary line of traffic, five kilometres long, Sunday picnickers out on a Father's Day drive.

By the time he reached Caesar's place, Donna told him they had already left. Podgorski left his wife and baby at Caesar's house. He jumped back in his car and sped off to Lance's place.

Turning into the driveway, Podgorski parked on Lance's front lawn. Leaving his club and chain in his car, he walked around to the back of the house.

Ray Denholm handed Podgorski a stubbie, and Caesar approached him as he took his first mouthful of cold beer. "You're a rover, mate," Caesar said.

"Aw yeah?" Podgorski looked up in surprise at the club's Sergeant-at-Arms.

"There's six or seven rovers, right? Look, we've had a discussion and certain blokes have got certain targets and the rovers are to bash anybody who is getting on top of our blokes."

Ray Denholm and Steve Hails, another nominee, were then sent to the Viking Tavern to check if the Comancheros had turned up. On their return, Hails said, "Walked around the carpark—couldn't see any sign of them."

"We'll go anyway to show other clubs we are not scared. If the Comancheros are there we will go ahead as planned," Snoddy said. "We'll show our colours and bash them."

"I hope the scumbags are there," Chopper muttered.

Bikes started up in the narrow driveway. "Get your bloody car outa the way, Bernie," Lance Wellington yelled. "I can't drive through it."

Podgorski pushed his car back a couple of feet. "That suit ya?"

The low roar of the bikes signified action. Roo and Big Tony went with Lance in his sidecar.

Outside in the street, Snoddy sat in his dirty white Falcon station wagon, a Bentley pump-action shotgun beside him.

Behind, in his white Holden station wagon, which was blowing soup-like grey smoke, was Stephen Robert, known as Bear. He had a pump-action shotgun on the floor under Tiny's feet.

Shadow sat in the seat of honour next to Snoddy. In the back were Lard and Lout.

"Wanna lift, Bernie? Jump in," Bear shouted to Podgorski. Bull started up his Holden, his adopted brother Chopper in the front seat beside him.

Bull's car led the eight bikes, carrying the rest of the men including Charlie Sciberras and Louie Cooper, down Pringle Avenue. Snoddy followed in his Holden. Then came Bear, his engine spluttering in complaint.

Their five-kilometre journey wound through non-descript residential streets and grey industrial areas.

The Bandidos were out in force.

8

The battle

Snoddy's car pulled up in front of the bikes when they reached Beaconsfield Street twenty minutes after the Comancheros' arrival. He signalled to Lance to slow down for the stragglers.

"Where is it?" Bull shouted.

"Just up the road to the left," Lance yelled back above the roar.

Roach spotted the Viking sign. Snoddy pulled into the carpark; Bull's car behind him. The bikes followed, Lance's first, slowing as it rose abruptly over the yellow striped speed hump.

The Comancheros were not prepared. The initial tension, heavy when they rode into the carpark, had eased. Jock, after prowling up and down the bitumen, agreed to a beer.

"Cunts aren't here," Dog said, stating the obvious after their reconnoitre. He had been wandering around the carpark with Snow.

A few Gypsy Jokers, Zeke, the Pres of the Fourth Reich, and a couple of Black Uhlans had been drinking on the hotel verandah, watching them.

"They've got to be joking," Paul from the Uhlans remarked after seeing the shotgun and baseball bat. "Who the fuck do they think they are?"

Jock was, in a sense, relieved. The Bandidos were too scared to show. When half an hour had passed and there was still no sign of the enemy, he relaxed. Foggy's ute was strategically parked at the entrance and he would keep a look out. He and Snow had the walkie-talkies. They would let him know if the enemy arrived.

Jock and JJ wandered around the back of the tavern. Jock's old rivals, the Mobshitters, had set up shop away from the crowd along the back fence.

From this position, the Supreme Commander of the Comancheros did not see the Bandidos ride into the carpark shortly before 2pm. His men were temporarily without a leader.

But some of Jock's men were prepared. Glen, Leroy, Snow, and Sparrow sprang to attention at the sound of the incoming Harleys. Foggy had left his ute and walked down to the hotel for a beer. The four had been sitting in

Glen's Cortina, which was parked in the centre of the carpark 30 metres from the entrance to the two hotel bars. Six Comanchero bikes were parked to the left of the Cortina. Sunshine's bike stood alone behind a Kingswood station wagon and trailer.

Snow stood up. "They're here," he whispered into his walkie talkie, but there was no reply. Foggy must have turned off his machine.

There was no time for any kind of bull horn ambush, no time to form a battle wedge as Jock had instructed them, no time to get ready. Snow hoped the others had seen the enemy arrive.

With his gun pointing at the bitumen, Sunshine moved off to the left of the others. He was closer to the hotel in front of a large clump of bushes, forming the left flank of the defence.

Kraut was still in the bar, drinking. Terry Parker was in the Public Bar toilets. His second bourbon and coke had made him more sick than drunk, although he had been drinking steadily for almost 24 hours. Alcohol had sustained him through the previous sleepless night. Old Morts stood beside him at the urinal.

Mike Langley was in the public bar talking when he heard the second throng of bikes enter the carpark. Instinct sent him outside. He pushed through the crowd and walked straight up to the Comancheros with shotguns, his heart pounding.

"What the fuck are you doing!" he screamed, but the men appeared transfixed. He followed their eyes, which were trained on the bikes riding in through the entrance.

Langley moved fast. He remembered the Sergeant-at-Arms was still at the bar. He turned, ran back to the door. He'll calm them down, he thought.

Snoddy saw the armed men who waited in a line beside Glen's car—familiar shapes through his mirror sunglasses—as he led his men down the driveway and turned right to the second parking lane at the western end of the carpark.

One line of cars separated them from the enemy. He swallowed. His mouth felt dry.

Behind him, Bull's brown Holden pulled up. The bikes fanned out behind, still in formation. Bear, whose white Holden had only just made the journey, parked his car on Beaconsfield Street ready for a push-start.

"Fuck, Snoddy, there's Commos out there and they've got guns!" Snoddy barely heard Lard. From the back seat, Lard reached for his pickhandle.

"The Commos are here, they've got guns!" Big Tony echoed from Lance's sidecar.

Snoddy reached under his seat and grabbed the club shotgun, the .22 pump-action Bentley.

Foggy was down near the public bar, out of position and weaponless, when he heard the bikes. Like Jock, he was caught unaware. The Bandidos had effectively cut him off from his weapon, his M1 carbine in the back seat of his black utility.

He had switched on the walkie-talkie too late to hear Snow's message. Static hissed back at him unsympathetically.

Within minutes of arriving, guns, sheath knives and iron bars of varying lengths were handed out from the Bandido cars. Big Tony had a baseball bat, Roach a pickhandle. The men moved down through the carpark.

It was Caesar, Zorba (George Kouratoras), the mountainous Greek, and Lance who formed the Bandido front line, picking their way through the parked cars and bikes, moving down swiftly to confront the armed men twelve metres away.

Bull—big and fearless—left his Holden carrying an iron bar. It was now or never. There was no more sniping at midnight or bashing in small groups, this time it was club against club, guns against guns. All out war.

Behind their front line, a second group of Comancheros waited, obscured from view. The eyes of the Bandidos were focused on their immediate opponents.

Snoddy remained at his car. He leant over its roof and trained the shotgun down the carpark, covering his men.

The only woman in the war was the first to break ranks. "Fucking Bandaids!" the thin woman in the black t-shirt yelled. Baseball bat and rubber truncheon in hand, she made towards the Bandidos.

"Get back here," Sunshine cautioned.

She held back, but not for long. "Cunts!" she screamed. But as the wave of Bandidos swept down the carpark, they pushed her aside and up on the bonnet of a parked car, forcing her to drop her weapons.

On the Comanchero front line, Leroy stood legs apart, his solid 103 kilo frame unflinching, a 12-gauge Bentley shotgun held across his powerful body.

"Put the fuckin' guns down and fight like men!" Zorba said, testing the feeling of the enemy.

"Let's sort this out without the guns," Lance shouted.

"Yeah, we'll sort it out," Leroy cocked his shotgun.

Caesar was moving towards Leroy when Sparrow stepped out from behind a car, blocking his path. He shoved the cold metallic barrel of a shotgun into Caesar's chest.

Face to face Caesar saw Sparrow's raw, frenzied excitement. Sparrow's skin was stretched taut over high cheekbones, his eyes were dark, and beads of perspiration appeared along his upper lip.

Caesar fought against his rising panic. He had to take control. He was aware of the others moving up from behind. He heard their voices.

"Put the fuckin' gun down, Sparrow," he said calmly.

Sparrow flinched. For a split second he wavered, but he kept the weapon pressed hard up against Caesar's chest.

Suddenly, without signal, the combat began. Like caged animals let loose, the two groups let fly at one another with fists, bats and iron bars.

Caesar grabbed Sparrow's gun, grappling for control. Moving up from behind, quietly and quickly, the way Jock had trained him, Snow pushed through and shoved Caesar in the chest with his shotgun.

Caesar heard the wooden bat slice the air before the blow sent him reeling.

It came from the left and the force threw him, spinning him away from the grasp of the two who held him.

Sparrow turned to tackle Zorba, pushing his gun into his soft, fleshy belly. "Put the gun down, you fuckin' idiot," Zorba said.

"Fuck off, turkey," Sparrow shouted.

As Caesar fell, Snow turned to Zorba and aimed the gun at his head. The woman moved up from behind and, holding the bat high with both hands, she brought it down across Zorba's back. "Fuck'n Bandaid prick!" she yelled.

The blow was ineffectual. Zorba turned swiftly and backhanded her across the face. She staggered back, but he lost his footing and Sparrow struck him in the stomach with the stock of his shotgun.

Gun still pointing skywards, Leroy's fingers closed on the trigger. The shot, the first in the battle, sounded like a warning, shattering all else. It was a signal.

Lance pounced on Snow forcing his gun into the ground, several shots firing as they struggled. Snow was no match for Lance's lightning karate strikes and within seconds Snow's face was a bloodied mess. He screamed in agony as Lance poked his left eye with two steel-like fingers.

As he stumbled, Caesar heard the explosion of gunfire through a blinding haze of pain. He realised men were going to die.

At the first sounds of gunfire a wave of panic swept through the crowd of people, sending them scattering in all directions, diving to the ground, crawling behind parked cars for shelter. One group surged towards the Public Bar for cover. Some stood at the windows, curious, unable to comprehend. Parents bundled children into cars. "Lie there, keep your heads down."

One man picked up his two-year-old niece and ran. As the shooting increased he threw the child under an old model Chevy and gave her an unopened can of beer to distract her. "Now you just keep your head down and see if you can mind uncle Stephen's can of beer, okay?"

Further down the carpark, a second lamb, abandoned, continued to turn on the spit.

Caesar shook his throbbing head and tried to correct his blurred vision. There were men moving all around him. He turned to his right. Snake, his brother, was sitting on the ground, his face contorted, his hands covered in blood, clutching at his stomach.

"Snake!" he yelled as he pushed Sparrow aside and made towards his younger brother.

He had run just three steps when the pellets entered his chest. He stumbled. He could see nothing but the vision of his brother's pained face. "Snake," he called a second time as he staggered, trying to reach him.

This time something hit him from behind. He fell to his knees and collapsed face down on the asphalt. He tasted blood as the pain intensified. He had no strength. He couldn't move. "Snake," he whispered as the black closed around him.

The Campbells had been gunned down in the first few minutes. Snake Campbell was shot in the abdomen as he left his bike at the top of the carpark. Whack Campbell, still up at Bull's car, got out of the rear passenger seat and was blasted through his right arm and his chest. He fell back down on the car seat, his feet sticking out of the back door.

"Christ, that's gunfire!" Eddie said to Joanne, "what the fuck's going on?"

"What are ya talking about?" Joanne asked, swaying on her feet, too drunk to panic.

"Get down, Jo, for Chrissakes!" he said diving to the ground.

A metre-high shrub beside Joanne snapped in half and a bullet bounced off Jethro's car door.

"Fuck, they're real bullets!" she said, instantly sober, crashing to the ground.

As the shooting started, Linda Motton looked up from her Agatha Christie book and saw a Bandido pointing his weapon in her direction. His third shot smashed the windscreen, the glass turning white. The slug, narrowly missing her, became embedded in the parcel shelf behind her.

Slivers of glass and lead pierced her face, arms and legs. Tiny red spots of blood formed on her arms and t-shirt, except for a neat rectangular patch across her breasts, where she had rested her novel.

The blood frightened her. She fell down across the seat of the Fairlane, paralysed with fear.

"Are you okay?" her boyfriend called as she slithered out of the front seat half on her stomach and made her way to the back of the car.

As the shooting died down, she realised the fright had loosened her bowels.

Edging carefully along the cars, she crept towards the incinerator at the back fence. But two men had beaten her to it. She caught a glimpse of their naked bottoms as they crouched near the fence.

Shadow was the next Campbell to be hit. He had moved quickly down through the centre of the battle, dodging bullets, Snoddy's Smith and Wesson shotgun by his side. He took cover behind a station wagon. It was from this point he had aimed at the Comanchero line behind Glen's car but missed, some of his pellets hitting the windscreen of the car where Linda Motton sat.

He was struck in the throat by a shotgun pellet, and, clutching the wound, he stood up and stumbled ahead several steps before he fell, blood oozing through his fingers.

Sparrow died almost where he stood, shotgun pellets spattering his right shoulder and upper chest close to his heart. Two pellets left holes on the right side of his face. He fell face down, a baseball bat underneath his groin.

Not all of the men had guns. Those accustomed to wielding the blunt instruments of normal bikie warfare used them with force. Tonka was set upon by a group of Bandidos. Davo, hitting him from the left, made a jagged gash down the side of his face. An iron bar came down across his arm and he fell to the ground. Curled up in a foetal ball, he felt the boots as they kicked his head and ribs.

Chopper was alone. Like Shadow he moved quickly, crouching behind a station wagon parked near bushes close to the Tavern. He was carrying Snoddy's .357 Magnum Rossi repeating rifle.

He caught sight of Foggy's sallow figure as he skulked down, making his way around the back of the fight. Fucking traitor. Chopper felt rage and hatred as he took aim at Jock's right-hand man. He was an easy target crossing between the two bushes, exposed on the bare bitumen. Chopper took aim and fired. As the bullet exploded through Foggy's body it struck and damaged one of the two M1 carbine magazines he had strapped to his waist.

He doubled over clutching his stomach, the bullet fracturing his ribs, severing the major arteries to his heart. He stumbled, dropped the walkie-talkie, and was propelled a few final steps by the sheer force of the bullet, which had killed him instantly.

Leroy was next, a sitting duck from behind. Chopper aimed, the stock in at the shoulder, left hand along the weapon, head to one side.

The bullet entered Leroy's back passing straight through his heart, leaving a neat one centimetre hole, exiting almost exactly in the centre of his chest. A litre of blood flooded his lungs almost instantly.

He fell heavily on top of Littlejohn, who was crouched beside him, dodging gunfire behind a car. Before he could do or say anything, Littlejohn was struck viciously across the head and he fell over the body of his dead comrade. He was punched continuously as he slipped into semi-consciousness.

Leanne Walters had been outside the hotel with Shifty, sipping her second vodka and orange when she saw a gunman with a Comanchero patch close to Glen Eaves' car.

"Look out, Shifty. He's got a gun," she reached over and pushed Shifty in the chest.

But the bullet which hit Leanne came from the top of the carpark, splintering the trunk of a nearby shrub before it hit her. There was no warning, just a faint whistle as it tore through the plant, its force lessened only slightly. It struck her on the chin, ripping her face open below the mouth, leaving the teeth in her upper jaw perfectly intact. The force sent her backwards through the air, lifting her up and throwing her to the ground like a battered mannequin. The bullet lodged itself in her right collarbone.

Blood and pieces of her flesh splattered Shifty's shirt before he hit the ground beside her. He saw her body twitch. He grabbed her arm and felt for a pulse. It was faint, and then it was gone.

Chopper had no idea he had hit the girl. He had been aiming for Sunshine. He fired again and Sunshine fell backwards, his shotgun clattering to the ground. Blood filled his eye and marred his vision. He ducked behind the car that had been his cover and wiped the blood from his eye. He waited 30 seconds and crawled to the front of the car, stood up and took aim. Blood dripped from his face onto the shiny red duco.

He fired twice at Chopper, peppering him with pellets. Eight struck his left side, several entered his heart, one pellet entering just below the left nipple, perforating his aorta. Two more left large circular holes on the arms of the Mexican Bandit he had tattooed on his chest.

Six of the pellets exploded out of his back leaving two tears in the tattooed woman who smiled like a genie, one breast exposed, the words "Black Magic" encircling her and the tattoist's trademark "By Jenny 1972". Two lodged inside his leather vest. He fell on his stomach, dying as blood flooded his chest cavities. Next to his right arm lay two spent cartridges from the weapon that had just killed three people.

The Bandidos retreated behind Bull's Holden, which became a shelter for the wounded. Those who were able offered basic medical help.

Roach was at the back of the car trying to push Whack inside.

Through the front window he saw Sunshine and Glen Eaves, guns trained on the car.

Charlie Scibberas called "Get down!" just as Lance reached the car.

Roach dived in the car on top of Whack, who moaned under the pressure. "It's all right mate, just lie still. We'll get you some help in a minute." Whack winced with pain and Roach smelt his blood.

Gunshots exploded above their heads as they lay pressed together on the car seat. Glass from the left cargo window showered them.

Pellets came over the top of the car and hit Lance Wellington in the forehead, the force throwing him back to the ground.

"Are you okay?" Roach crawled backwards out of the car over to Lance.

It was time to get the wounded out.

Snake was dragged up to the bushes, Charlie and Louie each taking a leg. Lance, bleeding from the superficial wound on his forehead, grabbed the shoulders of Snake's leather vest. They did it in stages, stopping at the bushes to wait for a break in the gunfire. They made it to the footpath on Beaconsfield Street, laying Snake on the grass next to the gutter.

Shadow was next. Roo and Ray laid him on his back next to his brother.

Shadow's shirt was bloodsoaked and in tatters. He was bleeding badly from his chest and neck, the blood matting his unkempt beard. His pupils were large jet-black circles, his eyes open in suprise. He was trying to breathe, but he was drowning, drowning in his own blood.

Lance turned him on his side, scooping blood from his mouth, clearing his nose. With his fingers in his mouth, he kept Shadow's tongue clear of his airways.

"Please breathe, keep breathing," he whispered.

A shotgun pellet had entered just above Shadow's larynx, cutting off his main airway. "Someone get an ambulance!" Lance Wellington felt his helplessness. "Where's a fuckin' ambulance?"

Less than five minutes had passed since the first shot was fired and six bodies lay dead in and around the carpark. The shooting continued, sporadic cracks sounding through the air. Behind the mustard Corona, the Comancheros crouched to reload.

Some of the Bandidos had broken through the Comanchero lines. Pig tackled Glen Eaves front-on, armed with a water pipe. Glen had been aiming his shotgun at Bull's car when Pig confronted him.

"Put it down, you bastard."

"Don't come closer. I'm warning you." Glen held the gun high, aimed at Pig's chest.

Pig stood still. "I said put it down."

Glen slowly lowered the gun, but stopped when it lined up with Pig's knee. He pulled the trigger. Pig's knee exploded and he fell without a scream, the pain numbing his senses. He crawled across to where his lead pipe lay, and used it to swipe at Tonka, who lay prostrate on the ground. Then he was hit himself by a woman, once on the back of the head and as he turned, across the bridge of his nose.

The Comancheros were using Glen's Cortina for shelter and treating the wounded. Tonka crawled to this refuge after the second attack and lay with his head on Snow's lap. Blood poured from a gash to his head, his left eye was closed and swollen.

Glen used the Cortina to reload, moving between his car and a Toyota Corona.

His energy was boundless, as he loaded and reloaded.

"Close the bar!" Mike Langley yelled to the bar staff as the shooting outside showed no signs of abating. "Quick, out the back!"

He ran into the office and pressed the alarm button which rang automatically at Revesby police station. He dialled the number and it answered immediately.

"There's shooting, bikies with guns. Hurry!"

Jethro started putting the money from the tills into the safe. Everywhere around him people stampeded, screaming, running into the hotel from the carpark. At first, he thought he had heard a Harley backfiring, but then as the crowd panicked he realised only too well that it was gunfire.

He locked the tills. "Get inside, you'll get hurt!" he yelled to the crowd.

"Go on, Deirdre," he said to Mike Langley's pregnant wife. "I'll do this. You go and hide. It's not safe."

Deirdre relinquished her task of unloading the tills. Jethro then locked the doors.

Inside the Norseman Bar "The Blues Brothers" movie was still running on the colour television.

It was into this bar that Kraut staggered, blood spurting from his arm which had been blasted open by a shotgun at close range. A flap of skin dangled from the soft fleshy part of his lower forearm; the blast had almost severed it from the elbow. "Jesus, somebody help me . . .my arm, ahh fuck . . .help . . ."

"Look out he's got a gun!" someone yelled.

Crying women gathered their children close, forcing some of them behind the sweet machines over by the door. A man threw himself over the bar, frogleaping across, scattering trays of glasses as he went.

Kraut staggered forward and fell between two pool tables. "Help me, get a doctor, help me," he was hysterical with shock.

Edward Nielson, a Black Uhlan, stood nearby. Kraut tried to grasp his leg, a pathetic gesture, as he pleaded.

"Get fucked. It's your own fight," Nielson said.

A man and woman came forward from the crowd after they ascertained the man in the black leather vest did not have a gun. The crowd watched, drawn by the strange spectacle of the felled bikie flailing on the floor.

Someone at the bar handed the man a long towel used to catch the beer drips on the bar. The woman got some iced water. Between them they attempted to stem the flow of blood.

The family who lived in the house next door to the Tavern, on the side where Foggy had parked his ute, were having a barbeque in their backyard for Father's Day. It was a large family gathering. Tony, the 23-year-old son, had nicked into the bottle shop to buy a cask of white wine and had returned, placing his purchase on the table outside when they heard the first sound of gunfire.

They thought it was a car backfiring, but the sound had not ceased, and a few minutes later the first head appeared above their high fence, which backed on to the carpark.

People frantic with fear, began clawing their way over the fence, pushing and shoving each other in their bid for safety, collapsing into the backyard where the family was gathered.

At first, Tony expected the gunmen to appear at the fence in hot pursuit.

"There's some guy on the ground being bashed with a baseball bat,"

Tony's brother-in-law called from the barbeque, where, peering over the fence, he had a good view of the carpark.

Tony's wife shepherded two women who had escaped into the yard into the house, along with their two children. She had found one of the women hiding petrified in the garage.

Tony had helped his brother-in-law get his invalid father into the house, pushing him through the increasing number of people who filled the backyard. The fish continued to smoulder on the barbeque.

Tony's wife dialled the emergency number. The woman who answered seemed to think it was a hoax. "How many dead?" she kept plying her with questions. In the end Tony came to the phone. "All right. I will put a report in," the woman conceded.

Up on Beaconsfield Street, Pig had been dragged to Bear's Holden by Gloves McElwaine. Davo was bleeding from a stab wound in his chest and had shotgun wounds to his head. Others bled from superficial grazes. Fourteen men crouched at the side of the car sheltering from the rage of bullets.

The two leaders, meanwhile, had taken back row seats in the battle. Snoddy had stayed with his car, only leaving it to help with the wounded. He shouted instructions to his men: " Stay down. They're coming back up the car park," and so on.

Jock, delayed behind the Tavern when the shooting broke out, had left his battle charge until almost the end.

As he came around the corner of the hotel, the gunfire was raging. He saw bodies falling, unsure whether they had been struck by gunfire or whether they were diving for cover. All his hopes for a strategic attack dissolved immediately. Everything was out of control.

If only the Bandidos had been there first, he would have had a better chance. He would have formed a wedge and led his men directly into the battle. It would have been a hard one, but he would have had a fighting chance.

Crouching low, he ran quickly across to Glen's car. As he ran, he heard bullets shave a clump of trees to his left. From the shelter of the car he glanced back across and saw the body of a girl, lying motionless near the trees he had just skirted.

In front were the men he hated, the men who had defied him, defiled the name Comanchero. He charged, holding his machete, with the words "Bandaid Hair Parter" on the blade, high above his head.

"Kill 'em, kill 'em!" he yelled, running into the line of fire, striking wildly in the air.

He lunged first at Bobby Watkin, the diminutive quiet Bandido who had recently got his colours. Turning in fright, Watkin stumbled down between two parked bikes. The blade narrowly missed him, wedged as he was between the two Harleys.

But Jock lost interest in this piddling trophy. Charlie Sciberras was running towards him. Jock struck and missed again and Charlie, seeing the crazed eyes behind the thick glasses, ran for his life. Lard came up behind Jock, swung at him with his baseball bat, and missed.

"Get him! Get him . . ." Jock yelled to a Comanchero gunman. Lard saw the gun pointed at him and ran, back towards the pub.

As he neared the building he felt the pellets enter his foot. He stumbled. His old work boots had protected his foot from being blown off. He sobbed with pain. Using his pick handle as a walking stick he hobbled his way up towards the Bandido lines.

The shooting, which had seemed to abate for a few moments, started up again.

Jock was isolated in the centre of the furore, just where his enemy wanted him, when the shotgun pellets entered the left side of his head and face, penetrating his brain, shattering his teeth. A second blast exploded in his chest and he could no longer breathe.

He collapsed to the ground. Lying face down, he was attacked viciously with a baseball bat.

In the distance he could see Glen Eaves crouched near his car. He closed his eyes and surrendered to the pain.

Several people had collected around Leanne Walters' body, some drawn by a morbid fascination, others making a bid to help.

Eddie from the British Motorcycle Club had seen her fall. "They've wasted the girl," he screamed, running towards her. "They've fucking killed her!"

As he reached Leanne's body, he saw her still twitching. "Julie, Julie!" he screamed.

Several BMC members tried to calm him, struggling physically with him, to contain his panic.

Eddie's wife Julie, a nurse's aide, felt for Leanne's pulse. The girl was dead. Julie found a hessian bag and placed it over Leanne's face, covering the hideous wound from curious eyes.

The gunmen were oblivious to the results of their rampage. Behind the Comanchero line, Old Morts, dressed in his black t-shirt with "Fuckin' juicy cunts" emblazoned across his chest, stood behind a Holden panel van directing the Comancheros' movements like a conductor leading his orchestra. A knife was hanging from the back of his belt. "Watch out behind you . . . Look out to your left . . ."

"How long is this going to go on for?" a woman called Jeannie McLaughlin surprised Morts, approaching him suddenly in the midst of the battle.

"I'm not quite sure," Morts replied with an air of a police officer dealing with a distressed member of the public.

"Shut your eyes and don't look," he advised.

Harry Ollerenshaw, Jeannie's fiancée, had been separated from her when the shooting broke out. Defying her wishes to leave, after they had both spotted the weaponry on the newly arrived bikes, he had left her with his Triumph 750 at the eastern side of the carpark. He was just about to buy a lamb sandwich when he heard the first crack of gunfire.

As he ran back across to Jeannie, crouching and weaving in and out of the parked cars along the fence, behind Comanchero lines, he saw Dog, whom he recognised as an ex-member of the British Motorcycle Club.

Dog had walked into a circle of three Bandidos who were beating John Bodt, a thin gangly Comanchero with thick matted blond hair. The men were planting their blows as if in a ritual, and Dog moved in to help Bodt.

As if in slow motion, Harry Ollerenshaw saw Dog double over and clutch his stomach after being shot at point blank range. Dog fell face down.

The pellets had entered his skull, causing a haemhorrage to his brain. Others entered his lungs, flooding them with blood. He died with his eyes open and staring, a slightly shocked expression on his face. The blood welled up on the right side of his face, covering the holes left by the shotgun pellets.

At the same moment Harry recognised Dog, he felt the pain on the side of his face. He had been shot, the pellet lodged in his left cheek. He rolled under a four-wheel-drive parked beside him, then crawled along under more parked cars until he reached the end of the carpark. He passed Linda Motton as her windscreen exploded.

"Jeannie. Jeannie!"

Then he heard Old Morts shouting. "Stay down. They're coming up behind you. Look out for that bloke."

Harry reached Jeannie and they crouched behind some bikes for cover.

Then, almost as unnerving as the gunfire, an eerie silence.

The shooting had petered out. Snoddy revved up his Holden and drove towards the bottle shop. At the same time Deirdre Langley noticed the bottle shop doors were open.

"Get down, they have got guns, everybody move back to the foyer," she yelled at the small groups clustered around the bar windows, mesmerised by the drama.

She ducked into the bottle shop. Deirdre Langley might have been pregnant and feeling a little vulnerable but she was not a lady who was accustomed to taking cheek.

As Snoddy's car approached, she pulled the roller doors down on the bonnet of his car. "No, we are closed," she said in a matter of fact voice. "There's guns," she added.

Snodgrass lifted his gun. It was a few centimetres away from her chest. "Open the fuckin' door or I'll blow your fuckin' head off."

"Okay." Deirdre remained cool. "But there are two bolts on either side of the door and I have to open them."

As she lifted the doors Snodgrass steered his car inside. As Deirdre pulled the doors down, she saw three men heading for the bottle shop, after their prey. She undid both bolts from the rear door, at the same time looking carefully at the man in the driver's seat.

He looked scared and his hair had not been brushed for a long time, she noted almost absent-mindedly.

He followed her movements with his gun, but as she released the second bolt, he lowered the weapon and put the car into first gear. She managed to lift the doors half way up as he sped under them and was away in the direction of Beaconsfield Street. But Snoddy did not get far. He stopped near Bear's car and joined his men on the footpath.

Joanne Caestro was sheltering behind the car when the woman limped towards them, holding her leg. At first Joanne thought she was an innocent who had been hurt in the fighting, but when she saw the woman's attentive audience of men, also behind the car, Joanne guessed who she was.

"Yeah, our President's copped all these bullets, the fuckin' Bandaids . . ." the woman was saying as the men around the car looked at her with hero worship in their drunken faces.

"So, you're involved in all this, eh?" one said. "Wanna beer?" he continued, much to Joanne's disgust.

"Look, just fuck off," Joanne cut in, glaring at her.

JJ appeared. "Go and get the car and the guns," he said to the woman.

He handed her a $20 note and she turned and left. JJ ran back towards the centre of the car park.

Joanne looked at the men around her. "Well, if you give her a fuckin' beer, you'd better give me one," she said.

Bull's Holden was the second car to leave the carpark. He had decided to get help for his brother Whack.

He picked up a gun, little realising the last person to hold it was his brother Shadow. Holding it by the barrel, he waved it above his head.

"Stop your shooting," he yelled. "Let me get my brother out of here. He's bleeding to death!"

He looked down the carpark and saw Sunshine and Glen Eaves stand up. "Get him out, we won't shoot," Sunshine yelled, his shotgun lowered to his side.

Roach drove. Bull pointed the gun out of the passenger window, the stock first, a symbol of truce.

"You fucking deadshits. Move your fucking bikes. He's shot bad. I'll fucking run over them if you don't move!" Bull shouted to a group of onlookers. People screamed, seeing the gun at such close range, fearing another outbreak of shooting. One man obliged, moving his car out of the way.

But the worst for Bull was yet to come. Driving along Beaconsfield Street, he and Roach saw the group of Bandidos sheltering beside Bear's car. Bull was out first, running to the prone figure on the footpath. "Noooooo!" he screamed. "Shadow!"

He collapsed on the ground beside him, cradling his brother's head, willing life back into him.

Down near Glen's car, Terry Parker lay over Jock's still body, weeping. When he and Morts ran out of the hotel after the shooting had started, the first thing he had seen was Leroy's dead body. His mind was dulled by alcohol, he couldn't understand. Leroy was his best friend, and he was dead. He sat there for a few minutes, then turned away and walked further up the carpark. He stumbled on Dog, and saw he was dead also.

His mouth was dry and he felt sick. It was like a bad dream. He was totally oblivious to the tatty little war as he walked slowly towards Glen's car. The car was something real, something concrete. There would be someone there to help. Before he reached the vehicle, he saw Jock's bleeding, battered body. He crouched down beside his leader and gently touched the face with his hand. Parker's numbness dissolved. "Don't die," he sobbed. The tears flowed freely as he wept for Leroy, Dog, and Jock.

Bernie Podgorski waited till the shooting stopped and ran up towards the footpath. A Bandido called Steve Owens—Hookie to his brothers—was dragging Caesar across the road. Podgorski ran over to help. Caesar was bleeding heavily from his chest and head.

Lout had spotted a woman he knew, driving a car that had pulled up in Beaconsfield Street and parked near Bear's car. Her name was Suzanne Worn. She and the passenger, Debbie Harvey, had decided that morning to go to the swap meet.

"He needs to go to hospital real bad," Lout said. Worn agreed to drive them.

Podgorski struggled with Caesar's deadweight body, pushing him into the back seat. Lout opened the front passenger door and sat next to the two girls.

"What happened?" Suzanne broke the tension.

"He's been shot."

"How come?"

"They've been shooting us," Lout blurted out.

"They are trying to kill us!" Podgorski and Hookie also answered from the back seat.

"Who?" Suzanne was confused.

"The Comancheros."

Caesar, slumped on Podgorski's shoulder, moaned. Suzanne did not ask any further questions. Debbie directed her to Bankstown Hospital.

All eyes turned as the three bikies and two girls carried Caesar into the ward and sat him in a chair.

"Excuse me, excuse me—wait!" a nursing sister came out from behind the reception area. Lout, Podgorski, Hookie and the two girls were heading for the door.

"Who is this man? Aren't you going to stay with him?"

"We gotta go . . ."

Podgorski took a last look at Caesar and ran out through the doors.

Suzanne and Debbie dropped two of the men at Lance Wellington's house and one at an address in Arncliffe. Then they drove back to the hotel.

Lance Wellington saw the white patrol car coming along Beaconsfield Street. "The pigs have arrived, Snoddy," he said.

"Put your guns down!" Snoddy yelled, waving a shotgun above his head. "It's over. It's over."

9

The aftermath

Detective Inspector Ron Stephenson finished his soda water and put down the remains of his t-bone steak. At 53 his trim figure was in part due to his careful diet. His age was difficult to pinpoint. Laughter lines had left their mark around his eyes and his dark hair, peppered with grey, was receding.

Soda water had become his drink since he had undergone open heart surgery three years previously. "Take it easy," he had been told by the surgeons.

"Very nice Louise," he said to his daughter as they sat by the barbeque in the warm lunchtime sun.

He looked at his wrist watch—2pm. He turned on his pager. Father's Day. He was on duty as the officer in charge of the regional crime squad south. After 36 years in the force he held the position of duty inspector.

The high pitched beep sounded almost immediately. Stephenson rang the communications branch. His orders were to go straight to Milperra.

"Got to go, love, business calls. I don't know what it is but it sounds big," he said to his wife Gloria.

Changing from his brown shorts and open-necked shirt into long pants and blazer, he made a rueful discovery.

"Sorry, Pete," he said to his son-in-law. "You wouldn't happen to have a belt I could borrow would you?"

Pete obliged. Although not a big waisted man, the 30-inch belt only just met around him. Holding in his breath, he joked, "Don't know how long I can keep this up, Pete."

"Take care," Gloria said kissing him goodbye.

It was a 20 minute drive to Milperra from Bonnet Bay, through Woronora and the newer suburb of Menai. As he turned the green unmarked Ford Falcon left into Beaconsfield Street, the spectacle made him slow down to a crawl.

The battle had drawn spectators like bees to a honey pot. They stood silently, craning to see the horror of it all. Several people were standing on the bonnets of cars to get a better view.

As Stephenson approached, he noticed several bodies on the ground.

But it was the gun scabbards on motor bikes which shocked him more than the corpses: shotguns, rifles, bats—savage weapons, artillery now being salvaged from the carpark by police.

Inside the carpark, tension was high. Both sides protected their wounded while attempting to assess the enemy's position.

Crouched behind the transit van where she and David Irving had sheltered after their windscreen shattered, Linda Motton took a small instamatic Minolta camera out of her handbag. "I'm not going to let those bastards get away with it. There are people here with kids—anyone could have been killed, the kids could have died . . ." Though her fingers were trembling, she focused on the armed men in front of her. She shot six frames, one from underneath the transit van, another from inside the driver's seat looking out.

She photographed Glen Eaves, gun in hand behind his Cortina. She watched as he laid the gun behind the car. Still in shock, she had not even noticed the fine slivers of glass from the windscreen embedded in her face.

Ambulance 601 had been returning from Liverpool mortuary when the call came over the ambulance radio. It was 14.01, six minutes since the first bullet was fired in the carpark.

"Person or persons shot. 601 proceed to Milperra, the Viking Tavern Beaconsfield Street."

"Christ, what the hell's been happening here?" ambulanceman Colin Burton said as he and his colleague neared the carpark. Muffled sounds of gunfire from deep within the carpark could still be heard.

"The ambos are here!" came a shout from outside.

As the two officers jumped down onto the roadway, a thin, dark-haired bikie approached. "Can youse come and check out one of our brothers? He's dead I think, but don't tell his brother Bull—or he'll go troppo."

"Right oh mate, where is he?"

Roach led the officer over to the two bodies on the footpath.

"Have a look at Shadow first," Bull strode up to them, his bulky frame and anguished eyes were menacing.

"Okay, mate, sure."

The men in leather parted silently. 31-year-old Burton, a probationary ambulance officer, went through the motions, placing an airway tube down his throat and oxygen suction over his face. In all his training he had never seen a bullet wound and he was surprised that the single wound to the throat, underneath the bushy beard, was not as severe as he had imagined.

There was a lot of blood though. He looked up at the faces hovering above, circling him.

"I'm sorry fellas, there's nothing more I can do. He's dead."

"Nooooooohhhh!!!!" Bull screamed.

As Burton placed a white cotton blanket over the body, Bull fell to his knees. Cradling Shadow's head, he laid his head across his brother's back. Closing his eyes, he stayed there for more than an hour, oblivious to everything around him.

Sunshine was being observed by a macroscopic eye from above. His every movement was monitored as he moved around his appointed spot in front of the hotel, shotgun held in both hands at waist level, pointing towards Beaconsfield Street. Moving the barrel in an arc from left to right, like a professional troubleshooter, he walked slowly across the carpark.

High above him, Constable Southey, wedged in the back seat of Polair 2, the police helicopter, watched him through binoculars. "Brown, looks like flannelette shirt, blue jeans, rifle in hand . . .moving in a southerly direction . . ." he relayed his observations to Constable Kohlagan, who sat in the front seat speaking into the police radio. The presence of the helicopter above the carpark at that time was something of a fluke. Polair 2 had been flying on its way to a public relations exercise at Bankstown.

Sunshine moved closer to Foggy's body and stood, shotgun still in hand, looking sombrely at the prone figure. Then keeping to much the same area he had patrolled during the battle, he moved down towards the rear of the carpark, near an old brown Holden station wagon.

Hugging the shotgun into his shoulder, his left hand steadied the barrel ready to fire up the carpark. Then three Comancheros joined him from behind a mustard Toyota Corona. Leaving his rifle on the roof of the Holden, the lone battler, as he appeared to Southey, walked across to the remainder of the men crouched behind the Toyota. Another Commanchero took over the shotgun, still training the barrel up towards the Bandidos.

"A number of people injured behind a yellow Toyota sedan . . ." Constable Kohlagan repeated the observations to the police radio operator at VKG. And later: "One police truck in attendance parked to the east of the carpark in Beaconsfield Street."

Southey watched the white caps of the ambulance officers, tiny figures near the entrance to the carpark . Then he saw the detective approach Sunshine.

Detective John Garvey and a uniformed officer had been ordered to move people out of the hotel through the bottle shop. As he pushed through the crowd people grabbed him, pulling at his jumper, shouting things about men with guns and rifles. He forced his way through the saloon bar and into the carpark, unaware he had walked into the centre of the battlefield.

"You're not coming in here with that fuckin' thing!"

Sunshine's gruff warning startled Garvey, the voice penetrating the stillness of the carpark. The detective turned and saw the tall, dark-haired gunman standing by the back fence, a shotgun trained in his direction. He was agitated, tense and ready to react to the slightest provocation. The left side of his face was covered in blood, his left eye closed, shotgun wounds on his cheek and forehead.

"I'm from the police. The blue's over. I don't want any trouble, I just want to help," Garvey shouted back.

"I don't care. You're not coming in here with a fuckin' gun!"

"Okay, mate, I won't, but I want you to put your gun down so we can help." Garvey kept the gun down by his side.

"The ambulance men won't come in until everyone's unarmed. I want you to give me that shotgun and any others you have," Garvey continued, his voice even-toned.

Sunshine said nothing. He watched as Garvey placed his SWOS shotgun on the ground, slightly behind him, near the uniformed officer who had followed him in. Garvey raised his hands above his head.

"I'll have to talk to the others," Sunshine said. He walked over to Glen's car. "The cops are here at the back of the hotel. They won't come in until all the weapons are handed over. What do we do?" he said to Snow, Morts and Tonka, who sat crouched behind the car.

"What about them?" Sunshine waved his gun in the direction of the Bandidos. "They've still got their weapons."

"Just give 'em the guns and get help in here fuckin' quick!" Snow, his head still bloodied, snapped back.

Ambulance officer Brian Everett radioed for help. "601 to 2KJ . . .we've got approximately six or seven deceased, and twenty to thirty injured, I'd say at least ten stretcher cases . . ." As he spoke, the second ambulance arrived, followed closely by a paramedic van.

Colin Burton picked up his first aid kit and oxyviver and moved over to Snake. He could see he had been shot in the abdomen, a cursory examination showed the wounds weren't serious, just messy.

Fred Fraser was in the second ambulance. The depression and gloom he had felt earlier as a lone parent on Father's Day, and thoughts of his unfinished coffee back at Bankstown station had vanished.

He saw Lard first, a pick handle for a crutch, wincing with each step,

Roach's bloodsoaked t-shirt a temporary tourniquet around his foot. Fraser helped him over to the area in front of the petrol station. "Here, mate. Sit down and we'll take a look at your foot." Lard sat in the gutter. His heavy black boot was pockmarked from shotgun pellets, and he'd lost a lot of blood.

Paul Vassallo, Fraser's partner, joined him, breathless, minutes later. "Brian says there's a about six deceased, but they're not quite sure. We're waiting for the all clear from police to go into the carpark," he whispered quietly to his senior officer.

Snow dragged himself over to the Corona, blood dribbling into his eye. He grabbed two guns off the ground from behind the car and passed them to Sunshine. Old Morts picked up two more firearms and went over to Glen, who was crouched by his car clutching a double- barrelled shotgun. "Can I have your gun now, Glen?" Morts reached down and placed his hand on the barrel. Glen pulled away, resisting. "Come on, son, they're all gone now. You can't get anyone now, give me the gun."

Reluctantly, Glen surrendered.

Sunshine and Morts walked over to Garvey, who took the weapons and passed them to a uniformed officer. "Are there any others?"

"Nah."

Taking out his detective's badge and with hands above his head, Garvey walked in behind the Comanchero line. He could see three more dead bodies, but no more weapons. He turned to the top of the carpark waving his hands in the air.

"Come in, come in!" he yelled.

After Sunshine's surrender, tension in the carpark eased considerably. Harry Ollerenshaw had seen the police helicopter as he crouched in a gully with his fiancée Jeannie. His cheek throbbed painfully from the shotgun injury he had received at the height of the battle.

"There's the cops," he signalled to Jeannie. "We're getting out of here."

Taking her hand, they ran across to his motor bike. He released the brake and kicked it from its stand. Freewheeling it, he pushed it on to Beaconsfield Street, where he was immediately searched by a uniformed constable, requesting identification.

"So that's the closest hospital, eh?" Ollerenshaw conferred with the constable.

"Yeah, Bankstown would be your best bet, mate."

Within ten minutes six ambulances, including two intensive care cars, had arrived. Crowds inside the bars trickled outside and stood watching.

"Are you all right?" an ambulance officer asked Linda Motton as she sat on top of a trailer. "Yeah, thanks," Linda said, thinking, "There's no way I'm getting into an ambulance with any of them".

"They're asking for ID," David said to her. "My licence has expired," he whispered.

"Well all I've got is me shooter's licence," Linda answered. "Let's give our names to one of the cops."

Sunshine walked over to the public bar and went straight to the red phone near the doorway. He fumbled in his pocket for loose change, dialled and turned to the wall, the earpiece hooked under his bloodied chin.

"Yes, it's Ray. There's been a bit of trouble and I just wanted to tell you I won't be home for tea tonight . . ."

Old Morts had discovered his leader lying face down in a pool of blood, his head almost under a car. Lifting Jock's head, he cleared his airways. "Jock's dying," Terry Parker said from behind. He was crying openly.

"Fuck, get the ambulances in here. Hurry up. Men are dying!" Morts yelled at the crowd at the verandah.

Snow saw Terry weeping and muttering to himself as he leaned over Leroy's lifeless body.

"For fuck's sake, Terry, get away from the dead bodies, keep out of the way," Snow yelled.

Outside on the footpath the number of onlookers had doubled. Red and white bunting blocked off both ends of Beaconsfield Street.

"It's a siege," one man said to another. "Don't know how many dead, but they say half a dozen."

Glen Eaves walked up to where the body of the young girl lay after he learned she had been killed.

There were three or four Rebels standing near her. He approached one of them.

"Hey, mate, I'm sorry about the girl," he ventured.

"Bein' sorry isn't fuckin' gonna bring her back, is it," the bikie replied savagely.

"Well, fuck you then," snarled Glen. "I was only tryin' to sympathise. We didn't kill her. Go and see those fuckin' dogs at the top of the carpark . . ."

Bruce Miller, the *Sydney Morning Herald* photographer, arrived at 2.50pm. The *Herald* car had been on its way to cover a soccer match at

Liverpool when it was diverted to Milperra. To most of the media, alerted shortly after the shooting by the police radio, the story seemed far-fetched, particularly for such a quiet Sunday.

Sneaking through the official tape, Miller crouched down, and using his zoom lense, he photographed Bull and his dead brother Shadow. Bull, lying half over Shadow's body, did not even open his eyes at the sound of the motor drive. Seven frames of his image were recorded by the camera.

Miller clicked opened the back of the camera and deposited the film in his sock as a precaution.

"If any of those fuckin' pictures appear anywhere we'll kill you," a Bandido yelled from the service station. "Fuckin' blow your brains out," one waved his fists to make good his threat.

"Get back behind those lines," a police officer yelled at the recalcitrant photographer. "Wait there with the rest of the media."

Detective Darryl Wilson heard the shouting and saw a man crouched on the road, several Bandidos over him, some still trying to hit him. He hurried over to see what the commotion was all about.

"Hey come on, that's enough," he said. I'm Detective Wilson and this is Detective Peter Whalan. Leave this man alone," he ordered. "Who's in charge here?" he asked.

Snoddy pushed through to the front of his men. "I'm Snodgrass, the President."

"Well tell your men to leave this man alone."

"He's just a drunken fuckin' trouble maker," Snoddy snapped back. "Get rid of him or we'll flog the cunt. He's fuckin' drunk and he's annoying us!"

"Can you tell me what happened here today?" Wilson asked.

"Yeah, we come to fight with our fists like men and these cunts were waiting with weapons, so we took their fuckin' guns . . . and . . ."

"Okay—now slow down—before you say anything more," Wilson tried to calm him. "I want you to clearly understand that you're not obliged to say anything and anything you say can be later used in evidence. Do you understand?"

"Yeah. It's war," Snoddy went on, "real war, too. That Scottish cunt, Jock, he caused all this."

"Where's this man Jock now?" Wilson asked.

"He's the Comancheros' leader. He's down there full of fuckin' holes." Snoddy waved his hand towards the middle of the carpark.

"There's a really badly injured man in the bar, behind the pool table. It looks like his arm's nearly cut off," a woman told the ambulance officer, pointing over to the public bar doors.

As Fraser stood at the open doors, stretcher behind him, he was confronted by what seemed like 200 bikies. "Come on chaps," he said to them nervously, "we need a passageway through here." The crowd parted and Fraser stepped inside, reluctantly followed by his junior officer, Vassallo.

Kraut lay on the floor near the bar. Despite shotgun wounds to his abdomen and the horrific injury to his left arm, he managed to smile at the ambulance officer.

"Okay, mate, it's all right now, we're here to help you. Now, do you think you could possibly sit up for me?" Fraser asked.

Kraut looked back, dark eyes blackened with pain. "For you, mate, I could walk," and he smiled.

Fraser smiled back reassuringly, and he and his partner managed him on to the stretcher. As they walked towards the door, the human wall parted once again to let the stretcher through.

Fraser placed a pressure bandage on Kraut's arm. He placed an oxyviver on the ground slightly behind him. "Hold this a minute, Paul," he said to Vassallo, handing him a drip. Then, when he reached for the oxyviver, it was gone. Behind, towering over him, was a tall, blond-haired bikie holding the 10-kilo oxyviver in both hands. He was ready to bring it down and crush Kraut's head.

"Look, mate, it's finished." Fraser's mouth as he spoke was dry. His hands were shaking.

"This will never be finished," he snarled.

"Well, it's over for today. Now put it down." Seconds passed.

The man lowered the machine, turned and walked away.

"Come on, Paul, we'd better get him out of here, fast."

The ambulance officers wheeled Kraut into the van and Fraser sat on the first aid kit next to him.

Vassallo sat in the driver's seat. Fraser liked Kraut. Despite his agony, he managed to talk. He was pleasant and amiable.

"I'm not only a biker," Kraut said from the stretcher. "My name's George Tomasian. I've got a good job at the Department of Lands where I've been for fifteen years. And I've got a wife and a house at Oatley."

"What made you go along to all this today?" Fraser ventured.

"I wouldn't have been game enough to stay away and now I think I've wrecked my life."

Kraut closed his eyes. Fraser felt for him. What would happen to him now? He could identify with him, the club thing. Maybe not bikies, but he'd thought of joining a club himself more than once since his own marriage had broken up.

Davo, Roach and Pig were treated over the other side of Beaconsfield Street. Blood seeped from Davo's armpit, soaking his leather jacket. As Mosely, a paramedic, made to cut through the leather, two Bandidos standing by intervened. "We'll take the jacket off, mate." Mosely did not argue. He stood as the two men wrestled the thick leather from Davo's arm.

As ambulance officers and police began to ferry the injured to hospitals, more and more police officers began to arrive. SWOS teams and specially armoured, armed Tactical Response Group officers were called in. In all, 197 police officers came to the Viking Tavern that day, some police breaking down some of the doors inside the Tavern in their enthusiasm to help.

Police in blue dust coats started dusting for fingerprints on a few of the parked cars. Gradually, cars were being allowed to leave.

David Ellis, a young paramedic, cut through Jock's green webbing belt to examine him.

"Do you know him?" Constable Lindsay McGillicuddy said to Parker, who was watching the paramedic, crying.

"Yeah. He's our President, William Ross," Parker's eyes were lowered.

McGillicuddy wrote in his official notebook.

"Can you identify that man over there?" McGillicuddy pointed to Chopper's body, which lay several feet away.

"Who gives a fuck about those cunts!" Terry snapped.

Parker held the drip while Ellis and Mosley lifted Jock's body into an intensive care ambulance. Jock regained consciousness but only momentarily, surfacing like a diver for air. He squinted in the harsh light and saw Parker, his face wet with tears. A shocking pain seared through his left side and he could not breathe. He lapsed again into unconsciousness.

"Your arm's broken son," an ambulance officer told Roach. "We'll take you to hospital for some x-rays."

As he climbed into the ambulance, Roach stopped and struggled out of the leather vest, the BANDIDO and the Mexican bandit proudly emblazoned on the back. They were Snake's colours. He handed them silently to Snoddy.

Snoddy looked down at the embroidered figure on the black leather jacket. What the fuck has happened, he thought as tears welled behind his eyes.

Gradually, he became aware of other people in the carpark—the hoards of onlookers, the press, the police, the Comancheros. As he stood with his men on the fringe of the carpark, he wondered who the dead girl was.

"Now I want you and your men to remain up here. Could you move them over to the service station?" Detective Wilson addressed Snoddy. They complied well enough, there were no objections, and no attempts to leave. They were dazed, not fully comprehending what had happened.

Lance Wellington was escorted by two police officers to identify the two dead Bandidos. He stood looking down on Bull's motionless body, overcome by grief, his eyes vacant staring nowhere.

"Get out of here," Lance spoke through clenched teeth, waving a fist at the cameraman who was filming him. He focused his anger on something at last.

Shadow's wife Joanne had arrived. Looking down at the body of her husband, she sobbed, her shoulders shaking with her grief as Dukes McElwaine and two police officers tried to comfort her.

As news of the deaths filtered out, relatives began to appear. A mountainous lady with olive Maori features in a hot pink sun dress comforted an older lady in a blue waitress uniform. Fat arm around her in a bear hug, the white straps of her bra riding up underneath her dress, the woman escorted her weeping friend from the carpark, daring any television camera to film them.

As the most senior officer present, Stephenson decided to deal with one problem at a time, not allowing himself to stop to think of the enormity of the crime. He set himself up in a mobile van, just outside the beer garden.

"It's not a pretty sight, we've got seven dead. Seems it was some sort of a war between two bike gangs, the Comancheros and Bandidos," Detective Garvey told him as he inspected the dead. "There's been a lot of abuse and threats between the two gangs," he continued, "they're still fairly hostile."

As he could not dismiss the possibility of reprisals, two senior detectives, Tees and Wilson, were assigned to each gang. "We'll keep them apart at all costs," Stephenson warned.

"You could organise that bar trading stops for the while till we get this sorted out," he told another officer.

"A few of the blokes are tracing the relatives now, we've got names for some of them, and nicknames for others," Detective Garvey said.

Dr William Brighton, the government medical officer, black bag in hand, arrived and was escorted through the carpark to inspect the bodies.

"After the scientific blokes have been through and the crime scene examinations finished, ring the morgue and organise for the bodies to be transported to Glebe," Stephenson ordered.

Identification did not look to be a problem. Many of the relatives were now at hand.

"And we'll need the photogrammetry boys to take aerial shots of the carpark," Stephenson continued.

Two hundred cars still stood on the bitumen. A team from the Motor Squad was already checking registration numbers, recording them so all car owners could be interviewed as possible eye witnesses.

Throughout all this, the belt around Stephenson's trousers kept nipping him uncomfortably. "They've exhibited their strength in front of the other bikie groups. Now, they seem fairly pleased with their actions. There's been no attempt by either side to disperse," Stephenson reported to the New South Wales Police Minister Peter Anderson, who had telephoned him at the Tavern.

"It must be a pretty unbelievable sight," Anderson replied. "It's hard to believe it's happened."

"We've had some legal advice," Stephenson continued. "It appears that the charge of affray is one course open to us—a common law misdemeanour—an old law not used much out here. No set penalty for it."

He and Anderson continued to discuss the legal implications of what was already being called a massacre.

A young, uniformed constable approached Stephenson. "You're wanted on the radio—it's headquarters, sir."

Stephenson's eyes scanned the collage of bodies and debris scattered before him.

"Have a good look at this son," he said to the junior officer, "because you'll never see anything like it ever again."

10

Nightfall

For a long time after the shooting, Snoddy moved quietly among his men. Despite his diminished stature, he stood out as their leader, comforting, crying with them, murmuring over their dead, mirrored sunglasses hiding his feelings from the outside world. A leader directing the clean-up after a battle. The orange glow of the sun setting in a cloudless sky lit his unkempt hair highlighting its redness. Red and yellow FTW ("Fuck the World") badges stood out on the black leather jackets of his men, a lesson to the innocents in the carpark that day. But without their machines, wandering around aimlessly, the men looked somehow pathetic. Snoddy mustered his reserves in a corner of the hotel underneath a sign saying "Skandia Valhalla Lounge Club Bar". The television cameras continued to film through a window, capturing the men's confusion, Big Tony standing next to a potted shrub dragging relentlessly on a cigarette.

A silence had fallen over the carpark. Police spotlights highlighted the corpses lying where they had fallen, one body in a black t-shirt, jeans and a studded belt lying face down without a sheet, between two cars, his arms clutched underneath his belly. The bright artificial lights lent a theatricality to the scene, like a film company setting up to shoot a major scene, the actors men in police uniforms still laying out weapons in the boot of an unmarked police car. Bikie magazines, old copies of *Easy Rider*, *Revs* and *Two Wheels* lay strewn on the ground. Signs lay where they had fallen: $5 pioneer speakers, EH dashboard gauges $50—cowling, reminders of the family day that had been planned.

By the back fence the lamb, hacked back to almost the bone, sat on top of a wooden trestle table. The proceeds of the sandwich selling had been stolen and the knife used for carving the dead beast had long since disappeared.

Rescue squad police climbed over the tiled roof of the hotel to set up more lights. Small details were highlighted, seeming even more ominous in the darkened carpark. A white cigarette lighter with a red top, the cheap disposable kind, sat next to two pools of congealed blood on the tarmac. Next to it, a beach towel lay near another patch of congealed redness. A pair of sunglasses from one of the dead lay next to where their owner had fallen.

There was a scribbled note on the windscreen of Al Smith's car when he and Joanne Caestro returned to the hotel: "Please see detectives about the number plate of a car you may have seen leaving the hotel".

When Joanne found the detective, he led her into the lounge, past the seven corpses, now neatly tucked into blue body bags awaiting transport to the morgue.

Joanne saw the group of Bandidos standing on the hotel verandah as she walked in. There were more inside, bandaged and solemn after their war. They were being interviewed in the lounge bar, which had been turned into a makeshift police office. Typewriters clicked away and police flipped out notebooks, interviewing men in lowered tones and scribbling down details.

"Who hasn't been interviewed yet?" Detective Noble addressed the waiting Bandidos.

"I haven't." Ray Denholm stepped forward.

"What's your name?"

Sitting at the table, Denholm relayed his date of birth, name and address. Noble wrote in a shorthand notebook. "How long have you been in the club?"

"I'm not a full member. I've been a prospect since February."

"What happened this afternoon?"

"The Comancheros were waiting for us with shotguns . . .I saw about four of them before the shooting started and later I saw one of them shooting . . ." Another detective photographed Denholm and Noble returned with a typewriter.

"I want to get a statement from you."

The Comancheros were being interviewed in the Norseman, the public bar.

The story of the war was beginning to unfold.

Joanne scanned the lounge as she was led through. She could see no signs of remorse, or sorrow. Sure, they were injured, but she could sense their defiance and it angered her. They snarled and stared as she walked by. She looked through the public bar door and saw a Comanchero with long red curly hair, a solicitor and a detective on either side of him. He was a big man, his hands spread around his corpulence. You fucking bastards, she thought, you should have all died.

She was tired and wrung out, but they would not intimidate *her*. Her eyes were angry and determined. Sitting up the back of the room, she told the detective every last detail she could remember. She felt proud, sitting in front of all those dudes, risking her life even. She was doing her bit for justice.

Later, up on the street, she found Al Smith and a couple of other BMC members.

"We were locked up in the hotel while the police started their investigations," one of them told Joanne.

"Geez, what did youse get?" Joanne asked. "You could have gone for the works—heaps of dough and piss?"

"No, mate," he said, laughing. "But we had three lamb sandwiches about this thick!" his hands were six inches apart. The two of them practically collapsed laughing.

"Youse guys are off," Joanne said.

"There's dead bodies lying in front of the spit and youse are there piggin' out."

Vanessa Ross did not register the news when it first flashed across the bottom of the Sunday afternoon movie she was watching: ONE PERSON DEAD, SEVEN PEOPLE BELIEVED SHOT IN A BIKIE SHOOTOUT AT MILPERRA. But Jock was at Liverpool. She felt comforted, but then uneasy, the words remained before her eyes as she closed them. There was little other news. She resolved to get Holly up from her afternoon nap. "C'mon Sharkey," she said. Their daughter looked like Jock, sprawled out on the bed. Jock's nature too, stubborn as a mule, Vanessa thought.

When she heard the names Comanchero and Bandido, and the reference to a swap meet, Vanessa knew at once with a sickening feeling this was the big one. No bashings this time—death. She sat watching as the Channel 7 news camera swept the carpark, showing the white shapes with the protruding feet of men she probably knew.

On the telephone to the police, she held her breath as the voice on the other end of the phone told her at least one person had died.

William Ross, she thought she heard the police constable say, but she realised it was just her mind playing tricks.

"That's all? Do you know about Jock Ross, the leader of the Comancheros—what's happened to him?"

"Nup, nothing yet, love."

She could do nothing but wait. Minutes later the phone rang. It was Joanne Warner, Sparrow's girlfriend.

"All I've heard is that one person's shot," Vanessa said.

"I'll go and pick up Lucy and we'll come over and see if we get any news," Joanne said.

Vanessa rang the clubhouse, but there was no answer.

Lucy, Littlejohn's wife, and Joanne arrived.

"I'm going to stay with Mum," Joanne said. "She'll be worried sick. If youse hear anything, give me a ring there. I'll keep trying the clubhouse and the police. Come on, Luce."

At 5 pm the phone rang. It was JJ.

"Jock's in hospital. He's shot up pretty bad, Vanessa. It doesn't look good." Sparrow, Leroy, Foggy, Dog and two of the Campbell brothers were dead, she was told. "Oh, and a young girl," he added. "I'll be over as soon as I can. We've got to let the women know, Vanessa, can you ring them?"

Vanessa looked out to the backyard where Foggy's five-year-old twins were playing. They were "grease monkeys", just like Foggy, from as young as three years old, climbing under the Harleys he used to take to pieces in their home at Heckenberg. You poor babies, thought Vanessa. Daddy's not coming home any more.

She began ringing the widows. "Could you come over right away," she said. No-one asked why. Some of the women were together, which made her task easier.

As she spoke to them, she saw the thong she had thrown at Jock some hours earlier still lying by the doorway. She saw his face, this ruthless man, a "hard man, a weirdo" she called him, brought up by the rule books. The man she loved and married, a man who meant well, her Jock, the father of her baby. She felt tears in her eyes and brushed them away. No time for sentiment now, no, he would want her to be strong, for she had a job to do.

She told each woman individually as they arrived. Dana took it the worst, Foggy's girlfriend. She stared at Vanessa, then ran from the house up the driveway and on to busy Pennant Hills Road. The cars whizzing up and down the busy freeway did not even slow down.

"Get back here, you silly bitch," Vanessa ordered. "That's not doing anyone any good."

"What's up?" a neighbour stood by her front doorway. Vanessa mumbled something and disappeared indoors with Dana, white, shaken and sobbing. The children were kept outside away from news broadcasts. One thing at a time.

Dr Tony Leece, the registrar on duty at Bankstown Casualty, did not get much cooperation from the middle-aged man in a leather jacket. There was a lot of blood.

"Me chest, it's me chest . . .and me arm . . ." he had gasped on one occasion. Caesar was adamant that they could not cut his leather jacket in any way.

"I'll get a stomping for it," he muttered to the perplexed medical staff.

Leece had therefore had some difficulty seeing the wound, which he eventually made out to be multiple puncture wounds over the man's shoulder, chest and right arm. The patient was having trouble breathing. It looked like shotgun pellets were lodged in the base of the wounds and there was a deep four centimetre laceration over his left eyebrow.

Nurses and doctors had appeared from everywhere when the alarm alerted staff to Caesar's emergency arrival. Several people stood around the patient, one had grabbed a crash cart another an IV trolley.

"100 over 60, doctor," one sister said.

"Okay, set up for an IV. Hartmans and Haemocell."

The doctor picked up the large needle from the trolley and inserted an intercostal drain in Caesar's chest between his third and fourth rib. When he withdrew it, the fluid was heavily bloodstained. "Better take this one to ICU," the doctor said.

By this time the ambulance officers had notified the hospital that there had been a shooting. They should expect more wounded. Numbers at this stage were not available.

Dr Newman Harris, the intern on duty, walked out to the waiting room. "We have been alerted by the ambulance control that we are to receive a number of injured people. Unless you have some major problem, it might save waiting time if you can come back later."

His announcement had little effect. Then the SWOS team had arrived, men in flack jackets, body armour and shotguns, pacing up and down the corridor looking for any signs of gang retaliation.

"Everyone who could walk left . . ." Dr Harris joked later, getting some mileage out of the story at dinner parties.

Forty minutes passed. Two more Campbell brothers arrived.

Two hospitals were required to treat the injured in case the rivalry continued. The Bandidos were sent to Bankstown; the Comancheros to Liverpool.

The theatre list at Bankstown hospital grew as the injured Bandidos were examined and prepared for surgery. At 5.15pm pellets were removed from Snake's abdomen; at 8.20pm Whack's right arm was operated on and pellets removed; at 11pm a pellet fragment was removed from Lard's right foot; at 12.15am a number of pellets were taken from Pig's shattered left knee.

But the listed names did not betray their bikie status: to the staff at Bankstown hospital they were Geoff Campbell, John Campbell, Tony Melville, Grant Everest: harmless everyday sounding names.

Comanchero John Bodt was aware of voices as he was lifted on to a stretcher and placed in the ambulance. By the time he arrived at Westmead hospital's casualty department he was fully conscious.

Blood had congealed through his dull stringy hair, underneath his black beanie. He was bleeding from the back of his head and his shoulder. A doctor sewed six stitches into his face, on the lower left side of his mouth. X-rays were taken of his elbow and wrist, the wound in his right shoulder examined.

"You've been shot in the shoulder and the pellet is still lodged inside," Dr Neil Warwick said. "We'll have to remove it."

Bodt was taken through to the primary care section and told to take off his clothes. As he bent over to step out of his pants, a large shotgun pellet fell out of the hole in his shoulder. Dr Warwick picked it up and put it in a specimen bottle. He looked into the wound. "Well, maybe we won't have to, after all."

At Liverpool hospital, the news of the massacre quickly spread among those waiting outside casualty. "The bikies are coming," they said, as nurses, doctors, ambulance and police officers hurried about giving and taking orders.

Four of the injured were turned away and Westmead hospital was warned to expect further casualties. Each injured bikie was assigned a police guard.

Flash, a bloodied bandage wrapped around his head, was rushed straight through to x-ray: "Large scalp haematoma and two lacerations on left side", his chart read.

Kraut was x-rayed, sedated, and taken straight to the ICU. He was weak. Doctors decided not to operate for a couple of days because he had lost so much blood. He had to stabilise. Several pellets had to be removed from his abdomen. "Set up an IV for antibiotics," the doctor said. "He'll need a skin graft for his arm."

Rex Walters switched off the Charlie Pride cassette he was playing as he neared Goulburn, the last stop before Sydney. It was just after 6.30pm, and bitterly cold outside. "We are coming into Goulburn now," he spoke into the microphone. "We'll stop here for 45 minutes. There's toilets in the park just here, and the Radnor Cafe opposite has great food for those who feel like some dinner. We'll see you back here at the coach at 7.15 and we should be getting back to Sydney by 11.30—12 at the latest. Okay? See you all in three quarters of an hour."

Rex turned the radio on to station 2WS. The news would be on.

"Sydney is still reeling tonight from news that seven people were shot dead this afternoon in what police are describing as the worst massacre in Australia's history."

Greg Henricks reports . . . "The shooting which we understand has left seven dead and as many as twenty men in hospital suffering terrible injuries—happened in the Viking Tavern in Milperra . . . When I arrived one body was still lying in the carpark, there was evidence of wild shooting . . . as far as injuries go, details are fairly sketchy although I understand that one of the victims is a girl aged 14 . . . the other dead, it still isn't clear just who those victims are."

Bloody idiots, Rex thought. Why on earth didn't they go out into the bush and shoot each other? A public place though, you wouldn't read about it.

The group of 49 skiers, tired and aching after their weekend in the snow, shuffled into the chilly winter night air.

"You wouldn't credit it, would you?" he remarked to one passenger. "The bloody fools."

"Aren't we stopping near there?" one woman asked.

"It'll all be over by now. The police have got it under control," Rex answered.

Lorraine switched coaches at Goulburn and joined her husband for the rest of the trip to Sydney. She now worked as a hostess for Calabros. "Terrible, that shooting," she said to Rex as she boarded his coach.

He nodded agreement. "Never heard anything like it."

It was almost midnight when he finally pulled up outside the Revesby Workers club, a five minute drive from Milperra.

"Do you want to go and have a look at the Viking and see what's happening," Rex said to his new wife as the passengers alighted. "Or shall we just go home?"

"Oh, let's just go home, love. It's not really my idea of something to do. There could be something there that we don't really want to see." So Rex drove on, straight back to the depot.

It was half past midnight by the time they parked the coach, swept it out and emptied the ashtrays and seat pockets. Then they drove to Rex's mother's at Leppington to pick up Peppy, their Yorkshire terrier.

Rex knew something was wrong as soon as he saw the house. Normally his mother only put the front light on when his father, the local fire chief, was out. But both front and back lights were on, and he saw Shifty's car out the front. As he pulled up, his father came out the front door and walked over to the car.

"You'd better come inside, Rex. We've got something to tell you."

His first thought was that something had happened to Cheryl. Rex said nothing but walked inside the house. His mother was there, and Cheryl was sitting at the kitchen table.

"You'd better sit down, son," his Dad said.

"You know the 14-year-old girl who was shot in the bikie massacre ..."

"It was Leanne, wasn't it?" Rex cut in before his father could finish.

His father nodded, tears forming in his red-rimmed eyes. "Oh my god, but how?" Rex said, his words trailing off. "How?"

There was a minute's silence.

"Who killed her? God! I'd like to get my hands on those bloody idiots—who killed her?" he demanded. Lorraine moved toward him and placed her hand on his shoulder. She began to weep.

Cheryl sat opposite, fighting back tears, her grandmother too was crying. Shifty stood by the kitchen sink, looking on, his hooded eyes dark and heavy.

Pamela Walters knew her daughter was dead long before her former husband. She had recognised the haircut just visible despite the blanket that covered the body, as the news camera had zoomed in for a close-up shot.

Mrs Walters was in Sydney for the weekend, staying with her stepsister, Maxine, at Hoxton Park. They had originally planned to leave for home after lunch on Sunday.

"Oh go on. Stay for tea, Pam, before you drive back," Maxine had said earlier that afternoon. Eventually she agreed.

"The bikies have been at it again," Stephen, Maxine's son, announced when the news flashed across the screen, shortly after 3pm. "There's been a big shootout," he said. Maxine and Pamela sat down. Cheryl had joined them.

"Six bikies and a young girl have been shot dead in the fighting which broke out in the hotel carpark at ..."

Pamela felt slightly uneasy when she heard the newsreader's reference to the young girl. She looked across to Cheryl.

"Do you know where Leanne was going today?" Pamela asked.

"Nah," Cheryl replied.

"Can you ring the Johns' house and see if she's there?"

Cheryl left the lounge and rang Melinda's house. "She's not home and they don't know where she is," she said as she plonked back down on the lounge.

Pamela still felt edgy.

At 6 o'clock everyone in the house gathered in the loungeroom to watch the news. There was silence as they listened in horror to the account of the shootout and saw the shrouded bodies.

"Police say they have not yet identified the young girl, or released the names of the six dead men . . ."

Pamela watched closely as the camera panned the scene. A body at the bottom right corner of the screen caught her eye. It was small and covered with a white sheet, the face turned away from the camera, brown hair showing from under the covering.

"That's Leanne," she said her voice shaking.

"Where? What are you talking about?" Maxine ridiculed.

"There," she said, pointing at the bottom of the screen, "I recognise her haircut. She's just had it done."

The camera had moved from the body.

"How can you tell? That's not her, love, don't be silly . . .What would Leanne be doing there . . ."

The protesting voices faded into a dull background hum. Pamela knew her daughter was dead.

She remembered their last conversation, yesterday afternoon at Madge's place. Madge Liddle was perhaps Pamela's closest friend. She and her husband Stan were next door neighbours to the Walters, and knew intimately of the struggle and hardship Pamela had endured bringing up three children without a husband.

Leanne had been late for Madge's grand-daughter Alison's fifth birthday party.

"Hello," Leanne had shouted, heralding her arrival in her usual "I-don't-care-what-you-think" manner. "Happy birthday, Al!" she had called across the room, demanding all attention.

But she came bearing gifts and as usual won Alison over, presenting her with a small neatly wrapped present: some brightly coloured plastic bracelets.

Pamela had forced a smile at her daughter that turned into a grimace as the girl forced a fistful of potato crisps into her mouth. "Leanne, that skirt's far too short, it looks disgusting. You might as well not be wearing one," Pamela had said. Her daughter had ignored the comments and bent over, exaggerating the movement for her mother's benefit. She put Alison down and pulled out a packet of cigarettes.

The afternoon slipped away, Leanne playing, happily enough, with the four and five-year-olds. Apart from a brief initial chat, the mother and daughter barely talked.

"Gotta go," Leanne suddenly said at half past six. "I'm goin' to a party tonight with Glen. When are youse going back up the coast?"

Note: because of the circumstances under which some of these photographs were taken, the quality varies throughout.

Right: Caesar, the Bandido's Sergeant-at-Arms, in full club regalia on a run to the New South Wales south coast two months before the shootout at the Viking Tavern. Caesar's Batman baseball bat, strapped across the front of his bike, was one of ten baseball bats recovered from the hotel carpark by police on Father's Day. (GRANT YOUNG) **Below:** Laughing, bearded bushmen—the Bandidos in happier times—pooling their strength as they gathered logs for a camp fire during a club run. (GRANT YOUNG)

Above: Lee (*centre*), Snoddy's old lady, talks with some of the other old ladies during rest time on a run. In a loving note he placed on the desk in his prison cell before he hanged himself, Snoddy told Lee he was sorry and that he would always love her. Old ladies, as the 'wives' were known, were invited to the clubhouse on certain days and attended club parties but were not allowed to be involved in club business. (GRANT YOUNG) **Below:** Knuckles, one time Commonwealth gold medallist boxer, on his bike holding his son Harley after a bike accident which led to him being in a coma for three weeks. Knuckles was the only bikie to be acquitted after the trial of both manslaughter and murder charges. He was convicted of a charge of affray and released on a good behaviour bond. His marriage to Wendy (*standing to his left*) split up before the massacre. (JOHN FAIRFAX AND SONS)

Above: The Bandido clubhouse at 150 Louisa Road, Birchgrove, now occupied by the Penfold family who have refurbished the old mansion. The upstairs kitchen window (directly above the clothes-line) was the target of two shootings at the Bandidos a month before the shootout at Milperra. (JOHN FAIRFAX AND SONS) **Below:** The peaceful, suburban backyard of the Harris Park clubhouse at 65 Harris Street, Harris Park. On Saturday nights the neighbourhood quiet was shattered by rock and roll music from Comanchero parties. The clubhouse is now a doctor's surgery. (NEW SOUTH WALES POLICE DEPARTMENT)

Left: The teenage memorabilia of Leanne Walters. Adulthood came early for Leanne, who sought approval and love from the supposedly worldly characters she met at the regular haunts of bikies and other misguided souls in Liverpool. **Below:** Jock Ross, the Supreme Commander of the Comancheros, pins a badge on his latest recruit, Raymond (Sunshine) Kucler, in a ceremony at the Harris Park clubhouse in July 1984, two months before the massacre. Kraut, on Jock's right, stands ready with a can of beer to pour over Sunshine as part of a Comanchero initiation rite.

Right: Snodgrass (Anthony Mark Spencer), President of the Bandido Motor Cycle Club outside the Louisa Road headquarters with the Harbour bridge in the background. Snoddy, an orphan from the age of five, found a family in his club brothers. (GRANT YOUNG)

Below: The Bandidos gathered at the turning circle at the end of Louisa Road outside the clubhouse. The neighbours were incensed that the bikies never appeared to be booked for parking illegally. Telexes were sent to the owner of No. 150 Louisa Road, Birchgrove, an advertising magnate, from the real estate agent after neighbours repeatedly asked for the bikies to be evicted. (GRANT YOUNG)

Above: Davo on his trike 'putting' along the highway. Davo's parents, Mummsie and Daddy Cool, attended clubhouse parties. Mummsie baked cakes for the Bandido children. Davo would dress up as Santa. (GRANT YOUNG)

Left: Mike Langley, the publican of the Viking Tavern in September 1984. Shortly after the shootout in his hotel carpark, Langley and his pregnant wife Deirdre left the Tavern after anonymous telephone threats. Langley moved to the inner city where he managed another pub. Deirdre Langley gave birth prematurely early the following year. (JOHN FAIRFAX AND SONS)

Above: Comanchero Snow (Ian White), one of the founding members of the Comancheros. Jock made him a life member of the gang. Snow's head was bandaged after he was bashed during the early stages of the battle. Police waited until all the weapons had been surrendered before ambulance officers moved in to attend the wounded. (NEW SOUTH WALES POLICE DEPARTMENT)
Below: The bloodied face of Sunshine talking to a detective after the shootout. Sunshine was confronted by the first detective into the carpark and organised the surrender of the Comanchero guns. After the battle, Sunshine rang his family with the message 'I won't be home for tea.' (NEW SOUTH WALES POLICE DEPARTMENT)

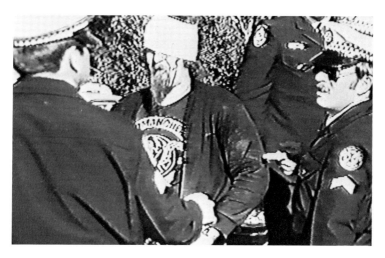

Above: 'Tonka' O'Keefe, Comanchero, after the shootout. He was relentlessly bashed with an iron bar as he lay prostrate on the bitumen of the carpark. He still carries a scar from the attack. (NEW SOUTH WALES POLICE DEPARTMENT) **Below:** Onlookers watch as police stand around the body of Leanne Walters in front of the hotel. The lamb, roasted on a spit by the British Motor Cycle Club, was reduced to a carcass by the end of the day. The large knife used to carve up the beast went missing as did the proceeds from the sales of the lamb sandwiches. (BRUCE MILLER)

Above: The bodies of Chopper (furthest away), Sparrow and Dog McCoy lie shrouded in sheets awaiting inspection by the Government Medical Officer. Chopper's wristbands protrude from under the sheets. Chopper killed three of the dead before he was gunned down himself by eight pellets, two of which cut clean through the Mexican bandit tattooed on his chest. (BRUCE MILLER)
Below: Bull (Phillip Campbell), a Bandido, lying on top of his dead brother Shadow (Greg Campbell). He lay there, overcome by grief, for more than an hour after the shooting had stopped. (BRUCE MILLER)

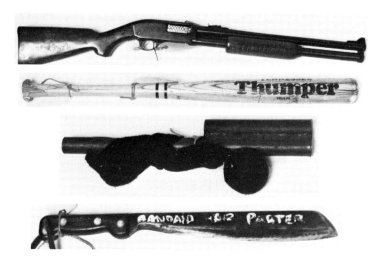

Above: Four weapons seized by police from the carpark. Nine guns were seized, ten baseball bats, some inscribed BANDIDO DUCK 1%er, Louisville Slugger and Thumper. Nine knives, seven iron bars and pipes, a knuckleduster and chains were also seized. Jock's Bandaid Hair Parter, a lethal looking wooden-handled machete was one of them. (NEW SOUTH WALES POLICE DEPARTMENT) **Below:** Police search Foggy's utility in the carpark, laying the weapons on the bonnet. The video taken of this event was later shown to police cadets at Goulburn Academy as how *not* to conduct a weapon seizure. (BRUCE MILLER)

Above: The Bandidos leaving Lance Wellington's house in Condell Park on the morning of the funeral, September 7, 1984. The funeral car is in front. The two Bandidos killed in the battle were buried at Rookwood Cemetery. Two of the Comancheros were buried in the club garden at Palmdale in the Central Coast, one Comanchero was cremated and his ashes laid to rest at Pine Grove Memorial Park. The body of Leroy (another Comanchero) was flown home to Townsville. Leanne Walters was buried at Leppington Cemetery near her grandparents' house in Sydney's outer west. (JOHN FAIRFAX AND SONS)

Left: Chewy and Kezra Lorenz at their wedding in the backyard of their Londonderry farmhouse. Chewy was arrested ten minutes after this shot was taken as the couple were filmed by Channel 10 during the ceremony. (NEW SOUTH WALES POLICE DEPARTMENT)

Following page: The new blood of the Comanchero Motor Cycle Club, men recruited after the massacre, assembled around the memorial garden of Sparrow (Ivan Romcek). They rode to commemorate their dead one year after the massacre. (BRUCE MILLER)

Left: Vanessa Ross, wife of Jock, the Supreme Commander of the Comancheros, outside Bass Hill Police Station after the massacre. She told the media there would be no retaliations. 'We wouldn't wanna cause any trouble for them burying their dead,' she said. 'I think there's been enough killing as it stands now they've got more of us. Surely they're satisfied.' (JOHN FAIRFAX AND SONS)

Above: Lee Denholm, Snoddy's 'old lady', comforts a young mourner outside the chapel at Pine Grove Memorial Park after Snoddy's funeral in May 1985. Only two of the Bandidos, Lard and Charlie, were allowed to attend, handcuffed. The Reverend Ted Noffs told the congregation Snoddy might have picked up a bit of formal religion along the way. . . 'For he was a spiritual man. . . Like Jesus Christ in fact.' (JOHN FAIRFAX AND SONS)

Right: Chewy Lorenz and Terry Parker at Long Bay jail with the Comanchero plaque made to honour the four men killed during the Milperra massacre. Terry Parker told the court he was in the toilet during the shootout. (NEW SOUTH WALES POLICE DEPARTMENT)

Above: Chris Murphy (*holding jacket over right shoulder*) and Phil Young followed by other Bandido lawyers arrive at the Penrith courthouse for the verdict on Friday, June 12, 1987. The verdict came after almost three years of court proceedings. (COLIN TOWNSEND)

Above: Lucy Hennessey, wife of Comanchero Littlejohn, is carried from the court by a relative after her husband was found guilty of seven counts of murder. Littlejohn's parents (his father was a shift worker) sat through all of the court proceedings. The Hennesseys left the courthouse via a side door but were spotted by a photographer and their car beseiged by television and radio journalists with microphones. (BRUCE MILLER) **Below, left**: Shifty, the adopted father of Leanne Walters, in his Rebel leathers. Shifty was 6 feet seven inches tall and Sergeant-at-Arms of the Rebels Motor Cycle gang. One of his favourite anecdotes was how he had run into a horse on his Harley late one night in a country lane. 'Had to slit the bloody thing's neck before it crushed me to death,' he said. (NEW SOUTH WALES POLICE DEPARTMENT) **Below, right**: Jock's home in Pennant Hills was used as the Comanchero headquarters from time to time. Vanessa Ross still resides there. The swimming pool (behind the wooden fence) was partially built by Comanchero nominees. (JOHN FAIRFAX AND SONS)

"Not until tomorrow night. I'll be at Maxine's place tomorrow," Pamela replied.

"Okay, then. I'll come over and see youse before you leave."

"Don't be too late. We'll probably leave before tea."

"Yeah, see ya's!"

Leanne kissed Alison goodbye and she was gone.

Pamela had watched as her daughter disappeared through the front flyscreen door into the cool spring evening. Madge had looked knowingly across the room at Pamela, and shrugged her ample shoulders . . .

The phone rang. Cheryl answered it.

"Shifty's been trying to ring me. I've gotta go home and wait for him."

She saw the tears in her mother's eyes as she turned to go.

No, it couldn't be Leanne she said to herself as she started up the car. But she had a gut feeling something was horribly wrong.

Shifty rang minutes after Cheryl arrived at his house.

"What's Shorty's last name, Cheryl?" he asked anxiously, his mind playing tricks with him, his memory failing.

"Why, what's happened?" Cheryl asked, sensing the panic in his voice.

"She was shot, Cheryl, Shorty's dead. Look, just stay there, I'll be home soon to explain, but what's her last name? I have to tell the cops."

"Walters, Walters . . ." she said as she lowered the phone.

"It was Leanne then, on the telly?" she said to Shifty's de facto, still unable to believe her sister was dead.

"I'd better ring mum."

Cheryl fumbled for a cigarette and lit it as she braced herself to dial Auntie Maxine's number.

Shifty arrived at 7.30pm. Cheryl noticed the blood splattered over his t-shirt but pretended not to see it. He went into his bedroom. Cheryl heard a muffled conversation and when he emerged minutes later, Shifty had changed his clothes. He sat Cheryl down and explained what happened.

"It all happened so fast, mate, there was nothing I could do. She pushed me out of the way, stopped me from gettin' hit, but there was nothing I could do."

Cheryl sat silently and listened, her cheeks wet.

Shifty rang Pamela and spoke for several minutes.

"Come on, mate," he said to Cheryl, "the others are going to Leppington to your grandfolks' place. We'll meet them there."

As Cheryl stood up, she burst into tears. Shifty drew her to him, encased her in his arms.

"It's all right, mate," he said. "Go ahead and cry, let it all out."

Debbie Lane, Foghorn's former wife, heard about the shootout on the radio, after she heard the sirens screaming towards the hotel not far from her home at Milperra. She left her new baby with her de facto husband and walked down to the hotel. She saw Foghorn's familiar black utility parked under the eucalypts at the entrance to the carpark. As if drawn towards him, she walked across the carpark to the hotel. His feet protruded from underneath a white ambulance blanket. She stared at the shape under the blanket, face down on the dark ashphalt.

"Okay, move along now," a uniformed constable came up behind her.

As she neared her house she began to cry. "Robbie's dead," she said as she burst in the loungeroom. "I'm going to go and get the twins," she told her new husband.

Debbie knew only too well the road to Jock's house. Jock had always figured in her life with Foggy. The two men were great friends. The jealousy had started as far back as five years ago, in the early days, when her husband started spending more and more time at the club with Jock and with his mates.

As Debbie drove along, the numbness gradually wore off. She felt sick and angry. That bloody club, she thought. "Well, was it worth giving up your life for, Robbie, well, was it?" she yelled out loud and she cried again, her vision blurred as she struggled to see the road.

She thought of their wedding day in April 1979, remembering him in his matching brown corduroy trousers and vest, his normally unkempt hair slicked down. He looked so proud and told her she was beautiful, she all of eighteen, in her long pink frock, and pink floppy picture hat.

She had been madly in love with this man on a motor bike, this merchant seaman, who had swept her off her feet. She remembered the happy crowd in the backyard of his home at Campsie. Jock was there. Snoddy and his former wife were there too. They were all good friends then.

God, how things had changed. Their first home was a bare housing commission house at Campsie. "You'd turn a jungle into a castle," she could hear his voice down through the years, the way he spoke when he was proud of her. With her antiques and bits and pieces, she brought a semblance of homeliness to his squalid life.

He had used his home to dismantle motor bikes, leaving the pieces, greasy and oily, on bits of ripped up newspaper. Robbie—the genius with numbers and an expert mechanic. He knew the serial numbers for every spare part on a Citroen. He had been the mechanical whizz of the imported car repair factory at Pymble, his first job when he left the navy.

It was her mother, Helen, who early on in her daughter's newfound relationship, had confronted Robbie over the shotgun scabbard permanently attached to his Harley Davidson.

"It's always empty, Helen," he had said.

"Okay, Robbie, I'll take your word for it," she had said sadly.

Helen McNeil heard the news while entertaining at her home on the New South Wales central coast. She and her husband Bob drove straight to Sydney.

"Robert Lane. Let's see, you think he was called Foghorn, you say?" a police sergeant at Liverpool police station wrote down the details and disappeared to make some phone calls.

He returned shaking his head, ten minutes later. "Look, I'm sorry, no one's received any information about a Robert Lane. You don't know if he had any other names, do you? There doesn't appear to be any deceased identified with that name. I don't think I can help you, I'm afraid. You could go down to the morgue. They might have some more information down there."

Helen went to the Ross' house to check on the twins. Satisfied they were all right, she and her husband went to the Liverpool morgue.

The reply from a policeman there was the same.

"No, there doesn't appear to be anyone here with that name. How would you describe him?"

"Well, I haven't seen him for a while, but Robbie's about five feet eleven, brown shoulder length hair, brown eyes, slim build, tattoos—you know, ones from the Navy . . .", Helen replied.

"Just a minute, ma'am."

The police officer took his clipboard and disappeared into a back room. He returned with a detective and another officer.

"There's no-one by that name here, but there is a man who fits the description you gave the constable."

Helen felt sick.

"Perhaps you'd like to have a look and see if you can identify him," he continued gently.

"No, I'll do it. I know him too, you wait here, love," Helen's husband took control.

Bob entered the morgue, the pungent smell of disinfectant piercing his nostrils. It was wet underfoot, cold and sterile.

He was led to a shrouded body, a tag, Body No 2, tied with string to a foot which stuck out from under the sheet. The detective said nothing as he pulled the sheet away. It was Robbie all right, Bob recognised him instantly.

He looked grey and cold, his eyes closed, revealing nothing. He did not look real, more like those mannequins that stand in shop displays waiting to be dressed.

He looks like he would last a million years, despite his death pallor, Bob thought.

"Yes, that's him okay," he said without emotion. He was not sad. It was difficult to remember him alive. "Those poor little girls . . ."

Bob's face said it all, when he emerged. "Yes, love, I'm sorry. He's dead."

Helen, sitting outside in the clinical waiting room, had been remembering Robbie's excitement last Christmas. He always spent Christmas at the central coast with his in-laws. He had brought out a big round plastic wash basket filled with presents all individually wrapped.

He always had a million things for them—brightly coloured umbrellas, dolls, make-up kits and toy cars—every one was wrapped separately. The adults would form an assembly line to wrap them. "I'm going to book into Nan's every year for Christmas," Robbie would say, laughing.

And now he was dead.

Jock Ross's Pennant Hills home had been set up like a fortress to protect the grieving women.

JJ had arrived and sat inside the dining room door, a menacing minder, rocking in his chair, a shotgun resting across his lap.

"I'm taking the girls with me," Debbie said as she marched into Vanessa's kitchen.

"Look, your mum's rung from Liverpool police station, she's on her way to pick them up, I think they should wait here until she arrives." Vanessa stood firm. She knew Robbie would not have wanted Debbie to take them.

"Come on, Deb, how long do you think you'd have them this time? You've got your new baby to look after, you haven't got the room for a start. They're staying here until Helen arrives."

Debbie argued, but Vanessa won. She left before her mother arrived.

Helen felt a cold shiver down her spine when she saw the gunman guarding the door. It would take many months before her grand-daughters settled into a suburban life with her on the sleepy central coast, far from what they were used to. But she had decided to take them home.

"We're calling in a couple of trucks. After the statements, we'll take the Comancheros to Revesby and the Bandidos to Bankstown," Stephenson told his detectives. "It should be around midnight, all going well. We're going to charge them with affray. Darryl's in charge of the Bandidos. He'll let you know when we're moving."

The Salvation Army mobile van had been stationed near the palm trees at the front of the hotel shortly after the shooting. A second Salvation Army trailer stood near the verandah. "Thank God for the Salvos" the red lettering on the side of the van read.

Detective Wilson had placed some Tactical Response Group officers, clad in soft armour and carrying TRG issued shotguns, in a perimeter around the Bandidos, effectively confining them to an area that spread out in an arc from the hotel verandah, as far as the Salvos' van.

"I hate bikies. That poor little girl—what did she do to deserve that. They should all be taken out and shot, second rate citizens, that's what they are, filthy things . . ." One spectator tried to rally others to his cause as they stood around the Salvation Army trailer drinking coffee.

"I used a Harley back in the fifties—but that didn't make me a bikie," a middle-aged woman in a Salvation Army officer's uniform retaliated. "Me and my stepbrother and a few kids from down the road—we got together and bought two or three bikes and made them into one. I used to ride it to the edge of town. I earned seventeen shillings and sixpence a week in those days. Had to save up a long time to buy it. But that didn't make me a bikie—no more than standing in the surf makes me a mermaid."

"But you're not saying these blokes should get off scot free," the man persisted.

"You don't need to go off half-cocked. Only some people had guns—not all of them . . ."

"Running around with tattoos and leather jackets terrifying people," the man continued.

"Don't brand people because of what they wear," the spirited lady in the uniform bristled. "I don't like tattoos. I hate them, but I have very fine friends with a tattoo somewhere, people who are in prison, who were there because of circumstances that started off beyond their control—they had tattoos." She recognised her opponent, after 36 years as an army officer, as the professional peeper, the ghoul attracted to disasters. "These men are innocent until proven guilty," she chided him, scolding him like a child. "It is not for us to judge—we leave that to the courts."

She remembered the Granville train disaster—everyone saying, "Stupid driver should have done this, stupid driver should have done that", mothers standing around ogling at the broken bodies with their two-year-olds. Poor little man, she thought of the driver. He is still living with the thought of the 83 deaths.

"Well, all I can say is someone's got to take the blame killing people in broad daylight like that."

The Salvation Army Major had seen the effect of the shooting on the so called gunmen—the grieving and the shock had started to set in. "Sit down here," she had ordered the bikies, seeing they needed guidance. "Get these chairs and don't do anything. Sit here and when the police need to talk to you, they'll bring you over one at a time."

A few of the Comancheros had meekly obeyed, sipping the scalding coffee, munching the biscuits, large hands around the polystyrene cups.

"We're worried about our safety," Zorba complained to Detective Darryl Wilson. "What are you doing about that, eh?"

"Look, the whole area is cordoned off by police. No-one can harm you here," the detective replied.

"Yeah, but we're worried about our families and our homes. Can we ring our homes?" Snoddy backed up Zorba's request.

Wilson made a phone available in the manager's office for one Bandido to use. Charlie was elected to contact relatives.

Later that night, Stephenson confronted the Bandidos in the lounge room bar.

"You're all under arrest."

"What's the charge?" Lance Wellington shouted. "Being a fucking target?"

Stephenson ignored the taunt. He had been expecting worse.

"You are all going to be taken to Bankstown police station and charged with serious alarm and affront. You two come with me," he pointed to Roo and Lance Wellington.

By midnight 28 men had been ushered into the waiting police vans. Snoddy had changed into a brown leather jacket, one strip of a nominee across it proclaiming him a Bandido.

As Zorba started to haul himself up into the back door of the paddy wagon, he paused. Struggling out of the leather jacket, he ceremoniously folded it and carried it into the back of the van. No-one wore their colours while they rode in a four-wheeled vehicle. Especially in a police van.

Outside the Bankstown police station, the now prisoners were led out of the van, a police officer accompanying each of the accused. As they filed past a red Coca-Cola dispenser, flashlights illuminated the participants in what was the biggest news day in Sydney for years.

Heads bowed, the Bandidos showed none of the aggression they had displayed earlier in the carpark. Tired and worn out, they merely trooped obediently into the police station to be charged with serious alarm and affray. Then, one at a time, they lined up to be recorded in the police files, faces, some still bruised and bleeding, staring at the police officer's camera. Zorba put his colours back on before he lined up for his mug shot.

At 2am Lee heard the car pull up. She hurried to the door and opened the squeaky wire frame. She could see the defeat in the approaching silhouette. His head was bowed and shoulders rounded as he came through the old wooden gate. Snoddy said nothing. He walked through the door and fell into her arms.

"They killed us," he sobbed. "Shadow and Chop are dead. They wanted to kill us, babe. They were trying to kill us." Snoddy buried his face in Lee's shoulder and wept uncontrollably.

Stephenson left the hotel shortly after midnight. The police command post shifted to Bankstown station. It was time to prepare a telex for the public, let the outside world have the official version.

He remembered he hadn't rung his wife. She would probably be worried.

At 1.41am, the telex machine at Bankstown police station began sending out the first official police statement.

Type of Occurrence:
Multiple shooting between rival motor cycle gang Comancheros and Banditos—7 persons deceased and 21 injured.
List of Deceased:
1. Campbell, Gregory, 67 Wentworth Avenue, Wentworthville. Bandido (Shadow).
2. Lane, Robert Francis, born 26.11.52, 9 Cabbamurra St, Heckenberg. Comancheros.
3. Cianter, Mario, (Chopper) 31 old, 49 Bradman St, Merrylands. Bandido.
4. Romcek, Ivan John, Born 24.3.60 12 Hazel St, Merrylands. Bandido.
5. McCoy, Tony also known as Ray, Derek Winfred, born 21,4,45 438 Erskine Park Rd, Erskine Park. Comancheros.
6. Jeshki, Philip, 654 Pennant Hills Rd, West Pennant Hills born 29.4.54, Comanchero.
7. Walters, Leanne, 14 years old, 117 Elizabeth Drive Liverpool. Associate of Rebels Motor cycle gang.

"Brief Details", the machine rattled.

About 1.55pm on 2.9.84 two motor cycle groups, the Comancheros and the Bandidos, became involved in an affray in the car parking area of the Viking Hotel, Beaconsfield St, Milperra. At the time there were approximately 500 persons in the car park area, consisting of motor cyclists from organised groups who were attending an organised market of motor cycle accessories. A number of firearms, clubs, machetes, chains, knives and other dangerous weapons were produced by the members of the two gangs resulting in the deaths and injuries as listed above . . .

The Bandido group is a breakaway party from the Comancheros and over the past three weeks there has been ill feeling between the groups due to the change of membership. This being the cause leading to the tragedy. All persons known to be involved in the affray have been interviewed and their statements obtained and as a result 28 offenders have been charged at Bankstown police station with 'causing serious alarm' and the common law misdemeanour of 'making an affray'. One offender has been charged with discharge of firearm with intent to inflict grievous body and firearm offences and one offender has been charged with indictable assault committed upon Det Senior constable John Garvey of the regional crime squad south whilst he was effecting the arrest of an armed offender. Enquiries are continuing to ascertain the identity of the persons responsible for the murders . . ."

Minutes after the telex was sent, the phone began to ring. There were endless media inquiries.

At 8am, Stephenson reported to the Deputy Commissioner Barney Ross. "I'm setting up a task force and you're obviously the man to head it, Ron. There's to be a full investigation and a fair amount of public pressure as to what's behind all of this," Ross said.

Stephenson thought about the job ahead. It would be the biggest brief he had ever handled.

He rang Gloria. "Yes, love, I'm fine but there's still a lot to do here. It looks pretty grim . . .maybe tonight, I'm not sure, I'll be home as soon as I can . . .I'll ring you a bit later."

"Why do you always get these jobs, Ron?" Gloria asked before she hung up, knowing she needn't expect to see her husband for at least another 24 hours.

11

The following days

"Got it bad this time, darls." Vanessa Ross was standing beside his bed in the intensive care unit of Liverpool Hospital the following morning when he showed the first signs of life. She had to bend close to hear the words, said in a hoarse whisper.

"He's on the critical list," Dr Kwok told her in the corridor outside. "Multiple gunshot wounds to the head, neck, chest and left arm. He'll need emergency surgery to remove one of the pellets lodged near his brain."

It seemed to her as she stood looking at Jock that the men in white coats who formed clusters around the ward had no interest in her husband. They expect him to die, she said to herself dispiritedly. "His lungs have collapsed," the same doctor told her. They have no idea why he is alive, Vanessa thought. And still she watched over him.

Plastic tubes ran from his nose and arms. Electronic bleeps magnified the sound of his heartbeat, but instead of being comforted, she felt depressed by the monotonous sound.

A bandage covered his chest. She noticed the sheets were splattered with blood. He had stirred just that once and drifted off again to somewhere where she could not reach him. Vanessa hung her head, one hand stifling her grief, the other on the lifeless arm that lay on top of the sheets.

"...Strathfield Car Radios—drive in and jive away, Strathfield Car Radios to-daaay . . ."

Karen Brennan awoke to the tinny jingle of the car radio advertisement blaring from the clock radio on her bedside dresser. She rolled over, squinting at the red digital figures. 5.58. Her shift began at seven. Just a few more minutes . . .

Half asleep, Karen listened to the news.

"..Police have identified the 14 year-old girl who was shot dead as Leanne Walters of Elizabeth Drive, Liverpool . . ."

Karen sat upright.

No, it couldn't be. She had seen Leanne just two weeks ago.

"You're looking great. You've put on weight," Karen had said. "New clothes too? You look really good, mate—finally decided to look after yourself, eh?"

Leanne had preened and strutted, pleased with the effect on the nurse. "Got a job, too," she had said. "Making curtains down at Smith's, you know, down Hoxton Park Road . . ."

Karen Brennan, barefooted and in her pyjamas, rang from the next door neighbour's house. "Is that the morgue? I wanted to check about a friend of mine, something I heard on the news . . . yes . . .Leanne Walters was the name I heard . . .is she? Yes, all right, put her on . . ."

"Hello, is that you Karen?" Karen heard the tired, high-pitched voice and a vision of the Pamela Walter's watery, vacant eyes crept into her mind.

She fell back against the wall for support. "How did it happen?" she said, biting her already chewed fingernails until they were red raw, listening to what Leanne's mother had to say.

Karen replaced the phone and slid down the wall, burying her face in her knees. She brought her arms over her head, blocking out the rest of the world, and began to rock, back and forth, slowly, like an autistic child.

Mrs Proudman was restless. She found the news particularly disturbing. Initially she had been shocked—shocked at the realisation that her own personal safety could have been in jeopardy during all those months they lived next door. After all, she had been living next to people who had been involved in murder, mass murder at that, and she found that particularly difficult to come to terms with.

The shock had soon turned to despair, and, this morning, as she gazed through her lounge room window at the house next door, she felt intensely sad.

She heard the dog barking, and saw Mick emerge from the garden shed to comfort the animal. Several Louisa Road residents had bought him food from the Darling Street butchers.

The phone interrupted her thoughts. She picked up the receiver and waited for the STD bips. "Lesley, it's David Connolly. I've heard the news. Are you all right?"

"Oh yes, I'm fine. Just shocked mainly. It's just so awful. I find it very hard to believe . . .those boys . . .surely they didn't shoot the others?"

"Perhaps you should go and stay with your daughter until this awful mess is cleaned up . . ."

There was no sign of the Bandidos until late on Monday. Earlier Mick had seen a female reporter from Channel 7 prowling around the garden and warned her she shouldn't go near the house until some of them were home.

"I don't think they'd like you snooping around," he advised.

But the cameras soon gained access to the house, as the cameramen realised that only one bikie was inside. They marched in past the No Turkeys symbol on the front door, filming the wooden plaque above the bar: Bandido MC 1%ers with the Harley eagle flying above it, the space invader machines, the red pay phone, the white plastic bucket seats.

Knuckles was the only Bandido there. "I'll call the fucking cops and have you up for trespassing," he had said defiantly but with no effect.

"Sorry to hear about your bad luck and everything, mate," Mick said, remembering Knuckle's son, Harley.

Later in the day Mrs Proudman saw more of the men arrive. There was something of a defeatist air about them; they were not the cocky, loud neighbours she had previously known. She walked across the turning circle and went up to the front door.

"Whaddya want?" One of them said abruptly.

"Do you want me to feed the dog, because I will if you like?" Mrs Proudman countered the cold stare.

"Well," one of the others said, "we'll have to ask Snoddy, see what he wants done . . ."

"No, that'll be okay," the first man interjected.

Shortly after, from her loungeroom window, Mrs Proudman watched as they loaded the dog into a car.

By 9am on Monday, a huge crowd had gathered outside the Coroner's court on busy Parramatta Road, Glebe. The seven corpses were to undergo post mortem examinations. Television vans ignored the No Standing signs and parked their vehicles askew on the footpath.

Camera and sound men lugged their heavy equipment up and down the footpath, shooting footage of the blue denimed skinny women, bottoms compressed into tight jeans, who clip-clopped up the steps of the court-house in high-heeled shoes.

Reporters watched, scrutinising everyone who approached. Others were inside the building, bickering with police and morgue supervisers. "Well, how come Liz Swanton from the *Mirror* got into the morgue if it's official policy?" one television journalist demanded.

Liz Swanton was unaware of the ugly scenes outside. As the permanent court reporter for the *Daily Mirror*, she was known and trusted by the senior supervisors of the morgue.

All the bodies were identified by relatives. Liz was familiar with the procedure. Each body was wheeled into a tiny viewing room, where a glass partition and curtains separated the corpse from the grieving faces on the other side. The curtains would be drawn back long enough for an identification to take place.

Liz and Jim, a senior supervisor, were walking through the mortuary to wait for the formal parade when the Government Medical Officer and police made their identifications before the post mortems.

As they passed the bier room, Jim said nonchalantly, "If you want to have a look at one of the bodies, there's one in here."

Before Liz could answer, he flung open the doors. The body of a young girl lay on a steel trolley, a sheet covering her body to her neck. The side of her face which met Liz's eyes was mutilated, beyond recognition as a human being.

Liz stifled a scream. She stumbled back and felt herself slipping.

"Oh, my god, I'm sorry, Liz," Jim grabbed her by the elbow and steadied her. He was genuinely surprised at her reaction.

"Are you all right? I'm sorry. I thought you were used to seeing dead bodies, I'm dreadfully sorry, I guess this one is a bit grizzly . . ."

"Yes, I'm fine . . .I have seen dead bodies before, but that's . . .half her face is missing . . .and she's so young . . ."

"Come on, I'll take you upstairs and get a coffee, I'm sorry, I should have realised . . ."

"No, no, don't be silly, it's not your fault, I just wasn't prepared . . ."

At 10am the grey cold bodies, still clad in jeans and shirts, lay on steel trolleys lined up for inspection. A detective stood by each corpse with a clipboard in his hand. Dr Brighton moved around the room, stopping at each one.

"Body Number 2. Robert Francis Lane, Born 26.11.52. Identifed by Bob McNeil . . ."

In the adjoining room, the forensic technicians joked among themselves as they waited to begin the post mortems.

"Piss off," a young mortuary assistant in a white coat laughed as his mate chased him around the room with a mini circular saw, which looked like a personal fan. It was the same implement that would soon be used to slice the top of Dog McCoy's skull, as neatly as slicing off the top of a boiled egg.

The seven bodies were stripped for examination. The flamboyant tattoos stood out, uniting the seven corpses in death. Dog McCoy's decorative eagle penned across his chest was smattered with shot gun holes. Now the excess blood had been wiped away, the small black holes, like scorch marks across his face could be seen. His eyes were open, his dark hair wild and unkempt.

Leroy's chest was opened up so mortuary technicians could recover any metal fragments still in his body. His two arms, one still covered in blood, were stiff with rigor mortis. They rose puppet like as one of the technicians moved his head forwards. A gloved hand with a pair of steel tweezers probed around inside the chest cavity and extracted a .357 bullet, which had been lodged in the backbone. The man handed the silver pellet to his assistant who washed it and held it up, a shade triumphantly, to be filmed close-up by the police video camera. The contents of Leroy's stomach were examined on the sink for further metal fragments, then returned to the empty cavity.

Six men, once bitter enemies, now lay together in death. A tattooed cockroach crawled up Chopper's calf, but the Mexican bandit on his chest had been shot straight through the heart.

In death, Leanne's face was frozen in a macabre laugh. Two bottom teeth were left protruding from the mess that was her chin and although her eyes appeared to be creased in laughter, a closer inspection showed they were bruised and puffy, reduced to slits caked with dried blood.

Mrs Johns sat on the vinyl studded lounge suite in the front room of her house in Elizabeth Drive, Liverpool.

Opposite, across the bare linoleum floor, Greg Grainger, the dark haired robot-faced reporter from Channel 7, sat with a practised sympathetic smile as Mrs Johns flipped through a garishly covered photo album that contained something Grainger knew no other television reporter had so far managed to get.

Mrs Johns looked down at the album, occasionally blowing her nose with a scrunched up white hankie. She was a plump woman, dressed in a red and white striped shirt style dress. She had opened a window facing onto the busy freeway outside. The breeze stirred the cheap lace curtains.

"Ah, here's some of Leanne," she said. The camera focused in on the page. A plump, younger Leanne had been photographed posing with a group of young friends at a swimming pool—her arm wrapped around a girlfriend, her face a broad smile. The camera panned to another shot of Leanne lying back in a hospital bed wearing a "Triumph" t-shirt, her head raised against plump white pillows. Again she was smiling. A tube was just visible entering her nose.

As the camera tracked over the page, it stopped at a photo of two bikies, long hair streaming in the wind, riding past a green field. Further down the page was a magazine picture of a trim neat-looking Jan Michael Vincent, Leanne's then heart-throb.

The last photograph was a badly reproduced black and white miniature of Leanne with some friends inside an instant photo booth. Their faces were squashed together as the three girls wedged themselves into the booth for the picture.

But it was the photograph of Leanne in the Triumph t-shirt that the television reporter seized on as an image to present to the world. It lent weight to the rumours she was a bikie moll who was at the swap meet selling raffle tickets and she was the prize. Yes, that would do nicely.

"Could we have a look at her bedroom d'you think, Mrs Johns?" Grainger had his photographs. He had nothing to lose.

"Well, yes I suppose so, she's got all these fluffy toys . . ."

The police had visited Vanessa Ross at the house in Pennant Hills Road two days after the massacre. Detective Darryl Wilson and another senior detective, Trevor Baker, spoke to Vanessa and JJ about the funeral arrangements for their men. Both detectives had spent a short time with Jock that morning.

"I also wanted to talk to you about some firearms belonging to your husband," Detective Wilson addressed Vanessa.

JJ produced two rifles. Baker then asked him, "I would like to speak to you further regarding the incident at the hotel. When would you be available?"

"After the funerals on Friday. I'll give you a ring at the weekend," JJ replied easily.

Leslie Andrews was more than a little concerned when he put down the phone. He remembered all the fuss at the only other bikie funeral he had directed—it must have been eight years ago—the red-faced panic of the bank manager across the way from his Markham Place funeral parlour, on the busy Hume Highway at Ashfield. Bikes had blocked the access lane where black funeral cars usually pulled out into the traffic, and the bank manager had been sure he would be attacked and robbed by the leather clad mourners.

What struck Mr Andrews as particularly strange this time was that the bikies wanted to dress their dead. On only one other occasion, when a Tongan family asked to dress a body for religious purposes, had Mr Andrews received a similar request.

Often he would dress the bodies himself, according to instructions from family members. Recently, two Japanese women helped to make up the face of their dead grandmother. But to dress the bodies themselves? Mr Andrews shook his head, perplexed. However, he had agreed to the request.

"Yeesss," he had said, pronouncing the words in his distinct, preacher-like fashion. "A private ceremony for both brothers on Thursday night—

yeeess, make it 7pm . . .that should be fine Mrs Campbell." He had calculated adequate time for the bodies to be released from the morgue.

Mr Andrews stood up from his desk and looked through the back window onto the lawn. His leg was aching. Although tanned and strong for a man in his fifties, the knotted veins on his left calf muscle were evidence of possible arthritis—the medical experts were uncertain, despite months of examination and different types of treatment.

The parlour bell rang. There was someone in reception. He looked back to the jotter on his desk. "No media at all—police informed and will co-operate."

Mr Andrews face was deep in thought as he limped through the smoked glass door into the main office.

"Ah, Mr Harvey, how are you? You've come to settle your bill then . . .good. How's the family coming along? It's nice to see you . . ."

Every day for two weeks after the massacre, both bike gangs had been besieged by reporters who swarmed to bikie addresses given by police, like seagulls fighting over scraps of food. They wheeled and circled, crouched in cars, knocked on doors and filed colourful paragraphs trying to decipher the mystery behind the massacre. Drugs, territorial infighting, the list was endless.

As the funerals drew closer, one newspaper printed that four Bandidos from the United States had been refused entry into Australia by the Australian Consul in Los Angeles. The men had wanted to attend one of the funerals.

One article hinted at the truth: "Dying for Jock" the headline in the *National Times* read. The reporter had found the Comanchero rules: ". . .he has complete loyalty from his 25 members. They talk of the four Comancheros 'dying for Jock' last Sunday . . .Sunday's bloodbath was a battle between men who used to be staunch comrades . . ."

Every night the television news would carry a new angle into the crime with graphic dinkas of Harleys, skulls and crossbones, chains and shotguns in scabbards attached to bikes.

"None of the bikies are prepared to venture outside their homes without weapons—baseball bats, knives or even guns . . ." Ross Symonds, eye-brows knotted in indignation, read on Channel 7 television. "Hundreds of bikies from all over Australia are expected to attend the funerals . . ." Behind him was the Milperra Massacre logo—a motor bike with a heavy chain wrapped around it.

The news fed off the fears of its viewers. There was talk of retaliation, more violence and more death, the viewers being warned in a "lock up your daughters" tirade, a theme that guaranteed the ratings.

Police Minister Peter Anderson in a suitably sombre dark jacket, navy tie spotted and striped, smiled as he was introduced on national television, reassuring the public that the police force was strong enough to cope.

"I can only indicate my disgust at what happened yesterday . . ." he adopted a serious face turning to the camera. "The community is not going to tolerate that behaviour . . .There are very significant penalties . . .It is not acceptable in the eighties to be contemplating what took place yesterday."

New South Wales Premier Neville Wran spoke of a better screening process for those who applied for gun licences and said tougher laws would be introduced.

Newspapers likewise took up a moral stance. An editorial in the *Australian* the day after the massacre warned: "If we are to ensure that Australia remains a fair and peaceful land, swift, firm action must be taken to bring within the strictures of the law those who have until now been allowed to live outside it."

And academics grappled with the sociological side. Dr Paul Wilson from the Institute of Criminology in Canberra was filmed in his garden. "The fact that it happened in the western suburbs doesn't surprise me. The people are disadvantaged . . ."

Bearded members of The Godsquad, a religious group of bikies, were seized as spokesmen for bikie gangs throughout Australia. They spoke of initiation ceremonies where a guy was "blind out of his mind" and other members "shaved his eyebrows and his hair". Tame stuff, hardly the sort of behaviours murders are made of, but they made good talent for the television stations.

Vanessa Ross stood outside the Bass Hill police station in jeans and a sweatshirt, with the words "Property of the Pres" across her chest, sounding more like an ordinary bereaved widow than the wife of one of the leaders involved in the massacre. "You can see how many we've got dead . . .Jock had even asked me and the baby and kids to go to the swap meet, so I can't imagine him asking me if he thought there was going to be trouble . . .He thinks he was shot twice, then he remembers taking off his glasses because they were smeared with blood, then nothing . . .He doesn't remember much of what happened—just being left for dead."

She was asked about retaliation. "We wouldn't wanna cause any trouble for them burying their dead," she said. "I think there's been enough killing and as it stands now they've got more of us, surely they're satisfied."

Foggy's mother wept on national television saying her son had been totally dedicated to the Comanchero club. "I think Robbie knew the consequences . . .but nobody deserved to die the way they did . . .If Robbie was here and I could say something to those people who did the shooting, I would say hang up your guns . . ."

But the pièce de resistance was reserved for JJ. Touted as the spokesman for the Comancheros while their leader was gravely ill in hospital, JJ permitted the television cameras into his home.

"So the Bandidos started it?"

"Yeah."

"What's the problem between yourselves and the Bandidos?"

"It was just a conflict of ideas . . .ideas on how a club should be run," he said, caressing his beard and dragging on a cigarette, the faint trace of an English descent apparent in his speech. A fine gold earring with a coin threaded through it dangled from his right ear. He looked like a gypsy, composed, deliberating on questions as if he was already in the witness box His long matted hair fell on to his checked flanelette shirt, under which he wore a dark coloured t-shirt.

But the pauses, the hesitancy, in between the questions and his answers did little to help the Comanchero cause. "So seven people died over an administrative dispute?"

"We didn't do nothing. We were there and all of a sudden we were fired upon . . ."

A baby cried in the background and the camera panned first to a double-barrelled shotgun lying on the carpet and then a copper clock, a Harley Eagle across it, with the word "Comanchero" across the top in a half-moon shape.

"I didn't kill nobody, I don't even know why they came. I don't know why they were shooting at us, I don't know why they blew the chick's face off . . .it just went crazy. They started shooting for starters . . . four of our blokes got shot at close range."

"You are sitting here in your loungeroom with a shotgun and pellets. Are you expecting trouble?" The camera panned again to the double barrelled shotgun.

"From what the police have told us they've stll got people out here in cars driving around with guns looking for us . . .out of the four men who died, we've got seven kids without a father and one woman with twins on the way."

It had been with some trepidation that Leslie Andrews welcomed his unorthodox customers into the entrance foyer of his funeral parlour, shortly after 6pm on the Thursday night.

They stood in front of the full length silver lurex curtain—six solemn faced bikies. Above their heads, hanging from the centre of the ceiling, was an oversized imitation cut glass chandelier, the artificial light softening their features. The room reeked of incense.

Mr Andrews shook Snoddy's hand and led the men through to the Chapel. Both corpses were outstretched on tables, covered with sheets.

The men spoke in whispers and as they began to dress the bodies in their Bandido regalia, they wept openly. A red and white scarf was tied around Shadow's forehead. In each wooden coffin, they placed treasured relics: a bowie knife, a badge: BFFB—Bandidos Forever, Forever Bandidos. Snoddy, whose emotional state was still raw, wept as he looked for the last time at Shadow—one of his favourite men, the man who had inscribed on his motor bike engine: "BFFB. Cut one and we all bleed. Shadow 1 percent." Gentle Shadow, popular with everyone.

After the bodies were dressed, Joanne Campbell came for one last visit alone with her husband. Staring down at Shadow's lifeless body, she felt nothing but resentment for the pointless way he had died, shot in the throat for a bunch of men who behaved like schoolchildren. She thought of her two children who were now without a father and she resolved that she would have nothing more to do with the Bandidos. The association would end here.

The funerals were to be the next media event, despite the press being unwanted guests.

One reporter, so rumour had it, had been warned off Jock Ross's premises with a shotgun.

It was under these circumstances that Eric Campbell, a D-grade journalist on *The Sun* newspaper, gingerly approached Vanessa Ross's front door, on the day of the funerals, under orders from his bearded, exuberant chief-of-staff.

He counted the seconds after the doorbell rang, then sprinted back up the steep driveway to the waiting car.

"No-one there, Steve," he spoke into the two-way, trying not to sound relieved.

"Try again, mate. Someone must know something," Steve Brien's voice came down the two way.

So far *The Sun* had no Page One pic and the *Mirror* was bound to be more organised. Mike Robotham, another reporter, had already spent a day sitting in the sun up near Gosford after a tip-off that this was where the modern day Mad Maxs would bury their dead.

"Nobody's home. I'm the babysitter," the woman who answered on the second ring told Campbell. "Nuh, don't know where they are or when they'll be back." And the door closed on his face.

After eighteen months working for *The Sun*, Eric Campbell, tall, skinny, in his late twenties with gold-rimmed glasses and a penchant for amateur theatre, knew this was the biggest story he had been assigned to. A later lead on that same day, about a police raid on one of the bikie's houses, took him to Lance Wellington's home.

This time, Campbell was in luck. He arrived while the police were still in the front yard. Twenty detectives and uniformed police were taking part in the raid. A wooden club, an empty rifle scabbard and a box had been seized from the boot of a car parked outside the house.

An alsatian dog had hold of one of the police officer's arms. One of the other policemen dragged him off.

Campbell, sitting in the car could hardly contain his excitement.

"Look mate. Just clear off will ya," another policeman came out of the house. "The bikies absolutely hate you guys. If you want to be safe I wouldn't be hanging around here, okay? Get the message?"

Campbell nodded sympathetically and beat a strategic retreat up Pringle Avenue. He had seen the *Mirror* car pull up outside the house and reporter Jack Doherty knock on the front door. He had the door slammed shut in his face.

Then, as if from nowhere, the sound of engines filled the air and black machines, like large dung beetles, poured out of the driveway of Wellington's house.

To Campbell craning out of the window of the car, they looked as though they were coming out of the house itself.

A souped up old car painted black—the mourning car—appeared, in the back was a wreath shaped like a tyre in red and yellow, the Bandido colours. As if on cue the bikie women congregated on the footpath, all dressed in black.

Bikes lined up in convoy along the street. Jackie Haynes, *The Sun* photographer, a hard-bitten woman in her forties, was in the middle of the road waiting. As she squinted through the lens, the Harleys, Triumphs and Nortons opened full throttle. They bore down on her, and at the last minute, motor drive still buzzing, she threw herself on to the gutter and out of their path.

The Sun driver was already pulling out to start the chase after the retreating leathered backs. As they drove down the road, Eric Campbell, speaking into the two-way, already filing copy, realised more bikies and the mourning car were behind them. The gleaming machines closed in on the left hand side of the car. The mourning car passed close by.

"They're trying to push us onto oncoming traffic!" Campbell's voice was high, almost hysterical.

"Never mind about that," Steve Brien's measured tones came back.

"Just file your story. We're going to be too late for the final . . ."

Back in the office, recalled from following the convoy to Rookwood Cemetery because the paper had gone to bed, Campbell was told to refile. "A caption mate, that's what we want for the photo. The whole thing's already been set."

" . . . A convoy of Bandido bikies lined up in front of the gang's Condell Park stronghold before the funeral procession heads off to Rookwood Cemetery to bury two slain comrades . . ." Campbell, defeated, typed the few paltry words into the VDT, his day of excitement reduced to a few paragraphs with no byline.

Meanwhile, the media waiting at Rookwood Cemetery were rewarded. Brian Bigg, anchorman for the ABC, had taken most of the morning trying to find a crew. Rumours had been circulating all morning, the strongest suggesting that the funeral would be at 11am at Rookwood.

"Why we've got a frigging marked car I've no idea," Brian Bigg had bemoaned to the crew when they arrived at the cemetery and saw the hire cars belonging to other members of the media. "If we don't provoke them I don't know what will. They hate us enough as it is . . .

As Bigg and his crew stood at the back of the car, discussing swapping the eyesore for something a little more subtle, they heard the roar of bikes coming towards them. The machines moved purposefully in two-line formation. The cameraman started filming.

Not one of the bikies took any notice of the offending car.

"We'll leave the car up near the chapel and walk down to where the grave is," said Bigg, as he strode down the hill. There the rest of the television cameramen had gathered, poised at what they had determined was a respectable distance.

As the service progressed, the cameras edged closer, sticking together in a tight gaggle.

"No knowing what they'll do," Biggs had said to a colleague. "Make sure you get a bit closer—we'll have to get something," he whispered to his crew.

Then the Channel 10 man made a bolder move, walking towards a side road, which brought him parallel to the small group around the gravestone.

The others followed, shuffling sideways like crabs.

A Bandido moved towards them. He had long blonde hair and wore leathers and jeans. "Give us a go. You've had your bit. You've got everything you want. What about giving us a bit of privacy?" the bikie paused. The media remained silent. "We don't want any trouble."

"Sure, mate, only too happy," Bigg smiled what he hoped was his most winsome smile as his cameraman and all the other camermen continued secretly to film. He had seen Channel 10 do the same. This was to be the closest they would get.

In the distance, a larger bikie, dark brown hair, muscled arms and a beer gut, ambled towards the small group of uninvited guests.

"Looks like the bloke from one of those 'Trinity' movies—Bud Spencer . . . time to go . . .", Bigg said.

Slowly the group moved back up the hill. Nobody wanted to be the first to go. "A funeral's a funeral," he observed to one of the other anchormen as they retreated. "I covered one funeral when this bloke wanted to shoot us all. Some underworld figure it was—they had guns . . ." Bigg related one of his favourite anecdotes.

Up on the hill in comparitive safety, Bigg faced the camera for his standup, his back to the mourners, their outlines a convenient shape over his right shoulder.

All the while, the group of television reporters kept watch for the promised shotgun salute, an event with a dramatic content that could not be missed.

And there was always the chance of more violence.

"We need some movement, get any footage of them moving off."

But Bigg knew his cameraman had already captured one bikie comforting another sobbing comrade. All was not lost.

"The service was closely monitored by police in plain clothes and a police helicopter circled above,.." Bigg spoke to the camera.

He had a 1pm news bulletin and they had to get some footage back.

The bikies' story led the ABC news for the first two weeks after the shootout. The funerals boosted the topic again when, by the third week, it had dropped to the third spot.

After the Bandidos returned to Lance Wellington's house, the police raided it again. This time they even checked inside the roof. Lance found one of them in his bedroom. Detective Sergeant Budge was standing next to his bed with a shotgun box in his hands. He had found it on top of the wardrobe.

"Where's the shotgun to this box?"

"It's not here. I gave it to a friend. They have hidden it. You won't find it."

"I want to take this box. D'ye mind?"

"I don't mind. It's only a box." The gun had been taken by Lance Wellington's sister. It had never been used at Milperra, Lance was adamant about that. His sister lived with his mother; he was not going to have the police raiding her house. The police spilled out on to the front lawn with their spoils.

Further west at Pinegrove Crematorium, Sparrow's girlfriend Joanne Warner wept as his ashes were laid to rest in the small tidily manicured garden surrounded by Australian native shrubs.

At the Palmdale Lawn Cemetery at Ourimbah on the mid-north coast 70 people had gathered for a private ceremony for Foghorn and Dog. There were no motor bikes, only station wagons, and no colours. The Comancheros did not have the requisite four sidecars needed to convey the dead in true club style.

Jock, still on the critical list, had requested the traditional seven-gun salute for the Comanchero dead. But the grand Comanchero ceremony did not eventuate. Two of the Comancheros were being buried elsewhere— Sparrow in his family plot, and Leroy in Townsville, his home town in Queensland.

"No guns of any description at the funerals," Superintendent Stephenson had insisted. "We're worried enough about reprisals, without the additional danger of firearms at the funerals."

Karen Brennan bought a half dozen long-stemmed red roses for Leanne and placed them carefully in the coffin with a letter she had tearfully composed the night before.

She should have been dressed in jeans and a t-shirt, the way I remembered her, Karen thought as she viewed the body in its long white lace dress.

Alabaster-like, Leanne looked like the young woman she never was— fragile, virginal. Light coloured freckles showed through the fine layer of make-up, which stopped before the pad that covered where her jaw fell away. Only her ears betrayed the secret of her violent death. They were bruised and blackened underneath the fine wisps of light brown hair that gently framed her face.

"What a waste, you poor baby. You never ever had a chance."

Rex Walters was outside.

"Hello," he said quietly, a sad half smile at the corners of his mouth. "I remember you from the hospital. You nursed Leanne didn't you?"

Karen tried not to show her anger. She drove alone to the graveyard at Leppington and followed the black Hertz to the funeral site.

At the end of the short ceremony the Salvation Army priest handed Karen the book from the service and the sympathy cards from flowers sent by wellwishers. He thinks I am the mother, Karen got some small satisfaction from his mistake.

During the ceremony, she had glanced around at the small crowd.

Bastards! All of you! You didn't give a shit about her when she was alive. She had noticed Pamela Walters' inability to find anything to do with her hands, Rex Walters' head bowed in contrition.

Shifty had ordered a leather plaque mounted on wood three inches thick, the leather secured by polished brass studs. A Harley Eagle was emblazoned on the leather. Leanne's name was at the top and an inscription was stamped around it. "Rest in Peace" it read. He had ordered it at a shop opposite Leanne's favourite hangout, The Las Vegas cafe. A few of Leanne's friends, including Vic the tattooist, had chipped in to pay for it.

From a respectable distance, Joanne Caestro and Debbie Larson watched as the brown wooden coffin was lowered into the ground.

Joanne and Al Smith had sent flowers from the British Motorcycle Club. It was the least they felt they could do. Al and Jethro had taken Leanne's death badly and no amount of comfort from Joanne could convince them they weren't responsible. Jethro planned to sell his bike. Joanne had decided to attend Leanne's funeral as a mark of respect.

As the coffin disappeared, Karen lost control. Her quiet, controlled weeping turned to hysteria.

From behind the burial site, Joanne watched as an elderly couple tried to comfort the distraught girl.

Karen Brennan drove to Leanne's grandparents home at Leppington for the funeral wake. She handed the cards and book to Pamela Walters.

"Oh, you've got them," Pamela was grateful. "I wondered what happened to the book. I was wondering why I didn't get one."

"It's yours," Karen Brennan said, avoiding the woman's dry eyes. She thought of the one friend Leanne Walters had in hospital who had not been invited to the funeral, a retarded man who had been in Liverpool hospital's psychiatric centre for as long as most of the staff there could remember. He had raped a woman, so rumour had it, but Leanne would smoke a Winfield cigarette with him from time to time, the middle-aged man and the 14-year-old girl sitting around the back of the hospital having a smoko, both misfits in their own way.

"Who is the president of the club?"

Kraut sighed and shifted slightly in his hospital bed. This was his second record-of-interview. He was getting tired.

"Jock."

"Can you tell us his full name?" Detective Roberts persisted.

"I don't know his full name." Kraut closed his eyes.

"Would it be right to say that some members of the Comanchero group left and formed another group called the Bandidos?"

"I was always of the opinion that it was Jock and us that left them at Balmain and went to Parramatta and that only afterwards they called themselves the Bandidos."

He moaned again, his dark hairy chest rising with resignation. The pethadine was wearing off.

"We have been told that since the separation there has been bad feeling between the two groups. Can you tell us anything about that?"

"It was general knowledge that—Oh shit! My drip has come out! Quick . . .call a nurse. Hurry!"

Blood spurted out of the small hole left by the plastic tube that had been inserted in Kraut's chest. The detective saw the panic on Kraut's face. He jumped up and called a nurse.

Roberts waited outside the ward while a nurse reinserted the drip and a doctor examined his patient.

He was used to interruptions at bedside interviews, but this time he had a feeling the delay could be lengthy, if the look of sheer fright on Kraut's face was anything to go by.

After two weeks in hospital and three operations, the veins in Kraut's arm had collapsed and the doctors had been forced to place a drip in his chest, in the sub-clavical artery. Kraut's doctors had told him that if the drip came loose, his life could be in danger. The threat hung over him throughout the weeks of recuperation, like a punishment for his involvement in the massacre.

Along with Jock and Caesar, Kraut had suffered the worst injuries of the battle. For him the first two weeks following the shootout was a blurred haze of pain as he slipped in and out of a pethadine-controlled consciousness.

He was oblivious to the emotional pain he caused one of his nurses, a slightly built girl with coal-black hair. Karen Brennan had been assigned to care for him for a week in the intensive care unit.

She performed her job to her usual high standard, but her hatred was not far from the surface. As she checked the intravenous drip and the figures which recorded his pulse and heartbeat, she secretly wished he was dead.

Caesar remained in the intensive care unit at Bankstown Hospital for a week before he was transferred to a ward where Lard, Pig and Whack were recovering. He was gravely ill, doped up on painkillers and for most of the time incoherent.

But the move to a room with his brothers helped considerably. He was comforted by their presence and managed short conversations with friends and the constant stream of visiting family members.

"Betcha I walk out of this place before you do," Lard, his foot bandaged and elevated, teased.

"Okay, mate. You're on," Caesar challenged, "I'll be out of here before you."

Each evening they sat propped up against their pillows ready for the 6pm television news.

One week after the shootout, Caesar, ashen grey, watched unbelieving as his home at Ashfield flashed on the screen as several armed TRG police officers raided it.

"Fuck, look. That's my house, what's going on . . ." Caesar watched the armed men burst through the front door and down the hall, searching his home for guns on national television.

He sank back into the pillow. He realised this was merely part of a growing nightmare in which he had been drawn and from which there was no escape—yet.

His mind drifted as the television reporter talked about continuing police investigations into the 1984 Father's Day massacre at Milperra. From his bed, Caesar saw a uniformed police officer walk by the door of the ward, and it was then that he vowed to make good his bet with Lard.

Jock lay on a steel bed, his eyes closed, two weeks of wiry grey stubble on his otherwise bald skull. His genesis, the Comanchero symbol, was splayed in blue across his shoulder.

Detective Sergeant Aarnie Tees was keen to interview Jock. The leader of the Comancheros, the "Supreme Commander", was emerging as the driving force behind the battle. He held vital answers.

Tees glanced around the single male ward. There was a phone on the wall behind the bed, a steel bedside cabinet, a tiny shower and toilet by the door and a wooden wardrobe. Next to the bed was a rented portable colour television and a radio.

It was 10.55am Tuesday 18 September, more than two weeks after the shootout. "We'll come back," Tees said to detective senior constable Geoff McNevin, who stood behind him nursing a portable typewriter.

Jock opened his eyes and looked at the two men by his bed. "It's all right," he said, several front teeth missing. "I can't read, but I'm all right."

It was his turn to tell the story.

There were ergonomic problems. McNevin, who stood at six feet three, had to place a footstool on the table top so the typewriter was at a suitable level for him to record the interview comfortably.

He and Jock soon discovered they both had served in Borneo in 1964, McNevin with the Australian Engineers, Jock the British Royal Engineers. Jock in Sarawak, McNevin in Sabah. It pleased Jock to talk about the army. Tees waited while they discussed the differences between the two military units before he began his questioning.

"As I told you earlier, we are from the Homicide Squad CIB Sydney and we are making inquiries into an incident involving motor cycle groups which occurred at the Viking Tavern Milperra on Sunday the second of September 1984. Were you present at the Viking Tavern on that day?"

At 12 noon, Vanessa and Jock's mother arrived and the interview broke for two hours.

As they pressed on through the afternoon, Jock became increasingly irritable. "When you meet trouble you can't be a coward and back off. I will not tolerate cowards . . ." he had answered aggressively to one of Tees's questions, while Kraut cried like a child from the next room.

Tees suspended the interview at 4.35 pm and returned the next morning at 10.25. Kraut was in Jock's room, unaware of the approaching detectives.

"What did you tell him?" Jock demanded.

"I didn't tell them anything."

"Well make sure you don't tell them fuckin' anything," Jock yelled back as the detectives appeared at the door. Kraut pushed his drip stand past the two police officers and retreated to his own ward.

As the questions continued, Jock became a little more cocky, boastful, enjoying the attention as he explained his fall from power and how things went bad when he split his forces. Aarnie Tees realised Jock believed he would not be charged with anything other than affray, simply because he did not have a gun at the hotel and he did not shoot anybody. He had answered most of Tees's questions cooperatively in his raspy Scottish brogue—a loud frustrated general who ruled his men with an iron fist.

"Coming to the actual Sunday the second of September, 1984, when the shootout occurred, I have been informed that on that morning a number of Bandidos again went past the home of Glen Eaves. Did the Bandidos in fact go past Glen Eaves' home?"

"I got a call from Glen to say that they went past the house. About ten of them."

"What did you do after receiving this call?"

"I phoned Leroy at the clubhouse. He told me that some members were going to the swap. There wasn't enough going. I went to the clubhouse and everyone had rung around to get more members to go. There was never enough to go in the first place. Foghorn, he is a hellishly brave man and so is

Leroy. I couldn't persuade them not to go. Some wanted to go and some didn't. Foghorn and Leroy were going come hell or high water and some of the newer blokes as well. We then had a meeting and I suggested to go low key and not in colours to find out what the other side was doing, but that was no good. Half of them were going in colours and it was decided that those on bikes would go in colours and the others in cars to support those on the bikes. I said we would go for one hour and they could have their show and leave because if they were there it would have been on for sure."

"Can you tell me this?" Tees continued. "What would have happened if the Bandidos were there when you got there: straight into them?"

"Yeah, I would say so . . ."

Kraut's moans from next door continued.

"I have been informed that you yourself were armed with a large machete?"

"Yeah, but in military terms it's called a gullocks . . ."

12

The dawn raids

Gloves was sleeping next to Sandy, sprawled comfortably on several large pillows on the loungeroom floor of Kid Rotten's Lilyfield home. Sandy was just pregnant. She slept peacefully, her breathing shallow.

Gloves was dreaming of his 1974 Harley Chopper, the motor he had had sent over from the United States, the chrome of the exhaust pipes and the gleaming metallic paint on the tank. He was going for a putt down the freeway, leaning back, feet up high, the bike surging forward . . .

When he first heard the banging he thought it was the big end, come loose from the crankshaft. "Shit, sounds like the big end knocking," he muttered, his voice thick with sleep. "Hope the crank's not buggered . . ."

He turned over, burrowing into the pillows, adjusting himself to avoid the gap in between the pillows and the hard floor.

Bang! Bang! Bang!

The noise was more insistent. Opening red-rimmed eyes, he saw the black shapes above him, heard the voices, knew that what had been feared was now a reality—he was being arrested. He felt the cold metallic barrel of the Smith and Wesson at his head.

Flicking his tongue around his dry mouth, he swallowed hard. He saw the handcuffs.

"You're under arrest."

"What the . . .what's going on?"

Gloves was dragged up against the wall in the hallway. The early morning quietness of the house had been shattered.

"What time is it? What the fuck's going on?"

He saw Kid Rotten and Opey to his right. All three were held up against the entrance foyer wall.

The wall was cold and hard. As his nose made contact with the brick he began to rely on sounds to work out what was happening. He heard the invaders turning everything upside down in the loungeroom and the other rooms in the house—cupboards, drawers—everything was thrown into the centre of the room.

"Don't move." The order begged no questions.

When he was turned around, Gloves saw Sandy, pale and frightened, coming out of the loungeroom.

"Get me wallet, babe, out of me jeans," he signalled to his hands which were handcuffed behind his back.

"There's a piece of paper in the back section that's got Murphy's phone number on it."

Sandy fumbled with his belt and undid the bulky iron chain that was strapped to his wallet. It was the chain he used to secure his bike. She handed the piece of paper to him.

"You're coming with us," a detective came out of the loungeroom.

"What's going on, mate?"

"We want to question you further."

"Where are we going?"

"Five Dock police station."

Holsworthy Army Camp occupies twenty hectares of dry land sprinkled with gum trees on the western outskirts of Sydney, far from the cooling eastern seaboard breezes. In summer the cicadas screech and the temperature is always five degrees hotter than in the city. The humidity is all engulfing. To combat the heat, officers and their families squash into a small kidney-shaped swimming pool set in a mock tropical garden outside the officers' mess, while the lower ranks, the corporals and the sappers, shelter in the small bar of their air-conditioned drinking quarters.

The Peelers Club in the Army's School of Military Engineering is a collection of rooms classified as the Junior Ranks Recreation area, which houses one of the more downmarket drinking holes at the base. A large, oblong hall is used for sappers' twenty-first birthday parties and end-of-course booze-ups, a big empty room where "they can wreck the joint and do little damage", according to one lieutenant.

Inside the adjoining bar, a photograph of Victoria Cross winner Lance Corporal W. Peeler reminds his young contemporaries of what war is all about. He stares sombrely out of the wooden frame, from underneath his slouch hat and World War I regulation dress, the rising sun badge on his jacket, "Australia" written in a boomerang shape on his shoulder.

Lance Corporal Peeler was awarded the Victoria Cross for "most conspicious bravery in Ypres on 4 October 1917." He killed 30 people, including a gunner, single-handedly, displaying "a fearless courage".

Above the pool table near Corporal Peeler's photograph is another nationalistic relic—a photograph of a young Queen Elizabeth II shortly after her coronation.

The Peelers Club was a fitting venue for the New South Wales police force to muster their ranks, inform their troops of the battle plans for Operation Hardwalk and brief them on what to expect from the enemy.

For three weeks, the police force had remained tight-lipped about the fate of the shameless participants of the Father's Day Massacre. The public began to think they had failed, that no-one would be brought to justice for the deaths of seven people. "Investigations are continuing" was the standard message from the police public relations department.

More than 100 detectives had been chosen to hear the secret instructions. Even those journalists close to the police, drinking buddies, fishing and golfing partners and old time mates had found it difficult to get details about Operation Hardwalk. The undercover assignment had been codenamed by Detective Sergeant Paul McKinnon. A tanned, nasal-voiced, seasoned detective approaching his forties, he was the head of SWOS.

At the Peelers Club on 20 September, black plastic chairs were arranged in rows and the floor length curtains were drawn across the glass doors to shut out the sun.

At 1pm, the team of plain clothed detectives began filtering through the entrance to the Club, past the pink oleander trees, red hibiscus bushes and the sappers' tuck shop in the foyer near the hall. Through the gaps in the curtains they could see children's swings and a dilapidated merry-go-round.

Operation Hardwalk—the opposite of Easy Rider—was a top secret series of simultaneous dawn raids. "H" Hour, entry time for all targets was 0500 hours, Friday 21 September.

Forty-four names had been decided upon by Detective Chief Inspector Stephenson's task force—16 Comancheros and 28 Bandidos who police could confidently charge with murder. Each bikie became a "target" and was bestowed with a name beginning with different letters of the alphabet. McKinnon had fun concocting the names from local Sydney football teams—Sharks, Roosters, Saints, Tigers, Eels and Bulldogs—when the alphabet was exhausted.

There were 144 detectives and uniformed police from SWOS, TRG, the Dog Squad and the Communications Branch assigned to carry out the raids.

The briefing, for detectives only, had been left until the day before the raid for secrecy. By 1.30pm all of the plastic seats had been filled. 2850 pages of photocopied orders were compiled into individual briefs for each officer.

The police operation was ambitious, one of the largest ever undertaken by an Australian police force. The police operations centre (POC) for the raids was located in the old hat factory on the corner of Campbell and Smith Streets at Surry Hills in the inner city.

Undercover observation squad detectives had been monitoring the suspects and their movements.

Photographs of suspects were placed in albums. Equipment was organised—sledge hammers, bolt cutters, soft body armour and shotguns for the SWOS members.

One police officer Geoff "Fluffy" McDowell, had been sent to Omaha, Nebraska for a convention on bikie activities in the United States. He had taken aids, slides and overhead projectors in case he was called on to speak. Australian bikies were now of international interest, the story of the massacre making headlines in England and the United States.

Intelligence on Australian bikies was sketchy. The Bureau of Criminal Intelligence had kept a file on criminal activities concerning bikies, but there was little knowledge of the activities of the outlaw gangs, how they structured their clubs or their lifestyles. They were a code unto themselves.

McKinnon's voice filled the hall: "Reading from the sheet, which you should all have in front of you . . .As a result of investigations 44 persons have been identified as being connected with these offences." He listed the offenders, and then handed over to Detective Inspector Stephenson, Commander Operations Hardwalk 84.

Stephenson began with the officers' mission: arrest the offenders. Upon entry, searches were to be made for weapons, ammunition, explosives, drugs and apparatus used for the manufacture of drugs, documents and photographs. Clothing, footware, any items with insignia and those articles which signify club membership, leather studded wristlets, and so on . . .

Stephenson had drawn information from the FBI to point his officers in the right direction. After all, many of them had had no previous dealings with bikies.

"If you see the number thirteen, that means the thirteenth letter of the alphabet—m—which signifies the man with that number on his jacket smokes marijuana.

"They call themselves the one-per-centers, which means they are members of an outlaw motor cycle club. They are the elite one per cent who pride themselves on the fact that they live outside the law.

"What to expect: Guard dogs . . .video cameras, wife or old lady as they are termed, booby traps, snakes."

Detective Barry Smith then addressed the police officers on the doctrine of common purpose. "We have had legal advice," Smith said. "Anyone who does anything knowingly in concert with someone else—that's a common purpose. They formed together to reach the common purpose . . . .

"You have to maintain an open mind—make your decisions as to whether you would charge or not based on this advice . . ." He outlined other features of the legal aspects of the charge.

After the general briefing, the detectives were divided into two groups, those arresting Bandidos were in the main hall, those in charge of the Comancheros were left on the verandah.

It started to rain. The Comanchero detectives were brought back into the second hall.

Detective Bruce Demmery had been assigned Davo Littlewood, Target name "Mike". Demmery woke up in his home on the lower slopes of the Blue Mountains at 4am, fifteen minutes after his alarm had gone off. He cursed into the darkness.

"What's up?" Sue Demmery fumbled across the rumpled bedclothes.

"I slept in," Demmery said, checking the clock radio. "It's bloody 4 o'clock and I've got to be at McMillan's place by 4.30 . . ."

"Well, get up then, you'd better hurry," Susie mumbled.

Standing under the shower, the initial coldness of the water helped revive him. No time for breakfast, a sacrifice for Demmery, who rarely missed his morning ritual.

He coaxed the accelerator of the Falcon, the unmarked police car, into submission, taking each familiar bend at just the right speed. As the main road down from the mountains, it was the route he drove every day.

On Lennox Bridge Road he cruised over the old bridge, coasted around another bend and straight into a large piece of sandstone that had become dislodged from one of the towering embankments sloping up from the road.

Surprisingly, there was little damage—only a flat tyre. Demmery cursed his continuing bad luck.

He looked at his watch—4.15am. He'd never make it to Parramatta Police Station where he was due to meet his partner, McMillan, by 4.30, not with a tyre to change.

"Damn! and I haven't got McMillan's phone number. Imagine being late for a raid."

On the police radio, he asked the operator to contact his wife. "Get her to ring McMillan and tell him I'll be late."

Snuggled back in bed again, Susie heard the phone ring. "Yes . . .okay."

She fumbled through the drawer for her husband's address book, quietly muttering. "No, don't know anything about a raid," Detective Chris

McMillan sounded a little annoyed at the early morning call.

Wrong McMillan. Susie tried again.

Demmery replaced the wheel on the Falcon, leaving the decorative covers off the wheel nut by the side of the road in his haste. He made it with time to spare. When he walked into the police station, some of the fellows were sitting around still checking their shotguns.

Back at Bass Hill police station, Stephenson master-minded the operation.

"Eagle in position.." the call came over the radio. Eagle was ticked off in the book.

Some time passed.

"Eagle back on. We've entered our premises. Target in custody . . ."

Operation Hardwalk was going smoothly. Stephenson permitted himself a small smile.

Terry Galloway from radio 2GB, dressed in his customary white shirt, beer belly from many nights drinking with his police contacts straining at the bottom button, stood by quietly. Occasionally he spoke into his two-way, filing copy about the dawn raids from the top of his head. The 5.30am bulletin broke the news to the Sydney public.

Demmery, now wearing his bullet-proof vest, an army-green flack jacket, blue slacks and black street shoes, was stationed outside the side window of 9 Hart Drive, Wentworthville, the address given by intelligence for Snodgrass. Davo, or "Mike", his target, was expected to be inside. In front of him was a detective from SWOS, shotgun aimed at the house.

"Open up!" McMillan, from SWOS, thundered on the door of the house, which stood back from the six lane highway, empty of traffic at that hour of the morning. The garden was overgrown and neglected. A dog chained to the verandah barked hysterically.

"Who is it?"

"Police . . ."

The door was opened gingerly. McMillan put his shoulder against it and forced it open the rest of the way. Several police followed him inside.

"The place is secured," the order came from one of the detectives inside the house. Demmery and the others who had been surrounding the house moved out of position. 'Mike' was not inside. He had been arrested at Five Dock during another raid.

"What is your name?" McMillan tackled the man who had opened the door.

"Ray Denholm."

"Were you at the Viking Tavern on 2 September 1984?"

"Yes."

"You are under arrest."

Demmery handcuffed Denholm and led him to the car. Lee, who had been standing watching, wrote the solicitor Chris Murphy's number on a matchbox and put it in her brother's pocket. She did not tell the detectives that Snoddy was staying at Murphy's house.

The raids happened simultaneously all over the city.

"I am Detective Duff and this is Detective Woods. Is Phillip Campbell there?" Christine had opened the door to the two plain clothed detectives.

"What for?"

"Is he here?"

"What's the baton for?"

"It's for a dog out there," one detective ventured.

"The only dogs here are mine and they are chained up. Put that baton away and I'll get Phillip." Christine Campbell, not quite five feet, frowned, her babyish voice growing as obstinate as she could make it.

Bull was getting changed as she walked into the bedroom. "The police are here to see you."

He went to the door still doing up his jeans.

"Hang on. I'll just put my dog out. She's just had pups."

Back in the loungeroom after locking the dog in the back yard, Detective Duff handed him a search warrant.

"We want to search the place. Where is the best place to start?"

Christine was angry. "Come back tomorrow."

"I wish I could." Duff smiled his reasonable smile.

"Don't you think he's been through enough now? His brothers are dead . . ."

"That's why we want to do it the best way we can. Can we start here?" Duff had moved across the small loungeroom to the door leading into the kitchen.

A colour photograph of Chopper stood on the laminated sideboard. The wooden house smelt of dogs. One puff and the whole lot would blow down.

"Yes, try not to make too much noise. One of my little girls is sick."

Duff turned to his henchmen.

"Try to put everything back the way it is."

Turning to Bull, he said, "I want the clothes you were wearing on the day."

"I had this shirt and a pair of black jeans on."

"No you didn't. You had a white t-shirt on."

"No. I had this shirt and a pair of black jeans. Where's my jeans?" he turned to his wife.

"They're in your drawer."

When he returned from the bedroom with his jeans, he saw the rifle scabbards in Duff's hands.

"Where's the guns that fit these?"

"They're Chopper's. They are probably in Merrylands gunshop getting fixed."

Duff fingered the shotgun shell, pausing a little.

"Who owns this?"

"It's Chopper's, and he used to own a double-barrel shotgun."

"Is this the girl's room?" Duff turned to Christine.

"Yes, that's where my little girl is who's sick."

"Don't worry about that room," Duff ordered.

"What's out the back?"

"A lot of of dogs," Bull answered.

"Don't worry about the dogs. I would like you to come to the police station with me."

"Is he under arrest?" again Christine spoke first.

"He is going to be charged."

"What for?"

"I think it would be better if you rang the police station and Phil tells you himself."

"Where are you taking him?"

"To Merrylands police station."

"What can I do?" she asked Bull.

He took the yellow Bandido courtesy card out of his jeans pocket. "We are the people your parents warned us about," it said in red writing. On the back he had written the solicitor Chris Murphy's number.

She borrowed a pen from Duff and tried to copy the number. "It doesn't work."

"That's the bloody government for you," Duff could afford to joke. He had snapped up his target.

"Here's some money, love," Bull pulled out two twenty dollar notes.

At Fairfield Police Station Duff offered Bull a cup of coffee.

Detective Woods had found the letter from Chris Murphy in Bull's wallet. "Phil, we are going to be fair dinkum with you. If you don't want to talk about what happened, you don't have to."

"I want to wait for my solicitor," Bull had been sufficiently warned.

On the phone to Murphy, Bull was given further instructions—do not say anything, do not sign anything. He would send someone to see him.

"Fair enough," Woods said agreeably. Then he tried a change of tack.

167

"You do a bit of pig hunting?"

"I do a bit."

"Where do you go?"

"Up around Sandy Camp."

"I used to go up that way myself. It would take a pretty powerful rifle to bring down one of them boars. What sort do you use?"

"I use dogs on pigs."

"What happened when you drove in the driveway?"

"I thought you said I didn't have to talk about that."

"I told you we was going to be fair dinkum. We won't talk about it."

Duff came back into the room asking for Bull's driving licence. "Is he talking?"

"He wants to wait for his solicitor."

Duff turned to the silent man hunched at the desk. "Phil, that might be too late. We are going to have to charge all you fellows. If you talk to us we can help you. If you don't, once you go over to the charge room it will be too late."

"How come we've all got to be charged?"

"There are seven dead people and somebody's got to pay for it."

In the small hours of the morning on the day before her wedding, Chewy's fiancee, Kezra, heard the phone ring.

"Kezra, it's Vanessa, is Andy there?"

"Jeezus, Vanessa, it's a quarter to five." Kezra's usually raspy voice was thick with sleep.

"Look, I have to speak to Andy, I've heard a rumour that one of our men has been arrested and charged with murder, but I don't know who."

"Christ, when?" Kezra was suddenly awake.

Rick Lorenz—Chewy—was staying away until the wedding tomorrow. But the police did not know this.

Ten minutes after Vanessa's call six armed TRG officers and two detectives burst through the front door of Kezra's farmhouse in Londonderry in Sydney's far west.

"Fuck, what are you doing? I've got my kids in here, show me your search warrant," Kezra's eyes flashed hatred at the intruders.

Outside, crack TRG men dressed in bullet proof jackets, long barrelled shotguns raised, broke down the old rotting shed door.

Andrew Thomas was bailed up against the loungeroom wall and hand-cuffed. More detectives surged through the back door.

"Where's Lorenz?" one demanded.

"Show me your search warrant," Kezra insisted, "and would you mind going out of my bedroom while I put some clothes on?" she said, with a characteristic flash of sarcastic coquettishness.

"There's no sign of him—don't think he's here," the detectives talked among themselves.

"Show me your fuckin' search warrant!"

Kezra was fuming. Her 10-year-old son Daniel slid through the door and hid behind his mother.

"Just tell us where Lorenz is," one detective insisted.

"He's not here and I don't know where he is, and you'd better show me that search warrant. I know my rights, you bastards!" Kezra had had considerable experience with the arm of the law. Two of her children had been taken away from her and fostered out by Youth and Community Services. Daniel was the only one left at home.

Detectives Farthing and Sweeney sat outside the wooden house in Pringle Avenue.

Lance Wellington had the foresight to ask for their warrant, but he hardly expected them to be unprepared.

"Is there anyone else here?" Farthing asked.

"Roo's in the other room with a girlfriend," Lance answered. "Are we under arrest?"

"Yes, for murder," Farthing said almost nonchalantly.

They searched the house first. Farthing found Tony Cain's colours in the kitchen. Lance Wellington, Roo and his acquaintance for the night sat in the kitchen drinking cups of coffee.

"We want to search the garage," Farthing addressed the group.

"Go ahead," Lance sounded obliging.

"You'll have to come with us. Would you chain the dogs up?"

"No."

"Why?"

"There's no chain."

"Well, how about a rope?"

"There's no rope."

"Can you lock them up in a kennel?"

"There's no kennel," Lance stared at the detective—sullen, uncompromising. "Look," he added almost as an afterthought, "nothing will happen unless you try to hurt me or make any sudden moves." It was his last attempt at mutiny before chessmate, a feeble attempt, but one which gave him an inordinate amount of satisfaction.

He walked to the garage, the dogs on either side of him. Once outside the garage, the police hardly attempted to conduct a search.

"Nice bikes," one detective tried to chat.

Then one saw the vintage car and the oily parts tidily stowed at the back of the garage.

"You do a lot of this sort of work?" It was a statement rather than a question.

"You let the main shooter out on a thousand dollars bail," said Roo, who had followed them to the garage.

"Who's that?" Farthing asked.

"Sunshine."

But Lance would not be drawn into any further conversation about 2 September.

Inside the house again, he and Roo were left waiting, powerless. Sweeney and Farthing went out the front.

"Look. I've got to ring my mother," Lance fronted the two men when they eventually came back inside the house. "I've got to open my factory up. People will be waiting to get in to start work. Can I ring them?"

"No, we're leaving now."

"What about the people at work?"

"Too bad."

"Where are we going?"

"Bass Hill."

"Why not Bankstown?"

"Because the Comancheros are there."

"Greenback on. We've entered our premises. Target in custody. Uniform also located—in custody also . . ." Farthing radioed back the information to base.

At Parramatta police station, Ray Denholm was being subjected to a barrage of questions by two detectives, McHugh and Reynolds.

"What clothes were you wearing on the second?"

"The same shirt, jeans and shoes that I have on now." Denholm was asked about his involvement. McHugh became more specific.

"Just show us on this map where you parked the bike you rode."

Denholm placed an X beside a bike. "I would only be guessing but I think it's that one."

"Don't guess. I want to know which one it is," McHugh said.

"All right. It is that one," Denholm decided, writing the initials RD next to the bike.

"What's that?"

"My initials."

"Write your fuckin' name," McHugh demanded.

The questions continued.

"You're in a ton of trouble," McHugh said. "You better make a record of interview. It's your only way out of it. We have people who saw Bandidos doing shooting and you're involved."

"I didn't see any of that," Denholm replied.

McHugh stormed out of the room.

"You've got him mad now. You better do what he says," Detective Reynolds said.

The Bankstown Aero Club attracts more locals than pilots, old timers who come to drink Reschs on tap and revel in the cool, dry air-conditioning while they exercise their biceps pulling at poker machines.

A few items betray the identity of the club, apart from the numerous runways seen from the windows of the clubhouse. Above the beer taps, stretching the length of the old fashioned wooden bar are blown up colour pictures of old aircraft—the Tiger Moth, Chipmunks and a Viney Vicar— historic military and civilian aeroplanes.

The only other flying paraphernalia is a notice telling of family flying days advertising flour bombing, spot landing, one turn spins, forced landing and streamer cutting.

Superintendent Stephenson chose the Club to celebrate the chain of arrests that morning because it was "tucked away and quiet" and the boys needed somewhere to release the tension accrued in three weeks of long, hard work. The last thing the detectives wanted was to be bailed up in a bar with curious members of the public, eager to expound their views on those bloody idiot bikies.

The boys in blue ate the club out of sausage rolls and pies, the only food on offer, and another order was placed for dozens more. No good drinking on an empty stomach. Some of the arresting detectives did not arrive until 4pm.

The new Police Commissioner, John Avery, a 57-year-old former licensing detective with a reputation for being squeaky clean, had been invited as a guest of honour. It was "Police Week" and he had been addressing the public at Bankstown Square, so it was convenient for him to call by.

Stephenson had rung his minions to pass on the invitation. "It'd be good for morale if he could be there," he told the Commissioner's staff.

Other important guests also turned up—the Police Minister, Peter Anderson and the then superintendent in charge of the CIB, Bob Bradbury.

Commissioner Avery was a serious man, devoutly religious. He had yet to make his mark—he had been Commissioner for only five weeks.

The mood was one of excitment. About 200 men filled the drinking area, pleased the day was over.

Most of them were dressed in casual clothes, dark coloured civvies worn at the time of the raids. Orders had been to dress casually but smartly, as if expecting to make an appearance in court. No jeans.

Avery put $50 on the bar and was the last of the three dignitaries to address his police force: "I am proud of the manner in which you have all held up the traditions of the New South Wales Police force." The speech ended on a somewhat sceptical note. "Let's hope the brief holds up," he said with a wry smile.

Stephenson left at 6pm, well pleased with the way things had turned out.

Christopher Murphy at 36 years old was solicitor for Sydney's underworld—one of the first to advertise his services on the back page of a daily newspaper—a daring move.

Handsome, solidly built, prematurely grey with black highly arched eyebrows and hazel-green eyes, he strutted before the courts as he did before the television cameras. Journalists were fascinated by him and his notorious clients. He was an enigma to the media and the public, a man with a circle of acquaintances who obeyed his every whim, servants who drove him to and from his destinations in a hired white Mercedes, running errands like valets, listening respectfully to his stock of earthy anecdotes, laughing at his punchlines, ever ready to agree with his theories on existentialism and the life of the underdog, whose lot Murphy felt he championed. In return, Murphy was ever-generous with his money, particularly after a successful day at the races—once he had won more than one million dollars in an afternoon.

Witty and clever, he was indispensable at parties. His charisma could win over even the most disgruntled of his followers wounded by his abrasiveness.

His fiery aggressive court techniques, coming partly from his Irish heritage, were unleashed upon unsuspecting mild-mannered magistrates. He would savagely attack personalities while cross-examining, honing in Rumpole-like on the victims in the witness box. It was not so much his knowledge of the law that gave him his reputation as a good lawyer as his ability to draw attention to himself and to unsettle the conservative confines of the courthouse, turning case after case into an Academy-Award winning performance.

If Murphy could not help you, no-one could. The waiting room of his Macquarie Street offices was often full of no-hopers, down and outs, shoplifters, prostitutes and petty criminals. There was also the occasional murderer.

Murphy, whose father was a police officer, albeit one reportedly fond of a few beers, hated the police with an intensity bordering on obsession. He had been hired by the Bandidos, bought for $400 on retainer, months before the shootout, for conducting club business such as traffic fines. He also acted as solicitor to another Sydney bike gang, the Black Uhlans, sometimes attending their parties.

He was about to rent a luxurious apartment, a two-bedroomed bachelor pad eighteen floors above Sydney overlooking Hyde Park, flanked by Police Headquarters and the Remington Centre, which housed Sydney's detectives. His red Honda Civic with number plates "VERBAL", was tampered with more than once as it was parked in the lane at the back of the Remington Centre.

Murphy had been living in what was to become his summer house at Collaroy, one of Sydney's far northern beaches. It was a roomy house on the beach front. The polished wooden floors gleamed from the practised care of Murphy's female friend who lived nearby and kept the house livable. She would often cook for him when he entertained, which he did regularly on summer weekends, arriving on Friday nights with an entourage of last minute guests.

It was to this venue several Bandidos came on 20 September, the night before the dawn raids. Unconventional to the end, half a dozen of his bearded clients, including Snoddy, slept in makeshift beds on the polished floors in Murphy's loungeroom. They had expected the arrests. Seven Bandidos spent their last night of freedom snoring on their solicitor's floor, oblivious to the sound of nearby waves crashing on the beach.

At 2pm on the day of the dawn raids, Detective Aarnie Tees walked into Jock's ward. It was his second arresting interview for the day. He was accompanied by Senior Constable Geoff McNevin, police prosecutor Bob King and a magistrate.

"I didn't shoot anybody," Jock grunted as they entered.

The detective walked over to the bed and stood beside the television Jock was watching.

"Jock, we're about to hold a bedside court and before we do I am obliged to tell you you are to be charged with seven murders which occurred at the Viking Tavern on . . ."

Jock seemed to pay no attention to the detective's words. His cold eyes scanned the crowd standing around his bed while Tees read him his rights and officially charged him with seven murders.

A uniformed constable took up position as guard at the door.

"After all the fuckin' help I gave you!" Jock shouted angrily after them as they disappeared down the corridor.

Kezra smiled when she heard the Channel 10 chopper hovering outside. She was applying the finishing touches to her make-up. That'll keep the fuckin' cops at bay anyway, she thought.

"You'll see it easily from the air," she'd told Bill Payne, her journalist friend from Channel 10. "Its got a corrugated iron roof with a swastika painted on it."

Kezra had found an ally in Bill. She had tipped him off about her forthcoming marriage to Comanchero Chewy, assuring him her Londonderry farm would be easy to find. There was a swastika on the roof all right, but Kezra failed to tell him it was painted white on pale grey tin. The Channel 10 crew flew around for 30 minutes searching in vain and was about to give up when the co-pilot spotted the vague outline in the distance.

Kezra blew gently on her near-dry nails and checked her face in the mirror. A plastic tray containing 30 bottles of nail polish in shades ranging from deep purple to black and crimson-red sat on her dressing table.

Sometimes, to while away the time, she would paint each nail two different tones—one half of the nail black, the other spotted like a leopard's skin. This ritual took most of a morning. Each false nail had to be put carefully in place before she painted it. For her wedding day, she had chosen a demure shade of pastel pink.

22 September 1984 was Kezra's third wedding day, but she had a feeling this one would be the most exciting.

She ran a brush through her layered blonde hair, which was cut cleverly around her face, softening her features. Kezra had the face of a woman who had seen a lot of life, hardened blue-green eyes and a thin, determined pair of lips, which she'd painted in matching pale pink. She was tall and slender, a narrow waist, small breasts and long legs, often shown to their best advantage in tight jeans. In her time, she had managed a brothel. She was well able to look after herself. She drove a white Mercedes, owned three fur coats and adored the limelight, a characteristic that led her to seek out the media.

Her wedding, although small, had become something of an event. One of the most important guests was Channel 10. Bill Payne had a news exclusive of the bikie wedding, planned the day after the dawn raids.

The bride fixed a garland of tiny white flowers in her hair and stood up from her dresser, checking her image in the mirror. She wore a soft, white cheesecloth dress and around her waist she had tied a long-fringed deep red and blue Indian-style shawl, the tassled fringe hanging long over her hips. A round, elasticised neckline showed off her sunbrowned neck and shoulders.

Picking up her small bouquet of pink orchids and clasping them with both hands, she smiled at her reflection. She was satisfied she looked beautiful.

As a final touch she chose her turquoise and silver bracelet and matching necklace, as well as two long silver chains, which she hung around her neck.

"The celebrant's here, Kez," said the bride's friend Mary, as she walked into Kezra's bedroom. "You look beautiful mate, just gorgeous."

Mary always said the right things.

Payne cursed Kezra as the chopper hovered above the farmhouse. Someone had laid sheets of corrugated iron to show the chopper where to land. It was one of the most dangerous landings the chopper pilot had attempted, as the iron could easily fly up in the downdraft and get caught in the blades.

"The crew can get out and we'll take off again. I'll come with you. That way the cops'll think we've gone. Get as many pictures of the ceremony as you can." Payne, a former policeman in England, directed his crew. "I'll piece together the story later."

Detective Senior Constable Wayne Poppelwell and detective Glen McNamara had visited Kezra early that morning, looking for her fiancé. "Look, he's not here, there can't be a wedding without a bloody groom, can there?" she had said.

But just after lunch Detective Poppelwell got a call at Bass Hill police station from one of the observation squad boys who had been watching the farm from an unmarked car.

"Look's like the wedding's going on," he said. "A few people have started to arrive and the Channel 10 chopper's in the air."

"Okay, we're on our way." Six detectives in three cars headed out.

The marriage ceremony was held outside. The cake, a two-tiered traditional wedding cake, with pink marzipan roses and a silver eagle stood in pride of place. Champagne glasses and cold bottles of Great Western champagne were at the ready, sitting on top of a Certificate of Marriage, waiting for the signatures of the happy couple.

Chewy stood at the table facing the celebrant and turned to watch his bride walk across the lawn in the early afternoon sun. Kezra's golden labrador sat nearby watching the ceremony with sad, soulful eyes.

Chewy had brushed his long hair and moustache. His black t-shirt had a large white slogan in old-fashioned printing across his chest—"Genuine Mustache rides 5c". He wore blue demin jeans, held up at his waist by a studded leather belt with an ornamental steel buckle that read "Live to Ride, Ride to Live".

He was uncomfortable with the television cameras. He kept his tattooed hands clenched together in front of his groin. "FTW" (Fuck the World) in heavy blue tattooed lettering stood out on both of his biceps. The letters HATE were tattooed on the four fingers of his left hand, one letter on each finger.

He smiled as Kezra approached, radiant for both her man and the television camera, which had begun to record the event. The pair held hands as the marriage celebrant, a middle-aged woman dressed in a tartan skirt, grey cardigan and soft white blouse, conducted the simple ceremony.

Chewy reached across and lifted a plain gold band from the small lacy pillow held by Mary. He slipped the ring over Kezra's finger, avoiding the long pink nail. They exchanged vows.

Kezra smiled as she held Chewy's hand, and together they sliced through the bottom layer of their wedding cake.

Poppelwell arrived just as the ceremony finished. The police were wary of the television cameras and made no move to arrest Chewy in view of them.

The small crowd moved into the loungeroom for a celebratory drink, and, satisfied the chopper was leaving, the detectives moved in to make their arrest.

As they walked through the front door, Kezra and Chewy were sitting on the lounge holding hands and drinking champagne.

Kezra leaned across her new husband to ash her cigarette in the ashtray beside him. She nuzzled up against his shoulder as she saw the police move in. He returned the affection, bowing his head, his long hair screening his face.

Poppelwell, with his short spiky hair and dressed casually in a blue woollen jumper, looked like a young football player rather than a detective. He walked over to the couple. As soon as he opened his mouth to speak, a cameraman appeared from the hall with a handheld video and began filming.

"Turn that off or we'll confiscate it," the detective said, his hand up to the camera. The cameraman held the camera upside down by his side but did not switch it off.

"You said you wouldn't come," Kezra said.

Poppelwell retained his cool. "I didn't say that, at all." Kezra began to argue and Poppelwell turned to Chewy.

"We've received further information about the events at the Viking Tavern on Sunday September 2 and we'd like to talk to you further at Bass Hill."

Kezra continued to interrupt and began directing the cameraman to film the arrest close-up.

"Yeah, all right. . .can I finish me drink?" Chewy, unlike his vitriolic new wife, seemed resigned.

"Sure," Poppelwell said.

Chewy did so, in one mouthful. "Can I go get a jumper?" he asked.

"Yeah, sure," the detective said, knowing there were three detectives out the back of the house just in case.

Chewy disappeared briefly and walked back in. "Can I just have five minutes alone with my wife?" he pleaded.

"Yeah, sure mate," Poppelwell said sympathetically.

Chewy looked over at his bride. She was holding court, directing the sound and cameramen as three wedding guests watched her.

"Let's go," Chewy said to the dectectives.

The television cameraman, who had followed them outside, continued to film as the officers showed Lorenz into the back of the green Falcon GL before they turned the vehicle around and disappeared in a cloud of dust up the unpaved dirt driveway.

"Where have you been?" Poppelwell asked Chewy as they made their way back to the police station.

"Went down the south coast with a mate to his place to do some fishin'."

Caesar Campbell developed a chest infection after his second week in hospital. By the time of the dawn raids, he was still too ill for police to conduct a record of interview. Two days later, a nurse placed a fan and a bowl of ice by his bed in an effort to bring down his temperature.

"Colin, it's Patricia. Can you hear me?" Patricia Gardiner, literary agent, a slender woman with features reminiscent of the Maori race, leaned over her brother's bed and wiped his burning face with the cold flannel.

Patricia Gardiner, née Campbell, had brains. She was cool-headed, dressed like a business woman and walked as though she had completed a course at the June Dally Watkins finishing school.

Now that the drama of September 2 had settled down, she had made it her business to find a legal representative for her elder brother to get him out of trouble. He had to get legal advice before he spoke to police. Up until now, because of his health, he had not given any statement to police and had therefore not been charged.

She had attended the hospital almost every day. Today, she straightened out his bed, fussed and soothed, but nothing seemed to help.

He was ashen-faced, breathing with difficulty, and on the odd occasion when he opened his eyes, the whites showed, the eyeballs rolling back into the sockets.

He mumbled incoherently.

"Shadow . . .Shadow," were the only words Patricia Gardiner could make out clearly. Caesar repeated his dead brother's club name over and over again.

As she sat on the hard seat next to his bed, Detective Sergeant Woods arrived with some other police. "Hello, Colin, I'm Detective Sergeant Wood. I was here yesterday. Do you remember?"

"He's not well enough for an interview," Patricia said. "Can't you see he's extremely ill."

Patricia had brought more flavoured ice blocks with her. It was the only food her brother seemed to be able to eat and it helped to keep his temperature down.

"I am going to continue inquiries into this and I intend coming back to see you tomorrow. Do you understand that?" Wood persisted.

Caesar's head moved but there was no reply.

A police guard had been placed outside the ward where Lard, Whack and Davo slept.

"Why are y' here?" Lard bellowed. "Are we gonna be charged with anything?"

"No, we are here to stop people getting in, not getting out," the young uniformed police officer answered. On 23 September, Lard saw the detectives talking to Caesar.

"Get out and leave him alone!" he shouted across the ward.

The following day two others returned. This time they headed towards Lard. "I am Detective Budge. This is Detective Ashcroft. How are you feeling?"

"Not bad. I've just had a skin graft for my foot."

"Can you walk yet?"

"No, not yet. They said I have to keep off it and stay in bed."

The talk turned to the Tavern.

"Then how come we are all getting charged with murder? We only had pickhandles and baseball bats. They were the ones with the guns." Lard complained long and loud.

"It was the same when Jock took over the Loners. He prepared an attack on them and then called a truce, then he got stuck into them. You coppers missed two cars loaded with guns. They left as soon as you blokes arrived . . ."

"Do you know what sort of car it was or what colour?"

"I can't remember."

A silence fell after Lard's account of the events.

"Have you blokes found out who shot the girl yet?"

"No, not yet but by the time we finish we will be able to tell."

Lard was charged with seven counts of murder at a bedside court at Bankstown Hospital on 4 October. He was then transferred to Prince Henry Hospital, near the sea, south of Sydney.

Some slipped through the official net. Lout—Rick Harris—a sallow-skinned, dark-haired Bandido with a mild stutter, in his late twenties, was one. Tatts, a Comanchero reportedly at the scene driving a Datsun, was another.

Lout decided to go to ground.

Like Caesar, he had not been at the Viking Tavern when the police arrived and no charges had been laid against him. He had been in the car with Podgorski and Hookie when Caesar had been taken to hospital. The police were aware of his existence, however, even as late as 21 September detectives had no idea that Bernard Podgorski (or Hookie for that matter) existed. As far as the police were concerned, Lout and Caesar were the only two outstanding men yet to be charged.

The police tracked Lout down. There was not a lot of evidence against him, but they believed he was involved. He appeared to be a cut above some of the others—married with a steady job behind the bar at the Royal Oak Hotel at Parramatta. He seemed a good candidate for the general police directive to offer indemnity to, a suitable potential witness who was involved in the massacre.

The week after his other brothers had been charged with murder, Lout was approached. Immunity from prosecution they said, in exchange for evidence against his brothers.

Lout agonised over the offer.

At his sister's wedding the following weekend, he faced the wet, reddened and disapproving eyes of his relatives across the wedding table.

The detectives never saw him after the wedding. Lout decided to bolt.

Bob Wood, his boss at the Royal Oak, sympathised. The two had been good friends for a long time, they had shares in a greyhound racer and both men shared a passion for the dogs.

Lout went north with Podgorski for the first few weeks after the massacre. Then, he moved to an island off Palm Beach on Sydney's far northern beaches, staying there for some months.

Even his wife was not told where her husband had gone, but Chris Murphy assured her he was fine and this was the best course of action.

"Has Campbell been moved?" the young nurse asked her superior, who was attending to another patient at the opposite end of the four-bed ward.

The sister saw Caesar's empty bed and ruffled sheets.

"It's time for his 9am medication," the younger woman continued.

"Not that I know of. You'd better check with the early morning ward sister."

Caesar Campbell had signed himself out of Bankstown hospital fifteen minutes earlier. It had been extraordinarily easy for him—no charges had been laid against him and he wasn't under arrest.

". . .Yeah, she had a red dress on, tall woman, supporting him all the way . . .looked like he was in a bit of pain . . ." Detective Sergeant Wood spoke to a man who had seen Caesar as he left through the hospital's front reception area. "Yeah, I was watching them, you know, he looked pretty crook . . . She helped him into an old Falcon, I'd say a '74 model, you know, a two door number. Took off pretty fast too, right out of the gates . . ."

It was 4 October. Caesar had won his bet with Lard. He too had slipped through the net.

Others avoiding the law were not so successful. Big Tony Cain had moved to a friend's place, a Black Uhlan, who lived in Brighton Le Sands near the airport. On 21 October at about 1.30pm there was a knock on the door. Tony had advertised his car for sale in *The Telegraph*. This was the first response.

"Sure we can go for a test drive," he told the prospective buyer. It was a hot day so he wound down the windows. "Bloody stifling," he said by way of small talk. The man in the driver's seat grunted a reply.

He had driven just two streets when two cars came towards them, flying down the wrong side of the road.

"Fuckin' hell . . ." Tony cursed.

Then he noticed they were police cars. Police spilled out of the front and back seats, guns in firing position.

More police appeared from behind fences and from unmarked police cars, which he saw parked along the roadside. There were fifteen detectives all told and all of them armed.

"Don't move a fuckin' inch," Detective Fennell rammed his pistol into Tony's temple, cocking it so that Tony heard the click as if it was inside his head.

Staring straight ahead he found himself looking down the barrel of another pistol as a detective lay across the bonnet.

He felt cold steel prickling the back of his neck—another police officer had leant through the back passenger door with a shotgun.

Tony felt his bowels loosen.

"I suppose this means you don't want to buy the car," he said feebly.

He was wrenched from his car, handcuffed and thrown into the back of a waiting police car.

"I want to call my lawyer, Chris Murphy," he said as the car headed for the police CIB headquarters in the city.

"You'll get a phone call."

Tony was taken into the interview room in the Homicide squad office at the CIB and the handcuffs were taken off him.

He took his wallet out of the back pocket of his jeans and pulled out a letter from Chris Murphy saying he didn't want to be interviewed without his solicitor present.

"Yeah, all right, I'll look into it," Detective Fennell said, reading through the typed note.

Detective McMillan came in with three cans of Tooheys Draught beer.

"Want a beer, mate?" he asked.

Tony accepted.

The two detectives left the room and locked the door behind them.

There was a homicide brief on the table, a box of papers relating to the death of a Vietnamese man, stabbed to death at Cabramatta.

Left alone for an hour, Tony occupied his time reading the police statements, looking at photographs of the dead body and drawing his own conclusions about the killing.

"Do you want another beer, mate?" Fennell stuck his head through the door.

"No thanks, but can I ring my solicitor?"

"We can't find Murphy, he's probably at the races gambling the money youse blokes have given him."

Half an hour later he returned.

"Look, why do you want to wait for Murphy for? He'll just take your money and run. All we want to do is make a record of interview."

"I will make a record of interview with you, but I want Murphy here first," Tony was determined to follow his instructions.

A further twenty minutes passed. Tony got bored with the Vietnamese murder.

"We can't find him. We think he's at the races but we can't get hold of him. Why don't we just do the record of interview, it will be easier for us and for you." They had both returned this time.

Tony was getting worried. He knew they were not going to get Murphy for him, especially after they told him Murphy had a greyhound racing that night and he'd be eager to make it to the track on time.

"Oh, all right then. I suppose it will be all right," Tony finally conceded.

On 30 October Detective Senior Constable Greg Bamford and Detective Sergeant Greg Nomchong set off to question another possible witness to the Milperra shooting.

Bernard Stephen Podgorski was expecting them.

He was working, labouring at the building site of a community hall in the backwaters of Richmond, a western Sydney suburb.

Podgorski was a Bandido, according to the old lady of one of the Comancheros. She had rung the police to tell them about his whereabouts and directed police to his photograph in the recently published glossy *The Aussie Biker Culture* magazine.

Bernie had been snapped astride his bike in his black riding leathers, a red and black bandana around his head and a tanned rifle scabbard attached to the left of his Harley.

It was the first time the police had ever even heard of Bernard Podgorski, but they thought they had better check it out.

It was almost 11 o'clock when they arrived at the site and the manager sent someone off to find him.

Podgorski, bearded and dusty, suddenly appeared before the detectives wearing a singlet and shorts, regulation hard work boots and scrunched down football socks. Detective Bamford watched as the man materialised from the bricks and mortar.

Both sets of trained police eyes fixed immediately on the familiar mark on Bernie's left forearm. The two officers glanced sideways, knowingly. The blue Bandido insignia was clearly marked on his weathered skin.

"G'day," he said, eyes averted.

One hour later, Bernie Podgorski was sitting in Bass Hill police station with his solicitor and Superintendent Stephenson.

Shortly after he was charged with seven counts of murder, he accepted a deal arranged through his solicitor in agreement with the New South Wales police force and Attorney General.

Freedom and an undisclosed sum to become the police star witness.

13

Prison

There are no obvious signs. Only a small white stone plaque with "Parklea Prison" set into a rock, which the passing motorist could be forgiven for overlooking.

Two turret-style decorations sit either side of the entrance, like those of a country mansion. Beyond the white picket fence bordering the prison grounds, horses graze, specks in the distance on the dry hilly grassland.

There are no wardens in sight, no sign that 200 people are being held against their will in maximum security behind those innocuous sun dried hills.

A driveway snakes up between the hills, the type that belongs on a ranch in Dallas rather than a prison in the outer western suburbs of Sydney. It leads to the jail. On the last curve before the carpark, a prisoner, t-shirt tied around his waist, freckled skin bared to the sun, rides a mini-tractor, cutting the prison lawns of the vast front garden on the 80 hectare site. From the visitor's carpark, the prison building on the right looks incongruous, like an oversized model. A tall tubular brick structure with shining corrugated iron arches gleaming, and sleek, white light posts, it has windows like a pretend "Playschool" building.

Architect J.W.Thomson designed this ultimate lock-up, the most modern jail in New South Wales, the first to have individual showers for prisoners, at a cost of $100 000, a waterless moat and other attractions. Outside, a plaque reminds visitors the prison was officially opened by the Minister for Corrective Services on 5 September 1984, three days after the Father's Day shootout.

Once past the waiting room, the niceties are dispensed with. Large double iron doors with wrought iron handles separate the inmates from the outside world. Each of the four parts of Parklea jail is sectioned off into its own wing. Everyone who passes from one wing to another does so through the formidable white bars of the control area. Civilians are escorted by warders. Upstairs in the control area the warders sit watching rows of television screens showing different areas of the jail.

The prisoners live in three wings, which border an open courtyard with neat trimmed lawns and curved cream pathways. A wide, grey bitumen strip like a miniature runway bisects the courtyard. Smaller paths branch off leading to entrances along the wing blocks. Manicured grass forms neat symmetrical patches between the paths. Arched walkway covers made from corrugated iron offer intermittent shade in summer.

A tennis court has been built outside Three Wing and opposite is a fully equipped gymnasium where prisoners can work out.

On each side of the path are flower beds—petunias and roses—each flower carefully pruned by men with time on their hands. Working inmates are paid from $9 to $22 for a five-day week plus a bonus. Non-workers are discouraged—they are not eligible for a TV, are only allowed one contact visit and one phone call a week.

Prisoners in green stubbies and t-shirts stroll across the lawns. Up above the courtyard from their tinted glass offices, wardens sit like eagles in an eyrie, chatting, ever-watchful for signs of unrest. Pigeons nest under the steel bars in the awning, leaving spattered white droppings to mar the warders' view.

The Bandidos were moved into this $40 million establishment on 21 September 1984, three weeks after the massacre. They had drawn the longer straw. Their enemies had been sent to Long Bay Jail, a much older, high-walled, cramped building in Sydney's eastern suburb of Malabar where sometimes as many as three men were forced to share a cell. Long Bay was also 85 kilometres from Penrith on the outer western fringe of Sydney—the town that housed the courthouse chosen for the committal hearing.

Snoddy, unable to see out, felt the police wagon slow as it moved over the steel grates, reverberating, sending shudders through the men seated in the back. It was his first experience of prison—"another fuckin' institution", he had said to Lee.

Three Wing Top, the right side cell block of the quadrangle was designated for the Bandido inmates, although some were still recovering in hospital.

Surprisingly, the New South Wales Government allowed the Bandidos to stick together—they moved in as a club, reinforcing their brotherhood. They held meetings in their common room before retiring each night at 7pm along to their cream painted concrete cells.

Each cell was ten foot wide with a single bed, a shower with hot and cold water, a toilet, eight shelves, a small table, one chair, a sink, mirror, a built-in radio, a bedside light and alarm system—the sort of cell the newspapers called "The Hilton". Individual showers, it was argued when Parklea was first designed, would cut down the number of homosexual attacks and reduce the number of wardens needed to patrol such a danger area.

When their beds were not in use, the prisoners could fold them against the cell wall to give them more room. Cleaning the cell was left to the prisoner.

The routine of jail made the Bandidos submissive, casting a dreamy quality on their memories of freedom, leaving no room for individuality. Institutionalism seeped into their veins, reduced their will power. Lining up for headcounts, they became mesmerised by routine. As the start of the committal hearing drew closer, they longed for a break in the daily rituals.

At 6am they were woken by a warder who unlocked each cell individually. All prisoners were counted, then allowed back into their cells for a shower. They dressed in their jail greens and then moved down to the common room for breakfast. One hour later there was a wing-muster roll call—all cells were expected to be clean and tidy. At 7.15am, all prisoners reported to their work area unless they had the job of a cook, assistant cook or sweeper. Lunch came early at 11.30am—sandwiches every day without fail.

At 2.30pm there was another works muster. The wings were then opened and phone calls allowed. At 2.45pm, all prisoners in their wings had another roll call. Tea was served in the common room between 4 and 5pm. The cooks were responsible for ordering food and deciding what to cook. Vegetarians were also catered for.

The evening muster, which varied in time according to the season, was held after tea. Phone calls were not allowed after 7pm. Although at Parklea the Bandidos fared better than most prisoners in Australia, after 7pm, all prisoners were expected to prepare for lock-in, a word the Bandidos came to dread. Weekends were a little less hectic with no work area to report to and visiting hours stretching across the afternoons.

The Bandidos did not work much at Parklea after November 10. Their days were then spent travelling to and from Penrith court, a ritual they came to hate more than life at Parklea. As winter progressed, they would get up in the dark and arrive back at Three Wing at the end of the day in darkness. The common room in Three Wing Top doubled as a dining room and a recreation area, and had a 60-inch colour television. The kitchen was part of the same complex, both rooms dividing the blocks of twelve cells, six a side in the narrow corridor.

From his first night in custody, Snoddy had trouble sleeping. Each day before 5pm he would report to the prison infirmary where a nurse would give him his prescribed dose of Rohypnol, a sleeping tablet many of the prisoners took nightly.

Most evenings, Snoddy would sit in his cell at the small writing desk wedged between the shower recess and the wall underneath the window, and, in his cramped, childlike scrawl, record his thoughts in a diary.

Jock had been discharged from Liverpool Hospital on 26 September, five days after his men had been arrested. He was sent to Prince Henry Hospital at Little Bay, which served as the State's prison hospital. It was close to Long Bay's Metropolitan Remand Centre, and Jock remained hospitalised, under guard, until he was well enough to join his men in incarceration.

The fifteen Comancheros had a different deal from the Bandidos at Parklea. Most of them had to share cells.

"Jump up and down and let's hear you rattle," Jock's men joked when he arrived at the jail, wearing his army green hat to protect his head from the heat and the sun. He still had fragments of pellets, more than 30 of them, lodged in his face and head. One was in his heart. He carried them as a soldier would, relics of a hard-fought war. His hat became his identity in place of his hair which was shaved several times in hospital. It grew back as thick, grey stubble, giving him a more sinister look, with his tinted gold-rimmed glasses and grey pallor from weeks in a hospital bed.

Vanessa and Holly-Anne would often visit on both days at the weekend. Prisoners were restricted to three visits at Long Bay, one at the weekend and two on weekdays, but once court started, Vanessa, along with the other Comanchero women, was allowed two visits on the weekends.

The visiting area reminded Vanessa of a school yard with brightly-painted wooden garden tables and chairs. One of the Comancheros built Holly a sandpit by bricking in part of the dogs' yard. There was not much sand, but it kept her occupied. She accepted Jock's new home, as most children of three adapt.

"It's Daddy's place," she would say each time Vanessa took her to visit her father.

"That's right, Sharkey, it's Daddy's place," Vanessa would answer.

Vanessa was glad Jock's mother, who had cancer, was not allowed to come to the jail. "The only thing that's keeping her going is waiting to see her William again," she said to Jock. "She'd crack up and go whinging and crying. I don't think that's a good sort of set up. Holly wouldn't know why Nanny was crying."

Penrith, a city that resembles a country town rather than a thriving metropolis, is the last major centre before the F5 highway leaves Sydney proper and heads towards Katoomba in the Blue Mountains.

It is a sprawling, relaxed town sprinkled with housing estates and middle-class dwellings with built-in backyard swimming pools. In the early 1980s the small city, which offered reasonably priced real estate to families eager to own their home, boomed.

In September 1984, Penrith became increasingly attractive to the detectives and members of the Crown preparing their brief for the Milperra Massacre case, because of its brand new, high-security courthouse.

The Penrith District Courthouse is a modern building. Air-conditioned, with sloping skylight windows, it stands in the main street directly behind Penrith Police Station, which is joined to the court by an underground tunnel.

The only disadvantage was its distance from Sydney, 70 kilometres from the city's central business district. It was a journey which was to become painfully familiar to lawyers, police officers and media who frequented the courthouse in the early long, hot months of the committal hearing.

At first, some chose to stay in the country town. One newspaper set up a press room, renting a fibro hut with one stifling room, a telephone and a single chair. Detective Barry Smith had organised a seven-bedroomed house for police, near the Nepean River.

Detective Smith believed the police should be awarded medals for their part in rounding up the men who had struck terror into the hearts of ordinary citizens.

"You ask anyone where they were when President Kennedy was shot and they'll tell you, just like if you ask anyone in Australia where they were on September 2 and I'll bet they can tell you that too," he would indignantly tell any interested party.

He felt some satisfaction telling about the New South Wales police force receiving a telex from West Germany saying they had 14 Hell's Angels on murder charges—what do we do with them?

He was proud of Operation Hardwalk, the biggest operation he had been involved with since he joined the force. The case had injected renewed enthusiasm into his work, a change from the routine murders he was used to dealing with.

Prior to the hearing, he had given up smoking. But as the court case started, he found himself reaching for the disposable lighter, a cigarette ready in his hand.

Early on, in the mornings before court started, he would chew on nicotine gum, but soon discarded that approach to beating his addiction. Dressed in jogging shorts, a t-shirt stretched across his paunchy middle, he would jog down to the Nepean River.

As the day neared for the start of the committal hearing, the police became tense over the difficulties of managing such a massive operation with the ever present threat of a breakout.

Lists of known members and associates of both gangs were printed and distributed to all police involved, stamped confidential. Addresses used by both gangs were noted.

The police had been told four high ranking members of the United States Bandidos intended travelling to Australia, including Ronnie Hodge, President of the Nomad Chapter, who had met Snoddy and Charlie Sciberras during their trip to the United States.

On 10 October, a month before the committal hearing started, the police were told there were negotiations between the Bandidos and the Hell's Angels in the United States to trade off chapter locations, which would allow the American Bandidos to have a chapter on the west coast of the United States and therefore easier access to the Bandidos in Australia.

They also discovered the new chapter of Bandidos that had been initiated in Griffith, a Riverina town south of Sydney.

Then in the first weeks of the committal, information came to police that approaches were made to certain people in Wollongong, the south coast steelwork city, and to others at the Commercial Hotel in nearby Port Kembla, to buy handguns at a cost of $1000 for both the Bandidos and the Comancheros. The handguns were thought to have been for members of both gangs still on the outside to continue their bitter feud.

All of this made the masterminds behind the police security arrangements—code named Operation Spartan—nervous. For the first few months 100 police were involved in the bikie hearing, at a cost of $2 million.

Seven units, including three back-up vans, transported the prisoners to and from the jail.

Eighty police, 30 of them TRG armed with shotguns, two-way radios, handguns and nightsticks, were rostered on duty for the first few weeks. The trade union for the junior police officers, the NSW Police Association, complained that the Milperra Massacre committal hearing was draining the resources of the other 10 000 police in the state.

Officers from metropolitan stations as far away as Cronulla, almost 100 kilometres from Penrith, were brought in for roof patrol.

A metal detector was installed at the front and only entrance to the court, screening everyone who entered the precincts unless they were lawyers, police or media, with authorised police passes.

Courtroom Number One was chosen, the largest of five courts. Reinforced perspex coops, like cages, were built for each gang at the rear of the courtroom on either side of the entrance. Microphones and speakers were installed in each coop so the defendants could hear clearly.

On the right hand side of the court, a large plaster model of the Viking Tavern carpark and hotel, complete with miniature bikes and cars, stood on a specially constructed table. The model was the work of a police officer who rushed frantically to finish it on the first day of his honeymoon. The model was never used. Objections were made by both defence teams that the model bikes and cars were not admissible as no evidence had been given as to their positions.

Chairs lined the doorway, hall and both sides of the court, three rows of four seats directly to the side of each cage. These were for officers of the New South Wales police force. Two men guarded the magistrate and a further eight were courtroom guards.

The mood among the press that gathered at the courthouse early on November 12 mirrored the tension felt by the police and lawyers alike.

There was the feeling of a big story in the air—television helicopters hovered, every Sydney newspaper had at least two reporters and an artist at the court, and many of the major interstate papers had flown in their own staff.

"Be there early, there's limited seats," was the message from the police media unit. As early as 9am, a group of reporters had formed a line at the courtroom door, giving their details to the police constable checking identification.

A hoard of photographers and cameramen swarmed over the steps outside the court, snapping pictures and filming legal representatives, policemen, and anyone who looked vaguely like a relative or friend of a bikie.

Sergeant Des Mussing from the police media liaison unit, organised the press at the courtroom door. It was first in first seated he joked, but it was obvious that more than half of the media would miss out on a seat.

He later compromised, announcing each media organisation was allowed one seat on the ground floor. The rest would be allowed into the public gallery, otherwise restricted to relatives of the defendants. There was no room for the interested public.

"Christ, we were here before her," one reporter shouted from the courtroom door as Sergeant Mussing gallantly allowed a female reporter from the New Zealand Press Association to jump to the front of the press queue.

"Okay, come on, you blokes. Let's move it," Senior Constable Brian Rassmussen opened the cell door and began herding the Bandidos out from the holding cells like sheep, one by one through the corridor and up the narrow stairs to the centre of the courtroom. The court was empty except for police, the heavy court doors guarded and locked while the prisoners were transferred.

The Bandidos were brought up first. Flanked by police officers, they were led into the left side coop. Wooden panelling screened their legs from the court. There was a small gap above the panelling, next to which the Bandidos would crouch awkwardly to talk to their legal counsel. Above the gap was the reinforced perspex screen, which stretched to a height of seven feet.

The Comancheros were led into court only after the Bandidos were secured. They sat in the right side coop, directly behind their lawyers—a sea of hairy faces in checked shirts and jeans, shorts and t-shirts. Two bore slogans: "Let the Comancheros Go" and "Comancheros 18th Anniversary, Long Bay Run '66-'84."

When the prisoners were secured, the doors of the court finally opened and a stream of lawyers pushed through, followed closely by the anxious faces of the press looking for the best of seventeen official media seats.

The defendants, unhandcuffed, sat in rows on plastic seats staring past the media who sat directly in front of both gangs. Several defendants smoked cigarettes while they waited for the magistrate, and some left their chairs and leaned up against the perspex partition to talk to their solicitors.

"All rise." The orderly heralded the arrival of the magistrate.

Mr Greg Glass, shiny pink face freshly scrubbed, wearing a navy suit with a muted pink shirt, entered the court and walked to his dais, bowing briefly before taking his seat.

He sat at the pinnacle of the proceedings, peering across gold-rimmed bifocals, his greying hair plastered carefully across his balding patch. Behind him an elaborate plaque reminded him of his duty "Dieu Et Mon Droit" (God And My Right) and scrolled around the Coat of Arms were the words "Honi Soit Qui Mal Y Pense" (Evil be to he who evil thinks).

Glass was more familiar with the quieter courts at Westmead, which did not attract such public attention. Greg Glass had joined the Attorney-General's Department as a junior clerk in 1953 and had worked his way through the system patiently waiting for an ultimate promotion to the City Coroner, ambition disguised under his unassuming countenance.

He knew nothing about bikies. The Attorney-General provided him with a hire car, a deluxe model Ford, which picked him up from his home every morning at 8.30am after his morning jog and a light breakfast. He would be dropped home at 5.30pm. He had ample time to read during the 100 kilometre round trip to court.

Sitting first as the Coroner, Glass took evidence identifying the deceased, the place of death, and he was informed about the persons charged with the seven murders.

He looked down on the sea of faces before him; he had never seen such a sight in a court before. So many solicitors, he mused.

The coroner's court adjourned, and, sitting as a magistrate, Glass began the committal hearing. Legal argument started, the difficulties of the multiple defendants becoming apparent immediately. One of the two Crown Prosecutors, Alan Viney, told the magistrate he proposed to make a public address. "It seems to me in a case of this nature where there are so many defendants and so many witnesses that to commence the case simply by calling the first witness, everyone in the court would be in the dark until the picture emerged."

Glass agreed that the Crown Prosecutor should give an opening address—he needed guidelines because of the complex nature of the matter. "No other judicial officer has been faced with a matter of this nature," he said, his face shining under the fluorescent lights.

An anonymous telephone call claiming there was a bomb in the court-house forced him to adjourn proceedings shortly after 11am so police officers could search the building.

"Yes, we've ascertained it was a hoax call, the building and surrounds have been checked again but we're satisfied it was a false alarm," Detective Chief Inspector Ron Stephenson told reporters twenty minutes later.

The large crowd filed back into the court and the defendants were again brought up from their cells.

Chris Murphy was on his feet almost immediately. Why, he demanded, was Kristine Duffy, who had been charged only with affray, allowed to sit behind her lawyer and not in the coop with the other defendants?

"Why be sexist about it?" Murphy challenged the magistrate. "She has played a part as strong as any and should be seated with the other defendants in their goldfish bowl without water. They don't have any privileges. She should not have any privileges. I don't want that woman sitting at the bar," his features fell into their best performance of a scowl.

A Comanchero lawyer, sallow-faced dark-haired Trevor Nyman, complained about the distance his clients had to travel each day from Long Bay Jail to the court. Both sides of the defence muttered about the amount of publicity the case had attracted.

Two hours after court began, the Crown Prosecutor finally rattled off his

his opening address in twenty minutes.

"The prosecution case is that the evidence will point to a common purpose among the defendants and others, including some of the deceased, to engage in a battle involving the use of weapons, contemplating that death or serious injury was a possible incident of that conflict."

The media began to leave their seats to file for midday.

Back in the courtroom at 2pm, the first witness of the hearing, Detective Constable Mark Charles Nicholls from the Ballistics Unit, Scientific Investigation Section, took the stand. "I was a passenger in the police helicopter and took some photographs," he said. He had a photogrammetery plan of the hotel and the grounds.

Viney had just begun to take him through his evidence when Glass was told a fault in the sound system prevented the defendants from hearing properly—they couldn't hear from behind their perspex partitions.

At that point, Mr Glass resigned himself to the fact day one was destined to be anything but smooth sailing. Faced with another adjournment and the prospect that adjusting the speaker system would take at least 45 minutes, he called it a day.

The list of injured requiring special transport arrangements was read out: Tony Melville (Lard), with his foot in plaster; Grant Everest (Pig), expected to be in hospital for six weeks with his knee injury; and John Campbell (Whack), who was "very sick and should be in a hospital bed".

"How many do you want tomorrow?" Charlie Goldberg, representing Jock and two other Comancheros, spoke through the gap between the perspex barrier and the wooden panelling.

"Winfield, coupla packets," Jock replied.

By the end of day one the security at the main entrance had one culprit—not a gun-wielding bikie but a woman who had been caught with hash-oil in her handbag.

The bikie case brought prosperity to Penrith, particularly to the sandwich shops on High Street. Scores of police officers bought takeaways for lunch, and counter lunch at the Top End pub became popular.

Some restaurants could count on at least one group of lawyers eating their lunches twice a week. And the local photocopying business, Instant Print, had new regular customers.

It wasn't long before several defence lawyers had individual accounts at the Courthouse Coffee Shop, where they notched up tea and vegemite on toast before court, open sandwiches for morning tea and lunch, and the occasional afternoon coffee. They would pay up at the end of each month, sometimes every three months writing cheques at the table with flourishing signatures. The Bandido lawyers spent around $150 a week which included the cost of their cigarettes. At least two were chain smokers.

Day two held promise. The Crown's secret witness was waiting in the wings. It was not known how the bikies would react to the turncoat who had broken every code of loyalty to the brotherhood.

Bernard Podgorski was driven to court by plain-clothed police officers. He lay flat on the floor in the back of an old model Holden. Under the Crown Witness Protection Scheme, only two officers knew of his whereabouts at any given time.

The police had also been informed that two unidentified bikies, probably American Bandidos, intended coming to Australia to "fix Podgorski". They could not afford to lose him.

He had spent the first few nights at the police station at Springwood in the Blue Mountains. His wife and child were allowed to bring him meals and the police turned a blind eye to him seeking solace from his wife by other means.

"Chris'll have his balls in the witness stand," another of the Bandido lawyers, Andrew Young mumbled to some of the men as they stood behind their perspex coop waiting for court to sit. From behind his Father Christmas beard, Young reassured them, "He'll keep him there for days".

Behind Young, the Comancheros shuffled up the narrow steps from the holding cells in single file. Knuckles watched as they were led into their perspex coop. Then the court doors opened and a stream of lawyers and journalists poured through. Knuckles saw Karen, her face red with effort as she leaned towards him.

"Hi, babe." Knuckles twisted around to face her, squeezing around the partition and stretching upwards.

"How are you today?" she forced a happy smile.

Her fingers brushed lightly with his own as she tried to reach him. Karen Martin was Knuckles' old lady, now that his former wife and the mother of Harley, had left him.

Karen, petite and young, had displayed a loyalty towards her man far beyond Knuckles' expectations, considering the infancy of their relationship. She had the sort of qualities a Bandido could expect from his woman.

Across the court, Kristine Duffy, wearing a tailored skirt and blouse, her hair dyed blonde, crouched by the glass partition and spoke to JJ through the gap.

"All rise."

The couple's brief intimacy was brought to a halt as the tip staff heralded the magistrate.

Knuckles watched as the small figure walked to his dais.

Knuckles sat down with his brothers. He felt the scrutinising of the media. He caught the eye of the cute blonde, sitting not far behind. He smiled at her. She blushed and looked away.

When Glass called for Podgorski, Knuckles watched the constable leave the court by the door near the witness stand. The seconds ticked slowly by. After five minutes, even the magistrate began to glance towards the door. The court was silent.

The door opened. Podgorski entered, flanked by two armed officers. He stood at the witness stand, with eyes averted.

"So help me God," he muttered. All eyes turned to the witness. He felt tiny rivulets of sweat trickle down the small of his back as he tried to concentrate on the prosecutor. His dark eyes remained downcast, as though he was studying the checks on his shirt. His red-brown beard was long and uncombed. His hair framed his face in long matted strands. He sat uneasily, despite the comfortable faded blue jeans.

"Would you please state your full name?" Crown Prosecutor, Peter Bodor asked.

"Yes, Bernard Stephen Podgorski."

"Can I have the spelling please?"

Murphy jumped to his feet.

"Can we have the people removed from the door? They are a distraction and I don't know what effect they might have on the witness, but I find them irritating. There is a Detective Smith and . . ."

Glass was indignant. "Mr Murphy."

Murphy fumed. "There are witnesses in this case that should be sitting somewhere, perhaps in a room.."

Glass dispensed a police officer to check whether the crowd at the back of the court were witnesses.

Podgorski did not have a chance to speak for his first half hour in the witness box.

Bodor attempted a beginning, "Mr Podgorski, as at the second . . ." Then Andrew Young intervened, with a number of objections. Chris Murphy, in a lengthy tirade, questioned the basis of Podgorski's indemnity.

"What are you asking the court to do, Mr Murphy?" Glass asked.

"Adjourn the matter, refer the matter back to the Attorney-General. Or deny acceptance of the indemnity within this court."

Knuckles was getting bored.

It was some time before Podgorski began his evidence in chief. His answers were soft. Bodor led him into the fray, hardly coaxing at all. It seemed that Podgorski was ready to speak.

"Were you a member of a motor cycle club on the second of September 1984?"

"Yes, I was. I was a member of the Bandidos."

"Can you recall on what date you joined the Bandidos Motorcycle Club?"

"Yes, about the thirteenth of November 1983."

"And on second of September 1984, where were you?"

"I was at the Viking Hotel, Milperra."

Podgorski went on to recount his history with the Comanchero Motorcycle Club.

" . . .you said you met a number of members of the Comancheros, is that correct?" Bodor asked.

"Yes, I did."

"Can you recall them by name?"

"Yes..there is Caesar, Colin Campbell, Shadow that was . . ." Podgorski had dropped his voice to a whisper as he named his former comrades.

Glass intervened.

"Witness, you will have to speak up. Start again."

Podgorski repeated the names, but only slightly louder.

" . . .and a bloke called Sheepskin Mick—don't know his second name."

"Did you have some sort of an association with these Comancheros at that time?" Bodor asked.

"Yes, I used to have a drink with them occasionally and see them at their houses and things like that . . ."

More objections followed, but Podgorski continued.

"I was invited to a few parties of the Comancheros I think—one down at Wiseman's Ferry. I was introduced to Jock Ross."

He recounted the history of the Bandidos.

"On November the thirteenth we burned our old Comanchero colours . . .Snodgrass—Anthony Spencer—was the leader of the city chapter . . .we had no contact with the Comancheros after the split . . ."

As Podgorski unravelled his tale, the defendants in both sides of the dock remained stony-faced. Some of them jotted down notes.

"Can you recall how long after the club was formed you became Secretary of it?" Bodor questioned.

"Probably a couple of months or so, I'd say."

"Now, I'd like you to take your time about this—go through the members of the Bandidos at the time of formation, first of all by club name followed by any other name that you knew the individual by."

"There was Caesar.."

Murphy was up again.

"I have no objection Your Worship . . .to him identifying the men in court. That might save some time. He can look at them and identify them."

"Well, it might matter for the witness," Glass hesitated but Bodor readily agreed.

Podgorksi saw the way in which Murphy had orchestrated this in a way blatantly designed to make him squirm.

"Bull Campbell," Podgorksi said as he met Bull's glare. Opey was next, then Zorba, Ray, Louie, Kid Rotten, Bear, Snake, Big Tony. On to the next row.

Knuckles was next. He followed suit, glaring at Podgorski. He felt Podgorski flinch as their eyes met momentarily.

"Perhaps if the front row stand up he might be able to see them," Murphy suggested.

Knuckles stood up and sat down again, feeling pleased. Podgorski was really having a hard time.

He identified five Comancheros—Jock, JJ, Snow, Kraut and Tonka.

Then he named the dead. "Leroy—Phillip Jeschke; Sparrow—I don't know his right name; Foghorn—that's Robert Lane, and that's all I know . . ." He tailed off, sat down and gulped from a glass of water.

Then he continued his tale, telling of the fateful meeting at the Bandido clubhouse. He fielded the objections like a horse leaping hurdles.

"Can you say whether all or less than all the members were present? I'm not talking about full members," Peter Bodor's voice carried across the silent courtroom.

"It'd be close to all, probably barring one or so . . .I think Bongo Snake was crook—he'd been belted up the week before that.."

"And he's also not before the court, is that correct?"

"No, he's not."

"And was there a speaker at the meeting?"

"Numerous people talked, Snoddy was talking . . .He was on the phone to Jock. He said, 'I have spoken to Jock on the telephone after these incidents that happened and. .'"

The atmosphere was oppressive. Glass interrupted several times, requesting him to speak up.

" 'And Jock Ross has informed me that we're at war'," Podgorski quoted letting it all out at once.

It was a fitting end to the second day of the committal hearing.

Knuckles watched the media record in shorthand notebooks the once-sacred secrets. Radio journalists hurried from the court, bowing quickly in the direction of the magistrate, falling over each other for what seemed the tenth time since Podgorski took the stand, determined to file the latest revelation. "A war declaration", good copy by any chief-of-staff's book, on the wires for the 4 o'clock news bulletin.

Knuckles felt violated.

He began drawing in ornate letters "B.F.F.B." on his court notepad. "Bandidos forever, forever Bandidos" ran repeatedly through his head.

Podgorski had been in the witness stand for six days, with two days off at the weekend.

It had taken until day four before the Crown was able to extract information from him without a stream of objections from the defence.

Roo had given up all pretence of listening. He was reading James Mitchener's *Centennial* as the legal argument droned on.

Now, like a bull terrier worrying its prey, Chris Murphy again tackled Podgorski.

"Now as a motor cyclist you were part of a—what you would describe—would it be called a brotherhood?"

"Yes." Podgorski's answer was barely audible.

"And in that situation loyalty to friends was something of high priority?"

"Yes."

"Doing the right things by your friends?"

"Yes."

"Not telling lies about them?"

"Yes."

"And that's very important to you?"

"Yes."

"You were at the scene that day?"

"Yes."

"Your physical appearance was then the same as it is now?"

"I don't think I had a beard as long as this, no."

"Did you remove the long beard for some reason?"

"No, it was just starting to grow then, I think."

"In relation to your body, do you have any marks on your body that distinguish you from any other human being?"

"I've got tattoos but that's about it."

"And what tattoos have you got?"

"I've got a Bandido tattoo across my arm. A couple of other little ones—that's about it."

"What other little ones? Or can't you remember?"

"I can remember but it's pretty hard to describe."

"Well, tell me what they say if words are written and what they look like, if they look like anything."

"One says Harley Davidson."

"Where is that?"

"On the inside of my arm."

"What else?"

"Heavily tattooed arms I suppose, up the top of the arms."

"What's on those tattoos?"

"All sorts of things."

"Well, how about telling us what's on them?"

"A couple of eagles and dragons, swallow, coupla things like that."

"Any other tattoos?"

"On me back."

"What's on your back?"

"Just a Harley motor and flames coming out of it."

"Yes, what else, any other tattoos?"

Yes, on the feet."

"What's tattooed on your feet?"

"There's a panther on one foot."

"Yes."

"Pair of skunks on the bottom of me feet."

"Underneath your feet?"

"Well, they don't tattoo underneath your feet, Mr Murphy."

"What . . .by skunks you means those smelly little animals? Is that what you refer to? Is that what a skunk is?" Murphy was in his element.

"Yes, I believe that's what it is, Mr Murphy. Yes."

"That's the lot eh?"

"That's correct."

"You have no other tattoos?"

"No."

"That's not correct is it? You've just told the court an untruth, haven't you?"

"Not really, no."

"Have you told this court an untruth in your last answer?"

"No, I have not."

"Have you got any words tattooed on your feet?"

"There's a pregnant skunk saying 'Hey you?' and the other one—it's got a skunk running away saying 'Who me?'"

Murphy changed the subject as quickly as he had raised it. Bodor said nothing.

"Remember the meeting at the club house when it was decided to go to the Bull and Bush Hotel?"

"Yes."

Murphy had won some silent admiration from the rest of the defence, who sat attentively, for once, looking at the witness box. He had also won a look of uneasiness from his prey, who started to drum his fingers on the table and scratch his beard as if seeking reassurance.

Murphy had tired of the Bull and Bush.

"The reason you are giving evidence in this court is because you enjoy an honest and loving relationship with your wife and child, is that correct?"

"That's correct."

"And that's a relationship of trust and honesty that you enjoy as a married man. Correct?"

"Correct."

"And as you're being honest with the court, you are honest with your wife?"

"Most of the time with my wife I'm honest, yes."

"Sorry?"

"I said most of the time with my wife, I'm honest. I mean everybody has their little side activities, don't they?"

"Yes, but it's the love of your wife and honesty that brings you to this court, correct?"

"Correct."

"Who was the woman you took down to Griffith on the back of your motor bike a few days before the incident at the Viking Hotel?"

"I can't remember the first name."

"Does it assist your memory if I suggest you stated to people you were only taking her because she had money and you could get her supporting mother's benefit off her. Does that jog your memory?"

"I beg your pardon?"

"Did you say to your friends you could bludge off her because she had a Commonwealth benefit?"

"No. I did not."

"Does it jog your memory if I suggest to you that you slept in Bear's bed with her down there?"

"We all do these things, Mr Murphy. I'm sure you've done that sort of thing yourself."

Glass coughed. "Witness you should answer the question. What you said is not an answer."

"I can't see how my sexual activity has got anything to do with the case, Your Honour. Everybody, you know, does these little things. I'm sure Mr Murphy's been in the same situation if he can find somebody who can handle him."

Glass was indignant. "Witness, there's no need to make comments like that. I direct . . ."

"Sorry, Mr Murphy. I apologise."

" . . .direct you to answer the question," Glass continued.

"You love truth and honesty don't you, Mr Podgorski?"

"Correct."

"And I suppose you told your wife about the activities there?"

"No, I did not."

Murphy had made his point. He moved on to Podgorski's fear of the Comancheros.

"And in fact each morning you lifted the bonnet of your car and looked under the motor to see if any gelignite had been placed there?"

"Hey, mate," one of the three courtroom guards sitting beside the Comancheros nudged his friend heavily. "Don't fall asleep."

14

The diary

"17-18th December. Went to Long Bay jail today for x-rays on my gut. Spent all day 17th in small yard. Got real pissed off. Then I was put into hospital for observation. Prison officers did not no what to do with me. Cause they thought there might be shit between me and a Comanchero. Seen none. Nite in hospital not too bad, but to be in Long Bay would send me round the bend."

Snoddy would start writing after 10pm just before he went to bed, chewing on the end of his pen, concentrating on the effort. After lock-up at 7pm he would chat to Roo from the cell door.

"You're in love, mate," Snoddy said to Roo one night shortly before Christmas. Standing at the window in a gap between the bars to the cells, he positioned the mirror until Roo's olive-coloured face appeared in the small oval shape.

"Aw yeah . . .," although Roo was non-committal the smile Snodgrass saw in the mirror told all. The mirror made talking all the more worthwhile. It gave you someone to look at, not just a disembodied voice.

"Davo's happy for ya," Snoddy said softly. He was like a mother hen sometimes, Roo thought, fussing over all his little chickens, soft-hearted. He remembered the time that Snoddy had burst into tears when Davo's mother, Mummsie Cool, had baked him a birthday cake one year.

"Val's taken a bit of an interest in Lee's sister so we'll see how that goes," Snoddy continued. "I'm bloody lucky I've got such a good family out there—Lee's mum and dad and all her bros and sisters."

"Yeah . . .What did you think of those movies?" Roo asked.

"Load of porno shit. Can't get any in here, eh?" Snoddy became morose again.

"No, mate, that's for sure. What do you think of her, eh?"

"Your girl? Good."

"She's not bad at all," Roo concurred. "Ya see that 62-year old junkie?" Roo tried a change of subject. "Told me today he had an eleven year lagging on another charge. Nothing else to look forward to, eh?"

"No, mate. Lee's having a shit time out there. I just can't see the end of the tunnel, you known . . .Best piece of medicine I've had all day was them coming to see me today—my lady and Joel . . ."

Roo was silent. Then he yawned and said, "Saw some foxes in the paddock again tonight. Out the cell window—clear as anything they were."

"Better get some sleep, bro, see you in the morning," Snoddy said.

Sometimes Snoddy would feel like talking for hours, sometimes Roo would call out and the returned conversation would be brief.

Snoddy's brothers accepted his solitary hobby, just as they accepted his emotional state. The diary became a form of release, a place where Snoddy could transfer the burden of responsibility that weighed on him—that of looking after his brothers—and the tormenting black thoughts that he was the one who led them to the Tavern that day.

Shadow's face was beginning to blur with time. He tried to conjure up his image. He could only think of him in the carpark, the blood seeping out from underneath his beard, his eyes open, gripped with fear. As the weeks passed at Parklea jail, Snoddy gradually became convinced that everyone who was close to him was tainted by him—he had a disease that infected those he loved so that they were the ones who suffered.

The proximity of Christmas made his heart ache. There was always the possibility of bail—the first time they had entertained the idea since it had been formally rejected in September—the word hung before him like the proverbial carrot.

But five days before Christmas that idea floundered. He had got up that morning imbued with optimism, showering with a sense of purpose, carefully soaping himself all over, permitting himself to daydream about what he would do with Lee when he got out. He would have a son of his own—they would start a family. He thought of Joel with his spiked haircut, similar to many of the sons of his brother Bandidos. He had grown to love Lee's boy as if he was his own.But Lee would have his child—his own son. He would see to that.

After the long ride to court in the police van, the Bandidos were placed in the holding cells briefly and then taken up to court to await the judge's decision. At 10 am bail was refused.

"Bail refused on grounds that the judge said that the safety of the people are at stake!" he wrote in his diary that night.

"Being put in a jail with cons is not what you would call doing justice to us. We are people that have not been in jail before and they put us in the most maximum jail in NSW. All it will do to us well me anyway, is make me bitter towards the people that put me hear . . ."

On 21 December, the weight of the depression intensified. "I feel like killing myself because I am being set up for a crime I did not do." He looked at the words on the page and wondered if he meant what he had written.

"I just wish I could talk to someone to tell them what really did happen. I don't know how much longer I can hang on to my sanity. I miss my lady and kid and this is fucking them up real bad. The same as all my bro's are going through, but I can't talk for them, each man has his own way of handling this thing. The Salvation Army came today and gave us a gift pack which was a real good feeling of at least someone caring for us in here . . ."

The Viking Tavern had lost business. Reception bookings for weddings had dwindled, one had even cancelled. Few people chose to stay there any more. It became known as a bikie pub. Busloads of senior citizens drove past, some of the more curious stopping to examine the bullet holes sprayed across the back fence, their fingers tracing the roundness.

Inside the public bar, Maxine, the tough, aging barmaid who stood just on five feet tall, entertained the lunchtime drinkers with tales of the hotel's new found notoriety.

"It was a showdown and that was it," Maxine rallied her audience, her face like a painted prune. "I was coming home from golf and on me way to the pub and I saw the Bandidos riding down with guns . . ."

Two older men sat with their beer glasses poised. They had heard the story before. "And the phone calls I've had. One said: 'I'm coming up to cut your tits off'—but I knew they were kids because they would have said boobs . . ."

"What about that girl—what was she about then? She a bikie moll?" a younger man in a check shirt asked.

"Yeah, she was a bikie moll living with Stretch, I think his name was. She lay there in the carpark like a little wooden doll with her arms stuck out . . ."

"Why did it happen here then?" the man asked.

"There's been two fights here in the last eight years. It's just not that sort of pub. We never had that many bikies—the Rebels and the Shitmuckers—that was about it. But when they got here," she nodded her head to emphasise the next sentence, "they got straight into each other. It was like a movie scene but the extras never got up." Maxine was pleased with the new image she had thought up and she paused, savouring its impact on her listeners.

Mike Langley and Geoff Coasby had left the hotel. Langley's pregnant wife had been receiving threats and he had had enough. He packed up in November and went to manage a hotel in the inner city.

Cliff Cartwright had taken over, a plump man in his thirties, his dark hair cropped in an oldfashioned pudding bowl cut. He wore loud clothes—orange shirts and cream jeans. Unlike Langley, he basked in the hotel's new identity. He stood behind the bar with Maxine occasionally contributing to the conversation.

"The day before I came out here a policewoman told me not to come. It's the roughest pub in the area. I know. I grew up 'round here."

The three in the audience nodded in sympathy.

"And Langley's wife's a key witness at the hearing, you know . . ."

During the first few months in prison, Chewy Lorenz spent many hours creating elaborate drawings on love letters he composed for his new wife, carefully filling in flowers and vines in pastel colours.

To Mrs Chewy! Well, my love. Here I am again hey! I'm really sorry about today about being shitty. I was just in one of those moods so again I'm sorry. I'll make it up to you on our next visit . . . I'm thinking seriously of buying a cheap caravan after we get back on our feet and put it down the south coast somewhere. Actually I saw one in the paper last week for $900 15' by 7' something like that will do us nicely with an annexe. It will be our own little hideaway or maybe a love nest hey! I'm not looking forward to going to court tomorrow only because of the shit drive in the cattle truck. The only good thing about tomorrow will be seeing you my love. If this thing goes okay when we all go to Penrith we should all be together soon—the Chewy family hey! . . .

Christmas Day came and went.

"25th December 1984. Merry Xmas Bandidos."

"Shit it was hot. It rained this afternoon. It was like someone, just watering a garden after a hot day. We all had lunch together not bad, but I missed my family."

Snoddy recorded the significant day in his diary. He had started writing a book on the massacre. The first chapter was almost finished. It was time the true story was told about the set-up in the carpark, he thought.

On Boxing Day he ran out of enthusiasm. "Same as allways", he wrote for the next two days.

The rain continued streaming down the window outside, a grey blanket of cloud covering the sky. The emptiness of the concrete waterless moat outside depressed him. It was visiting day and he would have to see Lee and Joel inside.

Some of the Bandidos began complaining about their lawyers. Nothing seemed to be happening.

"I feel like I want to resign as Pres but, when I say it to someone they always make me feel like I can't do it. I've got my own reasons to do so, so I just might," he wrote three days after Christmas.

Lee had a hangover on New Year's Day. She wrote Snoddy a note to tell him she could not make it. It had cheered him up—"poor babe, she was partying for two people", he chuckled to himself while sitting at his desk after lock-up.

There were no New Year celebrations at Long Bay Jail, but on the first Saturday night of the year a band came in to entertain the prisoners with a two hour concert.

Jock was starting to feel better. The first two months of prison life had been difficult and marred by pain, as he adjusted to his new home and recovered from his head injuries.

"You just get into your routine and carry on," he told his friends.

"I'd heard it was hard, you know, it is hard, but not to the same extent as people make out. I've seen more friction in an army barracks."

Whenever court was not occupying his time, Jock would be in the education centre, an innovation in the jail. There he would dabble in copper and leatherwork. He would sit at the precarious tressle table and tackle the raw leather, cutting a shape out of the skin, choosing dyes for tobacco pouches, wielding the swivel knife he had been given by the leatherwork teacher. He chose patterns from the books she lent him, traced around them carefully on to the leather. The room was a pleasant change from the starkness of the cells. It looked more like the art room of a high school. Misshapen pots, vases and lopsided animals lined the shelves on one side of the room. The prison did not have a kiln, but the teachers would fire the clay.

The Education Centre was always a hub of activity and offered courses ranging from English as a Foreign Language to Aboriginal Studies.

Jock enjoyed spending time there. He was impressed with the department. "It helps people adjusting, you know, they've got everything in here, all sorts of courses and crafts, it teaches a lot of people to work together," he would say.

He made handbags, belts and purses, sending them out as presents. He even made some tobacco pouches for some of the boys.

"They're not the sorts of things I would do outside, but you've got time in here and outside you're working for a living," he told a visiting friend.

"See, it's got lots of binding," he showed him a pouch that was on the table in his cell. "You do mostly thonging, weaving, you learn a lot of forgotten arts, things people don't do no more."

"The one good thing about education is you get people coming in here with skills that they can pass onto someone else, and you pick ups skills from others."

Vanessa Ross would visit twice during the week, parking her car on the wide Anzac Parade, and walking up the palm-lined bitumen. She would pass the medieval walls, the gates, the portcullis, the towers with the armed sentries. She would pass the message above one of the gates: Dieu et Mon Droit.

She would follow the concrete path past the office marked "Prison bail—fines, private cash", past the Central Industrial Prison, where Jock faced the prospect of ending up if he was found guilty.

He was aware of the strain on her, with Holly and the kids. He resented being totally reliant on his wife and others outside. But he learned to accept it, there was nothing he could do about it.

He had been to management meetings at the centre and drug and alcohol rehabilitation meetings. "You have to live from day to day," he would often say to his men. "At least we're in the remand centre and looking to a day when we'll be getting out."

His men had adopted their own ways of coping. Scott Dive (Bones) had taken up creative writing, JJ had reached grade four in classical guitar studies. Snow helped Jock reorganise the leatherwork programme. Glen Eaves was studying for his HSC.

Jock shared a cell for several months before he got a break and went "one out". The cells on the top floor had a view of the sea if you stood on the black plastic toilet seats and craned out of the window. He preferred his privacy and as soon as he moved into his single cell, he plastered the walls with photographs of his family and his favourite motor bike shots.

The remand cells were nine feet wide, 14 feet long, with a toilet, sink, one cold water tap, a bed, cupboard and small table. There were no bedside radios or hot and cold running showers. If the prisoners were fortunate, they had "a floater"—a television belonging to a former inmate who passed it on. Televisions and radios were a form of currency, those who had accumulated more than one televison or radio would rent them out. Sometimes drugs would be paid for the luxury.

The small brick cells were cold, freezing cold in winter, and stifling hot in summer. Not that the cold bothered Jock much. During the cold winter months at the jail, Jock would often be seen wearing a pair of grey shorts. "The cold doesn't bother me," he'd say. It was a Scottish boast. "You Aussies wouldn't know what cold was."

Lock-up would be after 3pm, when the prisoners would line up along a yellow line near the exercise yards. After this, they would be allowed to walk the length of the floor of their wing, visiting each other in their cells, stretching their legs along the narrow old-fashioned corridors. Skylights let in a small amount of light but the sky was hidden by the mesh across them.

Jock missed his wife's home cooking. But the prison food was familiar. It reminded him of what he used to eat when he was serving as a sapper with the Royal British Engineers.

Meals were served from the servery on the ground floor. Rissoles and roasts were common fare. Dessert would inevitably include custard, sometimes bread and butter pudding, tinned fruit and jelly. There were sandwiches in the afternoons.

Jock and his men had learned to be more tolerant of others. "You'll always get all races and creeds comin' up here: chinks, slopeheads, wogs—all different races—and probably before they came in here they hated each other's guts," he told his men one day. "But once you start working together and doin' a bit together, one teaches another how to do something, it creates a much more relaxed atmosphere."

The Comanchero Motorcycle Club also flourished inside the jail. They would meet sometimes in the yards. This was where some of the men spent most of their days outside the court, areas like playgrounds but bereft of trees and children. Murals lined the wall along which the prisoners sat at tables—escapist visions of a South American prisoner, so rumour had it, who had enthusiastically painted goddesses, Egyptian obelisks and colourful volcanoes.

One of the prisoners' favourites was a Pink Floyd-like vision of freedom—a heavy metal door, exaggerated padlock and bolt hanging loose as the door swung open to reveal the outside world, which was a turquoise blue, hazy vision that could be the sea or whatever the viewer chose.

3.1.85 Had a bad dream about Lee and Joel. Fuck it scared me.
4.1.85 Bad dreams still there, can't seem to tell what is a dream and what is real. Anyway see Lee and Joel tomorrow, that should make me feel a lot better . . .

Jail was affecting Knuckles too. When court started up again after the Christmas break on 7 January, he just sat in the front row and looked at his thonged feet, a vacant look masking his face.

He was sick and tired of the heat, the court, the jail. Sick and tired of the whole fucking thing. On Fridays, since the magistrate had agreed to sit a four-day week, he worked at the jail, hosing down the workshop. It was an easy job. The weekends were best. Then Knuckles would play rugby league and at night there would be videos—some of them were interesting if they weren't r-rated ones—one starred Bruce Lee and some of the comedies were quite funny. But then Monday would come along again and the whole ghastly nightmare would be revived.

He gazed blankly at the blurred print of the Jackie Collins' novel, *Chances*, in front of him. His head ached, he couldn't concentrate. His stomach rumbled noisily as he had refused breakfast. Today they might have Chinese—it was a treat they got occasionally.

He remembered the health-conscious breakfasts he had as a child—kelp tablets for iodine, followed by his mother's concoction of wheatgerm oil and molasses mixed with honey and lemon. And everyone at school knew the McElwaine children trademark, soyabean compound milkshakes for recess. For lunch they ate wholemeal nut butter, candied honey and sesame meal sandwiches. Knuckles remembered eating five oranges daily.

Dinner was invariably a vegetable dish and even their dog Bruno, a bounding, energetic black labrador, ate lots of garlic because Bob McElwaine said it was worm preventative.

He thought of his father, now an honorary Bandido. A one-time pub owner, health food shop proprietor, marathon runner, a would-be entrepreneur with a great idea for marketing his own running shoes, he had led his family through ever-changing health fads and business ventures.

On his visit to Parklea last weekend he had arrived wearing his navy blue t-shirt with the words "I'm Knuckles Dad!" proudly emblazoned on it.

It had hit him hard, this thing. Knuckles thought about his father's pain, the defeated look about his bowed shoulders, despite the cocky t-shirt. Three of his sons to whom he had devoted his life, were in jail. And two of those he had counted on to reach the top in the boxing world.

He remembered the daily routine—a four mile family walk, striding out along the streets of Newcastle hand in hand. Greg, Phillip and Mark had collected many trophies for swimming, boxing and running from as young as seven years old. He remembered the article in a 1968 edition of the *Australian Women's Weekly*. The McElwaines had been described as a model family "glowing with vitality, energy and general well-being". Knuckles was then ten years old.

Bob McElwaine had taught all his sons to fight and he knew enough about boxing to team up Knuckles with a good trainer. By the end of his junior boxing career, Knuckles had won almost 40 middleweight fights. He had also beaten his older brother Greg's three-time State junior title record, snaring the honour a fourth time and the national crown twice.

At eighteen he had been selected for the Australian Olympic team to go to Montreal. He remembered Bob McElwaine reading out the newspapers that morning at breakfast.

"Listen to this, son. 'Hailed as the best since Madigan', and because of you we're seeing the 'nucleus of a revival of Australian amateur boxing'. Isn't that something, eh, Phil?" McElwaine beamed at his son and read on. "They say amateur boxing has produced no real talent since Tony Madigan lost an Olympic semi-final to Cassius Clay at Rome in 1960. And now you're the best since Madigan. We'll show 'em, son!"

Phil Young, a short smiling man, formerly a solicitor with the public prosecutions branch, had given up the public service to represent five of the Bandidos. Now it was his turn to question Podgorski.

Podgorski had been in the witness box for about five weeks. "I called it a set up, yes," he was saying, being favourable to the Bandidos at last, Knuckles thought.

"The Bandidos were doing their best to get back to Beaconsfield Road?"

"Yes."

Young asked questions about some of the incidents prior to Father's Day.

"I heard one Saturday night—blokes at the club—telling me because of what was going on . . .they had information Jock had a hit list of four to five members of our club," Podgorski said.

Knuckles had heard it all before. He started reading a paragraph of his Jackie Collins' novel, but he found it hard to concentrate. He was still getting headaches, a nagging problem since his bike accident.

Dwelling on his fighting days at least mollified him a little. He closed his eyes and slipped into further reverie. Of course, there was his gold medal, but where was he? Ah, yes, the Olympics. He remembered his spectacular fight against five-time Romanian middleweight champion, Alec Nastac. Nastac, with 380 fights under his belt, beat him 3-2, but Knuckles won the praise and the hearts of his Australian fans.

Then came more fame. The following year, he was dubbed "the dancer" and "twinkletoes" by the Bangkok press when he fought for the King's Cup in Thailand.

But 1978 had been his year. It was the year he most liked to dwell on, when he represented his country at the Commonwealth Games in Edmonton. He won a gold—without lifting a fist. He was awarded the honour on a forfeit when doctors declared his UK opponent Delroy Parkes unfit.

"We had a feeling he'd win, but not like that. Of course we're disappointed," Bob McElwaine had said. "But he would have won the gold anyway."

When he returned from Edmonton, his father told him, "We sat there waiting for you, Phil. Your mum, and me and Joanne and Robin—we sat in front of the colour telly at the Terminus, there was a big crowd there, all waiting for the fight . . ."

The Terminus Hotel had been Bob's latest business venture at the time. He bought the pub—a tough inner-city early-opener in the middle of Sydney's wharfie district—and moved to Sydney with his family in November 1977.

I was happy then, Knuckles thought, looking back. He had been the famous figure working behind the bar. The Terminus was a popular drinking spot for ex-pugs and many colourful characters of the Sydney boxing fraternity.

Photographs of world famous boxers hung high on the walls and a pair of Phil's boxing gloves dangled from the partition between the public and saloon bars. A huge glass display case, filled with boxing trophies—mostly Phillip's—was a legacy of a father's immense pride and belief in his champion son.

His sons adored him. But some of the rot had set in. The McElwaine marriage was on the rocks.

"I took the gun on the second to defend myself," Podgorski told the court. Knuckles tuned back in to the voice in the courtroom.

"Not to set out to do anyone bodily injury?" Young asked.

"Not from my point of view—no."

The court adjourned for the first day back since Christmas.

Greg Glass prided himself in being methodical. He had the usual "in" and "out" trays in his chambers at Penrith but now he had worked out a method of filing at home. He stood in his study, polishing his gold rimmed bifocals, surveying his handiwork.

Two copies of the transcript were given to him each day. He kept one at his chambers, the other he took home. Every night since the committal had started, he would go through and dissect the day's evidence. It was a complicated case, the prosecution relying as it was on general evidence to establish common purpose. Anything he found relating directly to a particular defendant, he would put in a box marked with that defendant's name. He called them his pigeon holes. He would work diligently until 11 or 12pm going to bed exhausted. It was January and there was no end in sight. The court was up to the third witness out of a possible 200 to be called. He knew it would continue long after its predicted six months.

Snoddy was back to dreaming about his mother again. It was the same dream he had been having for as long as he could remember. He was in Tamworth, a country town in northern New South Wales where he knew he had been born. His mother's "face" rose up before him—an image with no features surrounded by dark shoulder-length hair. She always appeared to him this way, partly a childish reconstruction of an incomplete memory. His father, he always called the man his father, although he never knew for sure if it was him, sat at a table in the kitchen in a fireman's uniform. He was playing cards. His mother was cooking something on the stove. It always started this way—homely, comforting. His mother wore an apron. Then he was in the bedroom opening his mouth and screaming but no sound came out. She was lying on the bed. Her face was cold and waxy like the expression on a mannequin in a shop window display. On the sheets were splashes of red. It was sprayed on the walls, soaking through the pillow slip under her dark hair. He was transfixed. Her wrists and hands were the bloodiest. But her hand was what remained with him even after the dream was over. It lay lifeless over the bed, hanging limp, the blood caked inside each of her filed fingernails.

Snoddy would wake shouting, still drugged from the Rohypnol, clammy and shivering. As he opened his eyes he would see the cold concrete walls and the shower recess at the bottom of his bed. And he would remember where he was. The drug helped him doze off again, into the nether regions to grapple with the demons inside him.

Outwardly he tried to pull himself together. He was Pres. They had chosen him to lead them.

Chewy wrote letters to his wife every week. He had been concentrating on building muscle, lifting weights in earnest. He had lifted 250 pounds on the bench press, straining until he was flushed from the effort, lying on the red weight benches next to the Activity Centre. Less energetic prisoners lay on blue mats in one of the few patches of grass in the prison, sunning themselves. Others sat in groups of two playing backgammon seated at the tables on the lawn. The weights were in the cemented yard area. Benches had been placed in the shade.

To you Babe.

I just can't believe how fast time is travelling. It's over two months now that I've been inside on my little holiday. Let's hope the rest of my time goes just as quick. I've worked out what I'm going to do if I get a lagging out of this. I'm going to take up oil painting. I've done every other type of painting hey! and I think if I took it up it would

relax me while I'm in here like going fishing relaxes me out there
...Keep smiling for me always. To you and the kids. Love
always...

It was 33 degrees.

Lee sat on one of the hard chairs in the visiting area, by the wall, shaded
from the hot early February sun. Her brown, newly-shaved legs stretched
over Snoddy's knees. He pinched the skin on her calf between his thumb
and forefinger rolling it absent-mindedly as he chatted to some of the
Bandidos who sat at his table.

Prisoners sat outside under gaily-coloured umbrellas in the sectioned-off
grassy area for visitors. It was a distinct improvement on the old-fashioned
approach at Long Bay jail. Parklea inmates wore white, starched hard-
wearing overalls, a change from the jail greens. The scene was incongruous, like a happy summer gathering in a park, except for the surrounding
high walls and armed warders who stood around watching. A group of
warders checked all visitors before they met with the prisoners. Some
prisoners sat inside, their women sitting on their knees, kissing and
cuddling and murmuring to their menfolk. Maximum physical contact for
the two hour designated visit was important.

Lee was wearing a white Indian cotton dress with a lacy bodice low cut,
revealing her cleavage. The dress rode up her thighs showing off her long
legs. Her bleached hair, showing darker at the roots, was loose.

"I'm going to be in here in fifteen years' time, babe," Snoddy had
murmured to her when she arrived. Lee had decided it would be one of those
days.

Some days she would get there and he would tell her he would be home
soon. He would be chatty and expansive, relaxed and fun to be with. His
moods swung from one extreme to another. He hated the captivity. She
remembered from their life together how he could not sit still. He could not
be tied down. There was a sense of restlessness about Snoddy that even she
was unable to grapple with. Once he had gone to work, ridden off on his
Harley and then returned two hours later.

"Can't stand that arsehole telling me what to do," he had said when she
enquired about his return.

Often she would keep quiet about things so as not to worry him. He
worried incessantly, she knew that.

She had first met him in a hotel, three years previously. He had been
leaning up against the bar. Her brother, Tom, was a Comanchero at the
time and he and Snoddy had been close. Tom often spoke about him. Lee
remembered being interested in Snoddy from that first encounter. He had
something about him, a quiet assurance mixed with a softness and a need to

212

be mothered.

"I've failed as Pres," he had said to her once. "We're no good as a club locked up. And I can't do anything to get them out of here. I've told the solicitors I will say I killed everyone if you'll let all my brothers out."

She had tut-tutted, holding him close and trying to draw him into talking about the future.

"What about our trip to the States and the farm we'll buy?" He would brighten momentarily.

It worried her sometimes when he spoke of dying.

"I can't be there with you at night, that's the trouble, Snod," she said when he first mentioned it. "You need to be cuddled, that's what you need. You know how bad you took Johnboy and Bull's death. You've been hurt for too long."

Today, he was back to being morose again.

"The time I had with you and Joel was the best time in my life. I had a family then. I was a father and a husband. Remember our trips to the Colo River? We'll have a child, babe, won't we? I'll rub oil into your belly so you don't get stretch marks."

She laughed, rubbing the agitated fingers that still plucked at her skin.

There was silence.

"It's Shadow's birthday soon . . ."

"I know," she said.

Stevo, the cook, had asked to join the club. Roo nominated him at one of the meetings they held in the common rooms.

The mid-state chapter came to visit and were declared an official chapter by the Sydney Bandidos. Snoddy sorted out administrative problems. One of the members was fighting with another, threatening to stab him if he did not get the $3000 he said was owed to him. Snoddy decided to pay the debt. He did not want bad blood in the club and he could see no other way to sort it out.

The Bandidos were model prisoners. Police agreed they were far better behaved than the Comancheros. Roo was one of the few who was criticised. He had punched one of the inmates for trying to steal another Bandido's television. The inmate had required fourteen stitches.

Snoddy sought psychiatric help. He would visit the psychiatrist monthly. The psychiatrist told him he was suffering from a bereavement reaction— the sort of feelings experienced when someone close to a person dies. Someone had died. He had advised him to stay on the Rohypnol until he became more adjusted to life in jail.

1.2.85   This place is fucking up my mind real bad. It's hard for me 'cause I got to do what is best for this club. Joel started school today. I hope it goes well for him.

2.2.85   Let's not forget.

7.2.85   Bandido Shadow in loving memory of my brother Shadow. Happy birthday. Been off court for the last two days, cause of my back. I go back tomorrow. I've got this funny feeling that my relations with Lee is not too good. I think it is starting to get to her . . .I love her so much. I just wish I could do something to make her feel better.

10.2.85   I retired as Pres today because I feel that this is not the way I thought the club would turn out. Some men just don't give a fuck and others' just don't have the right attitude towards each other.

God said do unto others as you would do to them. Friends do to friends as a sign of love.

We as Bandits should do unto each other as is our right to do so.

I have a friend with dark green and brown eyes.

She is a long way away but she is so close. We meet as friends and then parted as friends. Then found each other again and became friends and lovers forever. Lee for me.

He signed off with crosses for kisses. Then he drew a Harley with bulky farings next to a cactus bush in his diary. Underneath the entry he wrote, "B.F.F.B. BANDIDOS FOREVER, FOREVER BANDIDOS."

The following day brought a sickening feeling to the pit of his stomach. He had received a card in the mail. He had opened it with curiosity. He knew it was not Lee's handwriting.

He realised right away it was a Valentine's Day card. Of course. It was only a few days away. He opened it, and read the inscription: "To Dear Snotty, All my love. Leanne Walters. PS: Wish you could be here with me."

His hands felt clammy.

"What's up, Pres?" Roo came up to him in the common room.

"Just some mother-fucker playing games," Snoddy folded away his secret into the back pocket of his jeans.

"Fuck that upset me," he wrote that night in his diary. "Can't understand why or who would send it. Fuck I didn't kill her. I just feel like killing myself. It's just getting me down cause I know I aint guilty."

His resignation as Pres was not generally accepted. Five days later he was back as leader.

"We'll buy our way out of here for $20 000," Snoddy said one day to one of the Bandidos.

214

"How?"

" . . .Could get wired up by Dave—Jenny's friend."

"Who?"

"Julius has a mate who works for Telecom." Snoddy never stopped thinking of the outside world and his freedom.

On 21 February 1985, Rhonda McHarg gave birth to Toni Jessica Elizabeth, Dog's baby daughter, named in his honour, although he never lived to see her. Dog had always longed for a daughter, Rhonda told one of the tabloids. She was a plain girl with long fair hair parted down the middle, and wide spaced eyes.

"He was always employed and simply loved bikes," she said, posing for the camera with her new baby.

"You could not have found a better man to be with. He loved his children very much."

Dog had left his widow with three boys—Kevin, 6, Richard, 3, and Michael, 2. They were among eight of the Comanchero children left fatherless after the massacre.

Toni, named after her father, was born almost five months after he was killed. Dog's parents only found out about their son's death through some friends sending them a sympathy card shortly after Christmas. They were in London and had not heard the news.

Knuckles was slipping further into depression. He was again prone to blackouts. Wedged in the plastic bucket seats in the coop at the back of the courthouse he became claustrophobic. Even the trip from Parklea to Penrith in a car rather than a police van had not helped. Some mornings he would lie in his cell and refuse to go to court. The feeling immobilised him.

On 19 February, he was taken to the hospital at Long Bay and treated for depression.

Snoddy kept writing in his diary. Sometimes he only wrote "Same as allways." He had some black t-shirts printed with the words "Bandidos in memory of Shadow and Chopper" printed on the back.

"21.2.85 Got real sick today and they ended up taking me to Long Bay. They thought it was my olser that burst, but I think someone slipped me a mickey. Some of the brothers think I od'd on sleeping pills. Well I tell you this if I was going to kill myself I would do it in my cell, so sit on that."

The Bandidos in Griffith were having their first party. Lee was going with Lout, who had still not been arrested.

"2.3.85 Got a letter from Lee and it started out ok, then finished by sticking up me like as if it were my fault she is going down there. She says that I don't trust her. Well I take that as an insult to me, so if that's her game it's up to me to feel bad. Fuck, I wish I was out . . ."

"Yes, Mr Crown, do we have a sick parade this morning?" Glass had settled into the routine of the committal hearing. It was March 20 four months down the track.

Often the defendants' illnesses would take up the first fifteen minutes to half an hour of the morning's proceedings. But Knuckles' complaint was more serious than the usual excuses for non-attendance, as Chris Murphy was at pains to explain.

"Your Worship, the situation in relation to Mr McElwaine is this . . .as Your Worship can see . . .this man is asleep. Your Worship, he's not sleeping out of boredom or disinterest. He is suffering gross brain abnormalities . . .If Your Worship notes . . .he doesn't know where he is, Your Worship, but he's in the court. Now he needs treatment urgently and I understand the report from Long Bay is that they must, to assess his situation, refer that issue back to his original treating doctor at Westmead. So what I ask Your Worship to consider is the granting of bail for him to be taken to Westmead Hospital, Your Worship . . .I don't think it's the intention of the law that his imprisonment should be a torture but it is a torture today . . .and if we just say, 'Well look, shovel him on the truck and take him back to Parklea' nothing's going to happen, Your Worship. Something's got to be done right now at this minute—an urgent application to a man who's in court and extremely sick." Murphy warmed to his topic. "And, Your Worship, in the interests of justice, this man does have a background of being somewhat of a national hero prior to this matter. He deserves to be treated a bit better than this . . ."

Knuckles was lying in his cell, a discarded boxing magazine lay next to him on the floor.

Mr Glass had granted that he be remanded until Friday, a short respite from the dreaded ritual of appearing in court. His reprieve had brought a spate of requests from both sides, and Roo and Big Tony had been granted similar breaks. Mr Andrews, a Comanchero lawyer, asked that his client, Tonka O'Keefe, be allowed to return to the cells as he was sick with the flu.

Even Andrew Young bore the marks of the length of the committal. The skin above his beard was puffy and unhealthy looking. The proceedings were beginning to take on a feeling that lasted the full thirteen months of their duration. There was a Kafkaesque depression settling in—the men in their perspex coops forced to sit there day after day while the lawyers lost hours in cross-examination, question after question leading nowhere. The massacre itself was buried and forgotten in legal jargon.

Knuckles was oblivious to the other prisoners' lot. He was gripped in an existential stupor. He had to struggle to remember the person he was before all this began. He lay staring at the ceiling, the whiteness dissolving into nothing before his eyes.

He went back to thinking about his father again. After the family moved to Sydney, Bob McElwaine spent endless hours training Knuckles, running twelve kilometres each morning to the top of the Gladesville Bridge, and sometimes accompanying him for the six-kilometre afternoon jog to Wentworth Park, and then on to a Newtown gym to watch his son spar and train.

He had special t-shirts printed that read: "Terminus Hotel Pyrmont Home of Phil McElwaine Australian Middleweight Champion" in a circular frame around a smiling picture of Knuckles, fists raised.

After his success in Edmonton, Knuckles had resisted attempts to talk him into going professional. It was a tempting offer. But Knuckles held out, he wanted more amateur fights.

He thought back, savouring the satisfaction of being at the top—immaculate physical form, a winner.

At what point had things gone wrong?

At 24, after a two year break from fighting, the lure of big money wooed Knuckles into the professional arena.

"I had close to 130 amateur fights and saw most of the world achieving what I wanted," he had told one newspaper. "In the end, I got sick of training six and seven days a week and thought I needed a good, long spell."

And there had been Wendy. It was a whirlwind romance that ended in marriage in 1978. She was beautiful. Knuckles was riding on the pinnacle of an Australian sportsman's success.

He had become a household name, an idol among the youth of Australia, their lavish Sydney wedding, courtesy of the groom's proud father, was celebrated nationally. Mr and Mrs Phillip McElwaine were happy—briefly.

In 1982 the Terminus Hotel began to change. Jock Ross and his Comancheros had found their way to the downmarket pub, which had acquired, as an added lure, topless barmaids. Framed portraits of savage scowling American Indian chiefs in full feathered regalia—Outlaw Comanchero Indians—now adorned the walls beside the famous boxers.

His two brothers' love of bikes filtered through to Knuckles, who, with less training and more spare time, got to know the pub's new clients, the Comancheros, who arranged their shining Harley Davidson motor cycles neatly outside the saloon bar doors for all to admire.

Bob and Shirley McElwaine's marriage was failing. It was at this time Bob had his "I'm Knuckles' Dad!" t-shirt printed.

Knuckles began riding with his brothers, who had joined the extended brotherhood. He grew to love the distinct dull roar that signalled the Comancheros were arriving, a group of men exhibiting a comradeship and strength he found exciting: something he'd never seen before.

Bob liked them too. They were a good bunch, rowdy, but good blokes.

Phillip was nicknamed Knuckles, Greg became Dukes, and Mark, Gloves. Knuckles told Wendy he was going to buy a bike and he called their baby son Harley.

Riding a Harley Davidson was the closest thing to the ecstasy boxing had brought to Knuckles, but Wendy did not understand her husband's newfound passion for motor cycles. The couple began to drift apart.

By July 1983, Knuckles had gone professional. He had won five professional bouts. Then the accident happened. He and Gloves had been riding along the Great Western Highway near O'Connell Street in Parramatta when a Commodore side-swiped them. The bike hit the kerb. The car disappeared.

For three weeks Knuckles lay in the intensive care ward of Parramatta hospital in a comatose stupor. Words and people floated in and out of his addled mind, and all he could feel was intense pain.

When he finally woke he told himself that if the pain went away, everything would clear in his scrambled mind. But the agony continued. Knuckles could not remember life without pain.

Months of unrelenting, blinding headaches tortured him from the moment he regained consciousness. Painkillers offered temporary relief and he stumbled through a drug-dazed veil, trying to understand why his wife was leaving him and why he could not taste his food.

He felt like yelling, screaming, but a searing iron poker in his head prevented him.

A wiry little man would sit at the end of his hospital bed each day and talk to him about big fights. When he got no response, Bob McElwaine would try another topic.

"The pub's not doing so good. But I've got a great idea for retailing my own running shoes. I've had time to think—what with Shirley gone, you know, Phillip . . ."

Knuckles did not know who he was.

His brothers visited him. The club had decided to get him better. Leatherclad, they trooped through the pink hospital corridors to the fifth floor, where Knuckles had lain suffering for two long months. He did not know them either, and responded to their jokes with vacant eyes.

Slowly, very slowly, the pain began to ease and he began to talk again. But Wendy left him and from that point on, he saw his son only occasionally.

That was when his life became a mess, he thought, swinging his legs over the bed. He walked over to the basin. Splashing his face with cold water, he looked up at his image in the mirror. His eyes were the first thing he noticed—dull and lifeless, hollowed into fattened cheeks, they stared back at him as if they belonged to another person.

He ran his fingers through his hair, forcing the short hair upwards, making it spiky, an effect he liked. But it did not change the waxy pallor of his skin. The rest of his long locks were out of sight, gathered loosely in a ponytail, which trailed down his back between his broad shoulders.

He was hungry again. Lately he hadn't felt much like eating, but his appetite was returning. He knew he was putting on weight and not doing enough exercise. He saw the flab where once he would flex muscle, but he didn't care. In fact, he didn't care much about anything.

Karen had taken over where Wendy left off. She was a friend of Pig's ole' lady. She had been both intrigued and touched by the failed boxer. She was patient with his forgetfulness. Sometimes, in the days after he got home from hospital, he would sleep sixteen hours a day or he would sit in the loungeroom and watch television, mesmerised by the colours on the screen.

Karen's parents offered their $50 000 home as surety if Knuckles was allowed bail. If any of them could get bail, it would have to be him, they all said.

But bail was refused, and Knuckles remained imprisoned.

15

The hanging

Karen Brennan was dreaming of Leanne Walters in the two-bedroomed fibro house in Ringwood, an outer suburb of Melbourne. She had been living there almost five months, since resigning from Liverpool Hospital on 5 December.

The decision to resign had been sudden. At 9 o'clock that morning, she had strode into the matron's office wearing her leather jacket, riding boots and her helmet tucked under her right arm.

Matron was shocked at her outfit.

"Here's my resignation," she said, handing a white envelope to the middle-aged woman behind the desk.

Then she climbed on to her Yamaha 250, adjusted the helmet strap under her chin and headed down the Hume Highway to Melbourne.

Ever since Leanne's death, Karen had had problems with her work. She visited the grave site regularly, talking to the young woman beneath the earth, telling her what was happening in the world she now knew nothing about.

As she worked through the rostered hospital shifts, Karen could not rid herself of the image of Leanne each time she walked up the hallway to B ward. She would sometimes blink to obliterate the smiling face from her memory, and then she would open her eyes and look at the empty bed, or a new patient, still expecting to see Leanne. But her friend was never there. She was gone forever.

The dream she had in Melbourne was a recurring one. Leanne would beckon her from the coffin. She was always smiling.

"Come and listen to Billy Idol. He's great. C'mon Karen, c'mon . . ." The cassettes she loved so much were clustered in bundles around the coffin.

"How are you?" Karen's question always seemed foolish.

"I'm great . . .just great . . .come on in . . ."

Each time the dream was the same, the music would intensify and Karen would panic, backing off in terror as Leanne began to smile, scared she would reveal the hideous wound Karen knew was there.

Karen had never been out of Sydney much before her trip to Melbourne. When she reached Albury, on the border of New South Wales and Victoria, there were so many traffic lights, she thought she had reached the Victorian capital. Then she realised she was only a little over half way there.

She had friends in Melbourne, a couple, who had a room they offered her. The house had a backyard. She found work through a nursing agency. She liked the work. It suited her for the time being.

Junior often drew in court, blue-biro cartoons of Bodor drinking super octaine rocket fuel, or skeletons pieced together in the shape of a Harley with macabre skulls and sketches of men with sombreros looking through jail bars crying, "Let me out . . .let me out . . ."

Snoddy alerted police about a man called The Rat, a longtime Comanchero and friend of Jock's who had just finished serving a term of imprisonment for manslaughter.

The Rat had appeared at court one day, creating consternation with his wild appearance, tattoos and leathers. He was the only one the regulars in the public gallery had seen who looked like a real bikie.

He had leant over the public gallery balcony to talk to Jock.

"He's a nut," Snoddy said. "He may kill some more people because he does what Jock says. Jock is mad and so is The Rat."

The Rat was evicted from the court.

"15.3.85 Joel has a bad case of tonserlites. Fuck I hope he's ok. I am a bit worried. I love that boy . . ."

"20.3.85 Well I guess I am just waking up to the fact that we aint getting out of this joint for a long long time. Beat Lard at chess three times today in the cell . . ."

Snoddy stopped writing in his diary for two weeks, gripped by more disillusion. Then suddenly he started again.

"13.4.85 I fucked it today. I walked out on Lee at the visit. I just had the shits and Lee just said the wrong thing at the wrong time. If I lose her it's my own fault because I acted like a real prick, I s'pose, but then again I am sure she would have done the same thing. If she comes in tomorrow I will apologise to her for being such a poonce."

On 19 April Snoddy requested extra activities for his men. He was becoming increasingly concerned about his brothers. They were dispirited, lacking in enthusiasm and fighting among themselves. He had the same old feeling it was his fault. He had got them in here and it was all going bad.

The Superintendent agreed that when the Bandidos were not required for court, they could use the sports oval if prison warders were available to supervise. Normally the sports oval was only used on the weekend or Wednesday afternoons. The Bandidos would also be allowed to use the gymnasium from 5 to 7pm every night after court. The gym usually closed at 5pm on weekdays.

It might give them the breather they needed, Snoddy thought. But the club still struggled with its identity, which was being smothered between the walls of Parklea jail. The boys had painted a mural of some Mexican dressed Bandidos against a background of canary yellow on the wall in the Common Room. Three Wing had become a type of Bandido clubhouse.

As the months passed, anger grew in many of the men. They needed to blame someone for the predicament in which they found themselves, and from which they could see no escape. The Milperra Massacre bikies were becoming the longest-serving remand prisoners in the country. A date had not even been set to test their guilt.

"22.4.85. I think sometimes if I died then things might have been better because then I wouldn't be called a Jock Ross—that hurt me real bad when people said it."

"I wish all this never happened to start with. God help me to sort it all out cause it is sending me crazy. I am seeing a split happening and then it's all over again . . ."

Andrew Cummings was drunk and had been trying to vomit near the side of his car in the Berala Hotel carpark at Auburn in Sydney's outer west. It was almost midnight on 25 April.

It started raining heavily, the huge raindrops were soothing but before he could relieve the queasy feeling and empty his stomach, Cummings decided to go back inside the hotel. In just a couple of minutes, he was almost soaked through.

As he stood up, he heard what sounded like a mild explosion a split second before the impact knocked him off balance. He was drunk and dazed, and his leg hurt. He hopped for cover between the hotel wall and the back of the car.

He sat down and pulled up the right leg of his jeans. Blood was running down his calf onto his sock.

He realised he'd been shot. A cold, clammy fear sobered him instantly and he remembered the phone threats at his Lidcombe home last November.

"May I speak to Andrew Cummings?"

"Yes, that's me."

"Talk and you will be wasted."

There had been a second call, three days later, and now this.

There was no way he was going to give evidence. Maybe now the police would believe him when he told them he feared for his life.

Cummings believed he had good reason to fear for his safety. He was at the Viking Tavern on 2 September and in his statement to police he had identified a Bandido he saw kill a Comanchero.

That same night, Snoddy sat up late in his cell, gazing out of his window at the rain. He had lost his woman, he was sure of it. And he had lost his brothers. He thought about his childhood years in grey concrete institutions after his mother had died, leaving him an orphan. Desperate attempts to track down his family and find out who he was had always failed. He would ask Lee to start at Tamworth Base Hospital where he knew he had been born, and try to trace his mother's name. He felt like closing his eyes and not waking up because sleep was the only release he knew. Except for the nightmares that plagued him . . .

He dreamt, last night, of the girl and the card he had received "from" her, luring him into the netherworld. Sleep was a temporary respite from the black depression, which now seemed to overcome him daily.

"I love my son and Lee," he wrote in cramped writing, quite different to his usual style. Then he looked out of the window again.

"And I feel that if it was different it might have worked out, but as it is I am in a situation where I don't want to live any more. I just want to be with Shadow and Chop. They died that day for the club and I will do the same thing for the benefit of the club. Maybe things will work out for everyone. But, I just can't take any more. It is killing me from within. And, it was good to see my son again and Lee, I hope she understands why and forgives me. She has all the rights to my estate and not my wife Joanne. Maybe it might help the rest of the men get out of jail. I love this club and all the men in it. Love Snotty. B.F.F.B."

He used to feel better in the daylight hours, being woken by the key turning in the lock at 6am, sensing the freshness of the dawn, mustering a feeling of hopefulness to encourage his men, but even this optimism soon became swamped by the drone of legal argument in the courtroom.

Lee came to visit him on Thursday. She saw straight away he was not in a responsive mood. She tried to be bright. "Davo's old lady thought she heard a gunshot last night."

Snoddy was startled from his state of lethargy.

"You know what it was," she said quickly because she knew how agitated he became. "A bloody car backfiring. I went back to sleep."

Snoddy looked straight at her. "If I'm not alive no-one will bother you."

She ignored the last remark. There was silence. He sat staring out of the window at the wintry day outside. Even the brightly-painted umbrellas had dulled in the weather.

She tried other topics. "As soon as you get out of here, we're going to the beach. And we're moving up to the mountains to get a little farm."

But he kept staring through her. The only time he showed any response was when he turned to look at Joel with a strange look in his eyes, almost a longing.

"I really love that boy," he said. "He seems like a real leader."

Lee had decided not to visit on Sunday. She was going to take Joel to the beach, if it was sunny. It might be the last time he would get to swim before winter set in. Snoddy seemed happy enough about her decision. Joel's father saw him every second weekend. Weekends had become precious to her.

"I wish I could come with you," was all Snoddy said at the end of the visit.

A power struggle was simmering within the club involving Caesar who, having eluded the clutches of the law, was living quietly in Perth. There had always been a rancorous feeling between Snoddy and Caesar. Now, it haunted him.

> 27.4.85. This club means a hell of a lot to me and I will carry it on into my memories forever. Shadow said that he was leaving because he could see that we were losing our brotherhood. Well, I feel the same, so the sooner I am with him the better. Caesar—I hope that he remembers the times I stuck up for him against a few of his Bandido brothers. I am the Pres and I wish people would think of me as a bro who tried . . .for the rest of our club.
>
> Snotgrass. B.F.F.B. One percenter.
>
> PS: If at some time I may die, this book goes to my brother and friend—Lard, Tony Melvell.

He signed with a flourish and added as an afterthought, "And all Bandido stuff I own goes to Lard. Lee is to get all my belongings."

He sat motionless at his desk, gripped by a helplessness that prevented him from doing anything. He despised himself. He could not even manage to kill himself—he could not even get that right.

On Saturday night, the boys had gathered in Lance Wellington's cell to listen to Gloves play guitar. "What the Fuck" was his latest musical composition, another fiery protest at the system.

Snoddy had called a meeting that afternoon and the club met, as usual, in the Common Room, gathered around the tropical fish tank under the Bandido mural.

They had talked about their families outside.

Bob Watkin's wife, Sylvia, a former apparel manageress with Coles had given birth to a baby who had never seen his father outside of the prison visitors' area.

Jamie Robert Watkin had been born ten days after his 31-year-old father, a "garbo" with the Parramatta City Council, was arrested. Bob Watkin had worn his colours twice before the shootout, having come up through the Bandido ranks as a nominee.

Gloves' old lady, Sandy, was due to give birth in less than two months. Gloves wanted to call the baby, if it was a boy, Jake Shadow.

The Campbells were always a worry. Christine was now a grandmother at 34, her eldest daughter, the child she had borne before she met Bull had given birth to a baby boy while still in her teens. Christine was still living in the scrappy wooden house in Ashfield with the five children, and now her son-in-law and grandson lived there too. She had been on the housing commission list for five years.

"Stephen's still upset," Bull said, the now habitual glower on his face. "He's still visiting Shadow and Chop's grave regularly and he won't go to school."

"How old is he now?" Snoddy asked.

"Thirteen . . .and these bloody neighbours have asked Chris to leave Bradman Street. They've formed a bloody protest group . . ."

"What's the time mate?" Snoddy interrupted Bull.

"Ten to five," Bull answered.

"Shit, who's going down to the clinic?" Snoddy asked. "Can you get my Rowie while I wind up here? Better go now as she closes soon."

"I don't think she'll give it to me Snod . . ."

"Tell her I'm on the 'phone."

Four of the Bandidos returned ten minutes later.

"Did you ask for mine?" Snoddy asked.

"Yeah . . .We told her you were on the 'phone but she said she couldn't give us any medication for another prisoner—stupid bitch . . ." one of the Bandidos replied.

Snoddy was not amused. He went to see the Wing Officer and relayed his problem.

The Wing Officer rang the nurse on duty. "Could you bring the medication to the wing please, sister?"

But even that request failed, the nurse insisting it was against the policy laid down by the Acting Director of the Prison Medical Service. Medication had to be picked up in person. "Spencer is getting a sleeping tablet, not a psychotic drug," she said.

Roo had set his alarm early, so he could go for a run. It was Sunday. He didn't have to rush to get to court.

As he opened his eyes slowly in the darkened cell, he recognised the low hum of drizzling rain on the iron roof.

"Damn it," he muttered. "More bloody rain."

He was not going to run in the rain, so he turned over and snuggled back into his pillow.

Before he could drift back to sleep the sounds of early morning began; the click of the cells doors as they were unlocked, one by one.

His ear tuned in to the familiar methodical sounds as the warder made his way down the hallway. The heavy cell keys jingled against his belt as he walked a few steps. Roo heard the key turn in the lock, the lock click and the door open. Then four steps to the next cell and each time the noise became louder, as the warder approached.

Roo heard the man stop outside his cell. The key turned, the lock clicked and the door was opened. Roo didn't look up from his bed. Three more clicks to go.

The feet shuffled on to Snoddy's cell next door.

The key turned, the lock clicked and the door opened.

But there the noise stopped. The pattern was broken. There was silence. Something was wrong.

Prison officer Peter Carruthers peered into semi-darkness of the cell. The first thing he noticed was the made-up bed.

Then he saw Spencer, standing at the toilet at the end of the cell. He noticed the toilet lid was down. His head was leaning against the wall, as if he was too tired to move.

He moved further into the cell, and saw Spencer's feet, outlined by the increasing daylight from the window. They were lifted a few inches above the white-tiled floor of the shower recess. He looked up. Snoddy was hanging from the thick steel shower rod.

Carruthers felt ill. His bowels threatened to open. He was paralysed with fear. He felt the coffee he had drunk half an hour earlier rising in his throat. He had the urge to run.

At the same time, he was drawn to the body, noting in a mechanical fashion that he was hanging from a pair of white long-johns, tied around his neck and up around the back of his head, carefully planned so that the head would not fall backwards.

He reached out and touched an arm. The skin was cold. Spencer was facing the wall. Carruthers reached for the cold hand. No pulse. He was stiff.

He tore his eyes from the grisly sight before him and, shaking, walked back across the cell and into the corridor. "Keep your cool, Peter," he told himself, as he pulled the cell door closed behind him.

"George. Come here, quick . . ." he called, trying to lower his voice, to stifle the mounting hysteria.

"What's up, boss?" Roo stood at his doorway in his underpants.

Carruthers looked into the dark Maori eyes.

"Spencer's hung himself."

Roo turned back to his cell and pulled on a pair of trousers.

He pushed open Snoddy's cell door and ran straight to the body. He lifted him to relieve the pressure on his neck, cradling the cold skin against his own.

He had seen dead bodies before, but never a hanging dead body.

Snoddy's tongue protruded from his mouth, grey and lifeless. Froth foamed around his lips. Roo felt like being sick.

Snoddy's legs were bent slightly so he could get the leverage he needed, as the steel rod was less than six feet off the ground. He had done it by stepping off the toilet seat, the longjohns tightening around his neck. The bent legs hurt Roo the most.

"You must have really wanted to die, Pres," he crooned softly into Snoddy's ear, holding him around his waist, taking the man's weight in his sturdy arms.

Clarence Dries, the Assistant Superintendent, had appeared so silently Roo did not hear him.

"Get a knife, Carruthers," Dries ordered from the doorway.

"It's too late, boss," Roo said, his voice thick with emotion, "He's gone."

Dries loosened the knot slightly and between them they eased the lifeless form out of the noose and on to the bed.

Carruthers returned with the knife and saw it was not needed.

The registered nurse on duty arrived with oxygen, a mask and a box of drugs. After checking for a pulse, he opened Snoddy's eyes and shone a torch into them. The pupils were dilated. He pulled out a stethoscope. It was a routine examination. He did not expect to find a heartbeat.

"We'll get on to the local police," Deputy Superintendent Jones decided. "Lock the rest of the Bandidos in their cells."

Several of the Bandidos started banging on the doors of their cells. No-one was sure what was going on. Usually, after the cells were opened and the headcount underway, they were allowed to go.

"What's up? Let us out. What's going on?" they demanded.

Carruthers told Kid Rotten what had happened. The word spread from cell to cell, mirrors were held up and quiet words spoken.

The Bandidos were taken down and locked in Three Wing bottom while the police visited Spencer's cell.

"Are we gonna get to see him before they take him away?" Lard asked.

The prison officers laid him out on a stretcher. Pulling a white sheet over Snoddy's body up to his chin, they wheeled him into the common room. He was still wearing his prison greens, green trousers and a green t-shirt, the clothes he wore when he died.

They came in groups of three, filing through the common room, those Bandidos who wanted to see their leader and pay their final respects. Some cried openly.

"Meat wagon's on it's way," Carruthers whispered quietly to another warden as the last man to visit Snoddy walked back down the stairs.

To you Babe,

As usual I loved seeing you again this weekend but the visits were short hey! Only cause the visits were underground babe and there was heaps of people there. Let's hope next weekend the weather is better. We might be getting a bit of time off from court this week cause of what happened to Snotty. I only hope babe that this all leads to us getting together pretty soon hey! I really think things should start happening now there's got to be some public outcry about what's happening. Still we can only keep our fingers crossed hey! I'll write the kids this week babe and you as well . . .

Loving You Always. Your Chewy. xxxx

Lee had seen them from the front window. There were six cars. Detectives I'll bet, she thought to herself. She had spent the day alternately crying and angry.

At first she had not believed it. She thought when she rang the jail that they would say it was a horrible mistake. But the other Bandidos wouldn't lie, would they?

She had broken the news to Joel as she sat on his bed, holding him.

"No, he's not coming back, mate. Not at all."

"But why mum . . .where's Snoddy gone?"

And now this. She peered through the curtains again and walked into the loungeroom.

"Dog, there's cops out there. We've got to do something . . ." Dog, one of the Bandidos from the Griffith chapter, had been looking after Lee and some of the other Bandido old ladies. He went to the front window. He could see the guns in the dawn light.

Then the hammering at the door started.

"Don't shoot for Chrissakes—there's kids in here!" Lee shouted.

The alsation chained to the verandah barked savagely.

"Get your fucking dog away or we'll kill it . . ."

The door threatened to give. As the police piled into the hallway, they bumped into Lee, who stood there shaking. The detectives ran down the hall, guns at the ready.

"It's only women and kids in here . . . what are you looking for? Leave my son alone . . ."

She ran into her bedroom, where Joel was sleeping. A policewoman was ordered to strip search her.

"I don't want them to have his colours," Lee said.

"Put them on and get into bed," the policewoman suggested, showing a momentary flash of sympathy.

Lee dressed herself in Snoddy's colours then stepped into a pair of his pyjamas.

The police ransacked the room. Three of Snoddy's guns sat on the wall—part of his antique collection.

"Better than collecting stamps," he had told Lee one day when she asked why he had such an interest.

They seized Snoddy's photos, his papers and boxes that she had kept in her room.

"Why are you doing this?" she asked from the bed, the bulkiness of the leather uncomfortable against her skin. "Because he's dead, is that why? None of the boys ever lived in this house. They've never even seen it. They're in jail."

Nobody answered her. They threw one of the photos on the bed and left the room.

Detective Grandidge had burst into the loungeroom. Dog was sitting facing the door with a rifle in his hand.

Grandidge was ready to shoot.

"I thought you were the bloody Commos," Dog said later, after the moment of tension had passed.

Lee was listening from the bedroom. "Who's this Spencer bloke anyway?" she heard one of the police officers asking.

Then she heard one addressing Dog: "Where's Caesar, mate?"

"Dunno. No idea . . ."

The detectives continued their rampage in the backyard. They searched the old shed up the back.

"Look at this . . ." Detective Steve Grandidge called to his partner.

"Bloody Nautilus gym machines and bikes . . ."

Two days later, Lee received a letter from Snoddy. It was in the letter box at the front gate on Tuesday morning. He said he wanted to go to the beach with her and Joel. She believed for a long moment that he was still alive, writing to her from beyond the grave. She thought back to their last meeting on Thursday. He was always at his worst at night; he did not have me there to comfort him. She thought of the intensity of the nightmares he had and shuddered.

Roo was going mad.

His sorrow had turned to anger. He would lash out at things, break objects within his reach, punch people. One of the nurses recommended he go to the Acute Psychiatric Ward at Long Bay, "the nuthouse".

"I hate you, Snod . . ." he would talk to himself at night, alone in his cell. "I loved you, you bastard—didn't you know that, huh? Well? We all did . . .Why did you do it?" he would ask the darkened room, his face creased and haggard for his 26 years. "You didn't think of us left behind, did you, bro?"

At the Bay, he was injected with 100 milligrams of Largactil, a powerful tranquiliser. The drug stupefied him, robbing him of the black rage inside, calming the torrents of abuse that welled up from within.

Roo had no concept of time or place. For two days he sat in a dry cell—just walls and a bed—and thought about Snoddy.

On the fourth day he heard the tinny drone of a portable radio, station 2UE was playing a song he recognised. He hated the lyrics. They were stupid and annoying. He knew he was back in the real world. Then one of the nurses began to talk to him, encouraging him back to normality.

She would play cards, and listen to his stories. She was cathartic, a sounding board on which Roo could test the thoughts that still plagued him.

He was sent back to Parklea. Looking up, as he walked across the quadrangle to Three Wing one autumn morning he saw Lard standing like a vision at the top of the ramp. Lard raised his fist and smiled down at his brother.

For the first time in days, Roo felt happy and safe. "It's good to be back with my brothers," he said to himself. He had been away for four days but it felt like a lifetime.

Six of the Bandidos were now receiving psychiatric help.

Snoddy's suicide note had been left on his desk under the cell window.

"I Tony Spencer,
do not want my wife to have any part in my life or death. Lee Denholm is my lady and Joel is my son and they get all my belongings.

Lee I am sorry for this but remember I will allways love you and my son.

PPS. I want my bros to not think of me as weak, but as tired of fighting for the well being of the club. I have failed maybe I don't no. But I do no someone will do the right thing for the club."

"Someone said to me this morning that now he would be riding the highways of the Cosmos . . ."

The Reverend Ted Noffs smiled down at Lee and Joel who sat in the first wooden pew of the small Pine Grove Memorial Park Chapel. Lee wore a black dress with a lace bodice, black patterned stockings and high-heeled shoes. The black was hard and sharp against the bleached blonde sheen of her hair.

Joel wore a tiny leather jacket, his blonde hair parted on the side and smoothed down. Lee was crying.

" . . .Snoddy, or Snodgrass, as he was known, loved the grass, the sky, the sea, the mountains, and the plains beyond, all his life . . .He was a deeply spiritual if not religious man and Snoddy has now joined that great spirit, whom we call God . . ."

The polished wooden coffin with gold trimmings sat on a stand in front of the pastor, piled high with red and yellow roses and carnations.

Four Bandidos from the Griffith Mid-State Chapter had carried in the coffin, resting its weight easily on their burly shoulders. The small round-shaped chapel was filled to capacity.

Only two of the 26 imprisoned Bandidos were granted leave to attend their President's funeral. Lard and Charlie Scibberas were chosen by their brothers to be given the honour.

They sat in the front row, handcuffed, and flanked by a team of decidedly uncomfortable looking detectives.

The Reverend paid tribute to Snoddy, whom he confessed he had never met, but knew his type through his work as pastor of the Wayside Chapel at Kings Cross. Reverend Noffs was a respected friend of the downtrodden, the dropouts, the misfits and the bikies, who in his view, were misunderstood.

As Lard listened to the eulogy, tears rolled down his plump cheeks, disappearing into his blonde beard.

"Snoddy, who was loved, and who loved some of you present here today, Snoddy, who was born 29 years ago in Tamworth, brought up in orphanages . . ."

The congregation was sprinkled with police, including many plainclothed officers. Trying to look inconspicuous, they undid their shirts and removed their ties while they patrolled the area outside.

Polair II sat quietly on a rise on the wet lawn beyond the chapel, like a big blue and white spider ready to pounce on unsuspecting prey. As the service continued, detectives noted the registration numbers of the eight Harley Davidsons parked symmetrically along the crematorium wall.

Young women in black with veiled faces wept alongside their biker friends. Sniffles resounded through the church. The Royal Oak football team in their yellow and black jerseys looked sombre and suitably moved by the service, as did the team of suited Bandido lawyers.

A large media contingent hung strategically rather than respectfully towards the back of the Chapel, so as to be first out the door for a good view of the crowd as it emerged when the service ended. It had been a while since the bikie story had made any headlines. The court case was now largely ignored.

" . . .Snoddy, who had no family and looked at the Bandido fraternity as his brothers . . .his family had become the people he rode with . . .

"Snoddy, who might have picked up a bit of formal religion along the way when forced to go to scripture classes. For he was a spiritual man like most of the bikie fraternity. Like Jesus Christ in fact. Christ, who was not a religious man, had trouble with religious institutions, but he was a spiritual man . . ."

Reverend Noffs read Psalm 23, from the fourteenth chapter of St John's gospel before Lard and Charlie were led awkwardly up to the coffin. Both men placed their handcuffed wrists on the top of the coffin fleetingly, as a mark of final respect before being led back to their seats.

President of the Bandido's Griffith Chapter, Burkey, paid brief tribute to his comrade.

He left his second row seat, strode to the front of the chapel and turned to face the congregation.

Balding, in his forties, his forearms tattooed, he wore studded leather cut-offs, the Bandidos Mid-State colours emblazoned across his back.

A fringed headband had been tied around his head, with tassles hanging behind. He wore demin jeans and a black jumper under his vest.

" . . .He loved his brothers, who loved him in return . . .he was a guy who loved life and lived by the club motto, 'Bandidos Forever, Forever Bandidos.'"

"Now darling, go on." Lee gave Joel a gentle push. The little boy set his face determinedly and walked bravely out of his seat and approached the coffin.

He lifted up the single rose and placed it on the top with the other flowers, and paused, for just a few seconds.

When he turned he was crying. He walked back to his mother and buried his face in her stomach.

The Bandidos gathered in their common room at Parklea at 11am, the time the service was due to begin.

It was a grey, wet day, not unlike the morning of five days ago when Snoddy's cold body was discovered in his cell.

By mid-morning the rain had eased, and, as though a sign from above, the sun broke through the grey for a few brief moments.

With heads bowed, the men observed a minute's silence. A cassette played in the corner. The mournful tones of the Hollies sounded. " . . .He ain't heavy, he's my brotherr-err . . .and I know-ow-ow, the load won't get meee dow-ow-ow-own, he ain't heavy-ey, he's my brother . . ."

Barry Smith was an efficient witness. He delivered his reasons as to why the five Bandidos should not get bail, his voice carrying authority across the President's Court on the thirteenth floor of the NSW Supreme Court, an imposing modern skyscraper in Macquarie Street.

It was 28 May 1985, four weeks after Snoddy's hanging. The court proceedings had continued unabated, only one day had been missed through his death. Life for the rest of the Bandidos continued as normal.

The committal hearing was into its seventh month.

The Bandidos of whom Smith spoke did not even make it into the President's Court. Whack Campbell, Knuckles, Gloves, Pig and Bobby Watkin sat spruced up in suits in the cells. "Security reasons" were cited for their non-appearance.

Karen Martin had not bothered to mow the lawn this time in preparation for the homecoming, since Knuckles' four previous attempts at bail had failed.

The women sat among members of the press towards the back of the courtroom, denied even a glimpse of the men they hoped would join them in their homes that night.

Smith pulled out his trump card. He told the court that "the hatred and antagonism between the two gangs" had not subsided and that "the protection of the community at large will be placed in jeopardy.

"Further, an eye witness, Andrew William Cummings, had received death threats to warn him not to give evidence and on the 25.4.85 at Berala he was shot in the leg by an unknown gunman.

"Bearing in mind the nature of the charges and the strength of the Crown case, we feel there is a real threat that if bail is granted further interference with witnesses may take place and also that any individual member granted his liberty may flee." Smith sat down forcefully, his mission completed.

Mr Justice O'Brien listened as Bodor told him that Cummings was now reluctant to cooperate in any way with the court.

"We don't know whether Mr Cummings is prepared to re-enter the witness box," Bodor said, emphasising the seriousness of the threats.

Justice O'Brien refused bail. No-one had really expected him to grant it.

Snoddy's inquest, on 10 July, was something of a non event with none of the sensational headlines that followed his death.

Chris Murphy grabbed the opportunity to blame the system. "Spencer had trouble sleeping in small rooms and had been taking sedatives to help him sleep ever since he had been admitted to prison," he told the press. Officers at the prison clinic had denied him the drug because he was five minutes late in collecting it.

"If Spencer had been granted bail, he'd still be alive."

But even Murphy's accusations paled into insignificance by the day of the inquest. No media were even present.

The nurse on duty that fatal evening was called as a witness. She repeated her statement, saying she had acted within the guidelines of prison policy in refusing Snoddy's emissary the sleeping tablet.

The medical report from the Government Medical Officer was read out in court. The coroner found that Anthony Mark Spencer had died from asphyxiation by hanging.

Gloves' cell was No 142. He would often sit on his own, preferring to be solitary, listening to the sounds of the evening. He would take out his guitar and experiment with chords and keys, composing more music, through which he could express his hate for the system. Jake Shadow, blond haired, brown-eyed, had been born in June. The thought of him and Sandy helped keep him going.

Gloves' body was in good shape, tanned legs well-muscled, and arms hard and strong. He weighed 71 kilograms at 26 years of age. He was 174 centimetres tall. He was forcibly fit by August 1985 through not being allowed to drink alcohol—his beloved beer and Jack Daniels. For breakfast he had the juice of three oranges and a lemon, followed by a Protein 90 drink.

Lunch was an apple or a banana, dinner was salad if he could get it, with fish or chicken. He also took multi-vitamins and five or six cloves of garlic after dinner. His old man was proud of him.

Gloves had started training in earnest, 35 hours a week. Kid Rotten was back to managing him again, planning his training circuits, massaging his tired body, stretching his muscles, boosting his confidence.

Gloves' black boxing outfit, a gown and a pair of shorts, had been hanging in his cell since he arrived at Parklea. He had cut his hair short, clipped around his distinct widow's peak, a rat's tail at the back.

Unlike his brother Knuckles, Gloves had handled imprisonment, and sometimes the fact surprised him. Sure, he hated the system, but he did not suffer from the sort of immobilising depression that had overwhelmed Knuckles.

However, for the past three weeks, Knuckles had shown some enthusiasm, training his brother five hours daily, injecting an ardour hitherto unseen into his new task.

"You have to make sacrifices," he told Gloves. Knuckles was always the McElwaine who had shown the most devotion to his career as a professional boxer.

Gloves had never quite made it to the top; after seven professional fights, albeit undefeated, he relinquished the boxing arena for parties and drinking bourbon.

But when his elder brother was chosen for the Australian Commonwealth Games team in 1978, Gloves decided to get back into boxing and take it more seriously. He had been primed ready to re-enter that arena 36 hours before Milperra, winning his first comeback fight.

Gloves was painfully aware that Knuckles could never fight again because of the head injuries he suffered in his bike accident, so he used his elder brother's success as inspiration, and returned to training and boxing to give him a new purpose in jail.

It had been meant to happen—this new lease of life. In July 1985 the Department of Corrective Services began a Sports and Fitness program at Parklea Jail. Seventeen prisoners had attempted a marathon of 139 laps of the prison oval; only two had succeeded.

On 20 August, leading gridiron players and officials conducted a training session, and a touch football competition had been organised for Friday. Rugby League players and coaches from Canterbury, Penrith, Parramatta and Manly had also visited inmates.

Gloves' fight, his return to the ring, became the star attraction in this burst of sporting fervour.

Crowded into the auditorium were 150 prisoners. Gloves had ten two-minute sparring bouts, the first with Australian number two light-welterweight Jeff Malcolm and the two Waters brothers, Troy and Guy, New South Wales amateur light-middleweight and middleweight champions.

"Knock 'im out, Mark," one Bandido yelled, in the otherwise quiet and respectful auditorium.

Gloves was light on his feet. A sharp left and quick footwork were his most potent weapons.

The bouts were hard fought and had given him a taste for fighting again. The runs had been worth it.

The memorial garden of the Romcek family had been well tended, like most of the other gardens of the Pine Grove Crematorium. This week-end, 2 September, the weekend mourners tending, were interrupted by the low throb of motor cycles.

Fifteen bikers rode up the bitumen road leading past the chapel on Harley Davidsons and Triumphs. The riders wore black leather cut-offs, beanies, bandanas, jeans and wrap around dark sunglasses. They sat low in their seats, hands high on the handlebars.

They bore the Comanchero emblem—the fierce grey Condor—on their backs. They were riding to commemorate their dead.

The pack dismounted beside Sparrow's garden, bowing their heads slightly to show respect, thumbs hooked into jeans. Commemorative ribbons were pinned to their shoulders. The ceremony lasted ten min-utes. They buried a poem under the white pebbles, telling their brother he would never be forgotten. The signal to leave was given and each man mounted his bike, starting up the ignition and going slowly back down the road and through the gates.

It was one of the first public runs for the Comancheros since the massacre. Many of the riders were new recruits, fresh blood in the club, which was thriving outside the walls of Long Bay Jail.

On Sunday 3 September, the same group rode up to Palmdale Memorial Crematorium near Ourimbah, the original Comancheros' stamping ground. They repeated their sombre task, standing in front of Dog and Foggy's plaques. R.I.P . . .

They had ordered plaques to commemorate their dead—shiny black marble with gold scrolled writing: "In Memory of Milperra 1984"; and in the bottom two corners, the victims: Leroy, Sparra, Foghorn and Dog.

In the centre the stylised Condor on the red wheel.

There were no surprises when, two days before Christmas, Glass told the court he believed that on the evidence before him, a reasonable jury could find the 41 men guilty of an indictable offence.

The defendants sat at the back of the court, showing no emotion.

"...I am not saying a jury would necessarily reach those conclusions, or probably reach those conclusions. The evidence and state of mind of the accused are matters for the jury to consider.."

Everyone had expected him to commit them to trial for murder.

It was just one more step in the nightmare, which, to the men in the reinforced docks at the rear of the court, appeared endless.

Just before 7.30pm, Glass picked up his scotch and water and walked down the stairs to his study. He flicked on the light and took a long look around the room in which he had spent most of his home time for the past thirteen months. He was thoroughly exhausted, but at the same time satisfied, with an enormous sense of relief. This committal hearing had been his most trying case. At times he had felt it would never end.

He remembered his thoughts when he first heard the radio news report of the shootings on Father's Day, last year—such a long time ago. He had tried to forget it, knowing the deaths would be reported to him, as Coroner. First thing on that Monday morning, which now seemed so long ago, he had received that report. He had then called for the reports setting out the circumstances surrounding the deaths.

It was an extraordinary case. Up until that point he had never let his work worry him, but as the committal hearing date approached, he was glad of his silent telephone number and the alarm system he had installed to protect his home.

As the months dragged on, the cost, too, had worried him. He wondered just how much of taxpayers' money had been spent in the thirteen months. It had been an expensive hearing—three times to the Supreme Court and one matter had been heard before a full bench of the Court of Appeal.

John Campbell's file lay open on the desk. Whack was the only one of the 41 men who had not yet been committed to trial. He was seriously ill with cardiomyopathy. He would have to be committed to trial at a special bedside court at Prince Henry Hospital tomorrow.

Then it would be Christmas.

From upstairs Glass heard greetings and laughter. His family had arrived for that long-awaited celebration dinner.

He closed the file and picked up his glass. Just one more day, he thought, as he closed the door and walked slowly up the stairs.

16

The verdict

Hookie approached the counter of the Social Security office at Bondi Junction at around midday,

"Yeah, I'm Steve Owens . . ."

He pocketed his fortnightly dole cheque and headed for the lift. Another man with crimped curly blonde hair and regular features entered the same lift. The doors opened at the lower level and Hookie got out. He was followed into the corridor by the other man.

Hookie became aware of him as he walked up the corridor. He tried not to panic.

"Are you Steve Owens?"

"Yeah . . ."

"We are police. Put your hands against the wall." Grandidge clicked the handcuffs into place.

"Where's your identification?"

Detective Peter "Silver" McErlaine showed him his police badge, flipping it open smartly.

"You are under arrest for seven counts of murder in relation to the Milperra thing," McErlaine said.

"Anything you do or say may later be given in evidence. Do you understand that?"

"Yes," Hookie was suddenly weary, "I've been expecting it."

He had spent a pleasant enough few months in Sydney working as a carpenter at various building sites. He was not the sort of person to keep his mouth shut and at one of the sites he was working at, Kambala, an exclusive private girls' school in Vaucluse, word got around there was a murderer working on the site. Hookie found the prospect amusing, chuckling quietly to himself. He had never killed anyone.

His dark hair fell in ringlets down his back, but he was far from feminine. He had a long chiselled nose, close-set brown eyes and an easy way of smiling.

His unexpected escape from the carpark, through taking Caesar to hospital, had provided him with more than a year of freedom.

His arrest on 6 February 1986 had been one of pure chance for the police. Grandidge had been briefed to attend the Social Security office at Bondi Junction by his superior, Detective Sergeant Paul Shiels. The police had found that Hookie used a Night and Day card and was making regular deposits from the electronic 24-hour bank, which amounted to the same as a fortnightly dole cheque. They knew he lived somewhere in Darlinghurst, that he was not having his dole sent to an address. Shiels took a punt he would collect his dole, not from his local dole office, but one close by.

Shiels could not spare his men for more than a day. But it was worth a try.

Grandidge had been waiting for a couple of hours when the Maori's familiar tapered waist, broad shoulders and black ringlets came into view. It had been a stroke of luck.

Hookie had been told by Murphy to say nothing to the police, but over the hours at the CIB his resolve weakened. He agreed to let one of the detectives take notes so as to have an accurate record of their conversation. As it turned out, it was the only evidence given that Hookie had been at the Viking Tavern when the shooting occurred. None of the handful of eye witnesses called, when his committal hearing eventuated in January 1988, could identify him as the man they saw at the carpark that day. Not even Suzanne Worn or her friend Deborah Harvey could identify Hookie as being in their car during the trip to Bankstown Hospital.

Chewy and Kezra were fighting. The tedious visits to the jail and Kezra talking to the newspapers had taken its toll.

She had been working in a massage parlour as a receptionist to pay the bills. Having been charged in court with neglect of her two youngest children, who had been taken away from her, she felt it was because of Chewy's involvement with the Comancheros.

During her visits to Long Bay Jail, she found Chewy vacillating between truculence and undying devotion.

About the middle of 1985 she had moved from the farmhouse at Londonderry into a brick house in Strathfield with some Comanchero nominees, taking her eldest child Daniel with her. It was the start of a tempestuous relationship between her and the nominees. To complicate matters, she had befriended an office bearer with the Black Uhlans.

Another rift in the Lorenzs' relationship began when Kezra spoke to a newspaper about the commemoration ride in September to the crematoriums, violating the club secrecy surrounding the event.

A Comanchero on the outside had abused her at the jail during a visit later in the year. Chewy did not defend her. It was a turning point.

"Why didn't you stick up for me?" she asked him later.

"Because he's my brother," Chewy replied.

Daniel asked Chewy the same question during the next visit. Chewy was angry at being confronted by a kid. "I don't want to see that boy again," he told Kezra on the phone.

"We're family. You accept either all of them or none of them."

After Chewy had not rung her for a few days, one of the nominees approached her. "You're not married to Chewy any more. You're not to visit him at the jail. You've got to move out of the house tomorrow."

The leaving had been messy. She ended up out in the street. By early 1986 she was back at Londonderry. Daniel ran away from home that Christmas at the age of fourteen. He was no longer her friend.

"Hey, looks like we're in business."

The room was suddenly lit up and a large silhouette was revealed by the changing glow of lights that indicated a television was turned on.

"Yeah, that's him all right, it sure as hell ain't no woman with a build like that."

The silhouette moved back across the room, stopping briefly halfway and bending over. He stood erect, then walked over to the doorway, reaching up to flick off the light. It was dark again.

"That's him all right, I'll go radio control."

The second observation squad officer yawned and pressed on the light on his wrist watch. It was 3.45am. It had been a long, hot night.

His partner returned.

"The chief's on his way over. Looks like they'll raid at five. They're organising the TRG blokes, we'll stay here till we get further word."

The two officers had been sitting in an unmarked police car opposite the house they were keeping under surveillance—number 95 Shakespeare Avenue, Mount Hawthorn, an inner northern suburb of Perth.

They had maintained an all night vigil, watching the rundown weatherboard cottage, waiting patiently for a sighting of their prey.

With a low brick wall as a front fence, and a bare front lawn, number 95 was easily the least salubrious house in the low-rent suburban street. A Hills hoist clothes line stood in the messy, overgrown back yard, along with a Holden panel van, distinct with yellow and black New South Wales number plates.

A tip-off had led the New South Wales police force to Mount Hawthorn.

Caesar, Donna—his real ol' lady—and their children had been living in Mount Hawthorn for nine months. He was the last of the bikies the police wanted behind bars.

Until they had received the tip-off in February 1986, the police had no idea of Caesar's whereabouts, although they suspected he had gone interstate. The former Sergeant-at-Arms of the Bandidos had not been seen since he walked out of Bankstown Hospital on 4 October 1984.

He had lain low for several months until he was well enough to drive across Australia to Perth. His lung, chest and arm were badly infected, his left arm had withered and he was still seriously ill when he arrived after the 4500 kilometre, 60-hour drive.

At Mount Hawthorn he felt safer, but he still lived in fear of the Comancheros. He was also worried about his health. Having experienced near-fatal injuries, he now took precautions, finalising his estate.

Irene and Donna can attend any B.B.Q given by a member or his ol' lady, they can attend the Xmas party, they can see the ole ladies of the club as much as they wish, but they are not to hop on any members motorcycle, go out with any member or prospect of the club or any male in general. If any member of the club sees them with another male, they're to bash him unless he's a brother or some such thing. I expect the same respect to be shown to Irene and Donna as if I was still there, for in my eyes they will be my ol' ladies forever and only mine. They are not to go to club nights or on runs.

Donna obediently wrote the instructions for her husband, who had found writing difficult since his injuries. All he could manage was a shaky signature, "Caesar 1%", at the bottom of the printed note.

As an afterthought she had added for her husband: "Chicago 'If You Leave Me Now' to be played at his funeral."

Caesar also prepared a layout of what he wanted written on his tombstone, in the event of his death.

BANDIDOS

1%   M.C

AUSTRALIA

CAESAR SGT AT ARMS

DATE:

COLIN FRANCIS CAMPBELL

BELOVED SON OF GEORGE FRANCIS CAMPBELL

BELOVED HUSBAND OF IRENE

BELOVED OL' MAN OF DONNA

BELOVED FATHER OF CHANE, LEE, PEGGY, SAMANTHER, DANIEL, LACEY

BELOVED BROTHER OF PAUL, PHILLIP, GREGORY, MARK, GEOFFERY, JOHN,

CHRISTOPHER
HOPEFULLY LOVED AND RESPECTED BY HIS BANDIDO BROTHERS
BORN A MAN, WENT ONE BETTER DIED A BANDIDO
TO IRENE AND DONNA YOU WILL NEVER BE ALONE
MY SPIRIT AND LOVE WILL BE WITH YOU ALWAYS
BLONDIE I'LL FIND MY WAY HOME
B.F.F.B.
CAESAR

An instruction in Donna's handwriting was tacked on to the bottom of the page: "If either Irene or Donna arn't my ol ladies at the time of my death, their names don't go on the tombstone."

One blow from the heavy hammer and the front door fell open.

Caesar's heart leapt into his mouth as four dark figures burst through the front door into his loungeroom.

They encircled him, four shotguns pointed at his head.

Caesar had been sleeping, lying on the loungeroom floor, dressed only in a pair of white underpants.

The terror in his glazed eyes lessened when he realised the intruders were police officers. When he finally found his voice, he muttered: "I thought you were someone else."

Noting the elaborately tattooed panther snake on his lower left arm and the mole in the centre of his forehead, one of them told him, "Colin Francis Campbell, we have a warrant for your arrest . . ."

Caesar got dressed. He was then handcuffed and taken to East Perth police station.

When the charge was read, the first name on the list of seven dead was, by a cruel twist of fate, Shadow's name—Gregory Campbell.

Caesar sat, ashen and silent, as he was charged with feloniously and maliciously murdering his own brother.

The following morning Detectives Paul Shiels and Steve Grandidge woke in their respective hotel rooms with aching heads. They had really let themselves go the night before, celebrating with the Perth boys after Caesar's arrest and court appearance, which had gone off without a hitch.

They had been drinking until 2am. And they had not recovered from sleep lost on the flight from Sydney. So it was with a dull pounding head and dry mouth that Shiels visited Caesar in the East Perth holding cells on 21 February.

"I have warrants here for your arrest for seven counts of murder and one of affray," he told him. Shortly after 10am, a magistrate ordered Caesar be extradited to New South Wales.

Both TAA and Ansett, two of the domestic airways, refused to carry Caesar back to Sydney.

"What? Why the hell won't they let us?"

"They say they won't carry him because they're bloody well scared of the Comancheros—can you believe it?" Grandidge broke the bad news to his partner.

"Christ, what are we going to do?"

At least Ansett would negotiate. They held a pilot's meeting, and made a conditional proposal for Caesar to return to Sydney on Flight 1221, due to leave at 8pm:

1   Caesar was to remain handcuffed at all times.
2   There was to be no alcohol consumed by the prisoner or the police officers during the flight, and neither police officer could have the smell of alcohol on his breath when he boarded the plane.
3   They had to board an hour earlier than the rest of the passengers, and alight an hour after they landed.

Shortly after 7pm, Caesar was smuggled up the rear steps of the plane from the back of a service van, after the aircraft had been thoroughly searched for bombs.

The three men sat in the back row on the left hand aisle. Grandidge took the window seat and Sheils sat on the aisle. Caesar, handcuffed to Grandidge, was wedged between them.

The pony-tailed bikie was sweating, nervous and jittery.

"Well, you blokes have made me do something no other man could ever do," he said to his escorts.

"What's that, mate?" Sheils said, turning to the worried face beside him.

"Made me get in a bloody aeroplane."

As the plane surged down the runway, Grandidge teased: "Have a look at the acceleration of this thing, mate—oh, we're up now. Have a look!"

At the end of the flight, after the passengers and staff had alighted, a police van and three police cars drove slowly up to the aircraft.

Five SWOS officers armed with shotguns got out of the cars and waited at the bottom of the steps.

Detective Paul Shiels, bearded, dishevelled, wearing jeans and a t-shirt, was first down the steps. He had barely put his foot in the ground when he felt a the cold metal of a shotgun barrel pressing into the side of his head.

"Into the truck!" the voice said.

He decided not to argue as he was shoved in the paddy wagon, but laughed with the embarrassed officer who helped him out after Grandidge and Caesar appeared at the top of the stairs, handcuffed together.

The Bandidos were playing one of their favourite games to help pass the time. When night fell at Parklea jail, rats would emerge from the drain holes in the moat outside Three Wing, or along the jail's brick fence, scavenging for edible scraps.

The men would lie in wait in their cells with honey jars, and other missiles at the ready. It was a form of hunting, albeit rather different from the pig shooting and fishing they were accustomed to on the outside. Still, it required the same attributes: cunning, patience and a good aim.

On Monday night, 10 March 1986, Roo was feeling lucky. The honey jar he hurled down towards the fence hit home with a dull thud, trapping and squashing one furry rodent as it scuttled along, trying to avoid the missiles exploding around it.

Roo jumped up and a cry went out among the Three Wing inmates. "It's a good omen, brother," one yelled down the corridor. Roo felt a surge of excitement. He believed it.

Zorba had been released that day, the murder charges waived, and there was a strong rumour more of them were to be released soon.

The following day, by order of the New South Wales Attorney General Terry Sheahan, murder charges against nine other Bandidos including Roo, Snake Campbell and Pig, and two Comancheros, John Bodt and Andrew Thomas, were dropped. They were released on bail and remanded to appear at Penrith on 23 April each charged with affray.

Zorba's parents, diminutive respectful Greeks who had stood close by him since his arrest, attending court regularly and visiting him in jail at every opportunity, hugged their mountainous son. He went home to his mother's cooking, a treat denied to him since the early stages of the committal hearing. He had been imprisoned for eighteen months.

When Roo walked out of the Penrith police cells, he sniffed the air still warm with the smell of a fading summer. He stopped, drinking in the simple things before him: cars driving down the road, the people in them intent on their destinations, oblivious to the impact they were having on a man whose freedom had just been returned. He watched the people walking past outside the police station, chattering lightly, saw the shops displaying goods for sale and the man in the service station across the road joking with a customer. It reminded him somehow of his trips to Australia from his native New Zealand as a child, the sort of days when the family would set out to explore Sydney—where everything seemed so fresh and new.

Freedom—so this is it—he savoured it, standing still with his hands in the pocket of his jeans.

The party that night had a feeling of recklessness. It took some time to realise they were actually free. Pig, Roo, Sparksey and Steve Hails had partied until 2.30am, propped up on the old bar they had salvaged from the Louisa Road clubhouse. They partied as Bandidos, even though just hours earlier they had agreed as part of their bail conditions not to associate. It was a good party.

One week later, two months after his arrest, murder charges against Hookie were dropped. He too was left to face the charge of affray.

"You have probably often heard it said that the law is an ass. No-one knows it better than those who work in it." Mr Justice Adrian Roden made the pronouncement on 28 April on the first day of the trial, to the five startled jurors, the first five people to be selected—and later dismissed.

Small and spritely for his 60 years, Justice Roden was soon nicknamed The Rodent. While there was nothing imposing in his physical stature, it was apparent from the first time he sat in the high-backed swivel chair behind the polished wooden bench, that Roden commanded total control of his court. Futile legal argument and paltry excuses from bumbling public solicitors would not be tolerated. Nor would the daily sick parade. He ordered all defendants to be present in court and all excuses on medical grounds had to be certified. Only in exceptional circumstances would leave be granted not to appear.

His narrow, angular shoulders jutted out from under his cumbersome red robe. A coarse woven wig sat squarely on his head, its lines repeated in the square silver-framed glasses, which sat evenly on his long, thin nose. A grey and white speckled beard and moustache framed thin red lips, which occasionally curled upwards from the corners, creasing his face in a smile—often tinged with sarcasm.

His eyes were small, but dark and piercing below arched eyebrows. His voice, via the stereo microphone system, was clear and compelling. Adrian Roden had nurtured his cutting wit and quick intellect as a debater, a hobby he developed during his Sydney University years, when he studied law.

In 1948 the Sydney University student council threatened to axe his job as newspaper editor of the student newspaper *Honi Soit*, for publishing "blasphemous and obscene" material about Jesus's private parts.

His wit and way with words became apparent after he established himself as a champion of the English language and captained the combined Australian University debating team in 1949, and later as President of the New South Wales Debating Union from 1975 to 1978. As a schoolboy he had starred in radio debates with Neville Wran, later Premier of New South Wales.

By 1981 the outspoken Roden held office as Commissioner of the New South Wales Law Reform Commission.

He was chosen by the Chief Justice of the Supreme Court, Sir Laurence Street, to head the so-called bikie trial.

So it was that on April 28 he took his first long hard look at the six prosecution and 30 defence counsels. The court had been modified further since the committal had ended in December.

Additional wooden panelling had been built on to the dock cages. Wooden hinged doors now replaced the rope gates. It completely obscured the Bandidos and Comancheros from each other.

A glass partition had also been built on top of the jury box, adding height to the division between the jurors and the press gallery on their right. The glass enabled the jury to look over the top of the press and straight into the dock areas.

Most of the Bandidos had chosen suits for the first day of their trial. Knuckles wore his official State boxing jacket, and several Bandidos wore ties. Their hair was neatly combed and tied back.

Only three Comancheros wore suits. JJ had undergone a transformation. Gone was the scraggy matted hair and unkempt goatee beard. His hair was short and neat, and he sported a grey lightweight woollen suit and matching tie. He looked like a trendy Darlinghurst businessman en route to work in the city.

Tonka O'Keefe could have been mistaken for a timid Commonwealth Bank teller, in grey trousers, a shirt, picture tie and tailored leather jacket.

Morts had chosen a dark navy suit and tie rather than the black t-shirt with the gross obscenities emblazoned across the chest. Chewy sat in the front row of the dock, chewing gum, a cardigan over a t-shirt and trackpants.

The judge glanced up to the public gallery. It was full of relatives of the defendants, a field of colour.

Of the 1252 candidates chosen as potential jurors, 563 had been led into court and seated in the dock.

Mechanically, like a factory processing line, they rose one by one, were challenged and whisked from the court—all but the twelve finally chosen. Roden told them:

I am aware of the extent jury service in this trial will upset the normal course of your lives. The community should play a significant part in the making of those decisions, even when it involves serving for a long time on a trial of this nature . . .you are a very special jury. Your task is only just beginning.

If you need assistance or guidance in relation to the trial, the only person from whom you can seek it is me . . .Above all, it is a very, very important rule that it is your verdict—yours and nobody else's . . .

Roden adjourned the court early, to allow the jurors time to come to terms with their new job. By the end of the third day, the Comancheros had followed the example of the Bandidos, rising each time the jury entered and left the court.

The following day, Roden issued a series of instructions to the jury.

This is a trial in which 31 separate, distinct individuals are charged with seven offences of murder and one of affray. I want to stress the importance of your recognition of the fact that you will be considering the positions of 31 separate individuals. Since the charges were first laid, this has continually been referred to as the bikies' trial, and in two groups, as the Comancheros and Bandidos. The events have commonly been described as a massacre. I am concerned that the use of those terms be not allowed to prejudice the trial or the position of any of the persons charged. Each will be considered as an individual, on the basis of his participation, if any, in the event . . .

There is not to be and there cannot be a collective trial of the bikies, or the Bandidos and the Comancheros. Such concepts are foreign to our laws. Each defendant will have his trial considered separately and on his own merits . . .

At 3pm, Alan Viney began his opening address to the jury. " . . .It was a fine day, a number of vendors had set out their wares in the carpark. A lamb roasted on a spit . . ."

Lard yawned. They had heard it all before.

In the holding cells during adjournment periods, the Bandidos soon reverted back to one of their favourite ways of amusing themselves— annoying the Comancheros. They mimicked Jock's Scottish accent in voices loud enough to be heard in the cells directly below, occupied by the Comancheros.

In the months that followed, the jury listened patiently as 250 witnesses paraded before the court, the bulk of whom were eye-witnesses to the incident.

The defence case did not start until 4 November, when Garry Annakin— Peewee—delivered the first statement from the floor.

" . . .I'm here because I'm a member of the Comanchero Motor Cycle

Club, not because I've committed any crime . . ."

It was the first time the court had heard a defendant tell his own version of what had happened in the car park.

None of the 31 men chose to give evidence from the witness box and risk cross examination. Their lawyers advised them to read statements from the dock.

Bob McElwaine gave evidence on behalf of his son, Knuckles—a tired and jaded Bob McElwaine, his once spritely form dissipated. Now a small man, he limped to the witness box supported by a walking stick. A car had hit him while he had been out jogging at night, ironically within metres of the same spot where Knuckles had had his bike accident in 1983. He gave his occupation—invalid pensioner.

He told the court about Knuckles, how his bike accident had affected him.

" . . .Knuckles sat and watched TV nearly all day. His brothers came round. They used to try and get him to go out.

"He was always easy going and very nice to everybody. He forgot to clean his teeth. I used to take him into the bathroom . . .

"The mother of one of my friends rang me up to tell me about the trouble at Milperra . . ."

Other witnesses gave evidence for Phillip McElwaine. There seemed to be no shortage of people willing to come forward. Kevin Wynne, a Sergeant of the New South Wales police force for 23 years who supervised the police boys' club spoke of him as "a monument to the police boys' movement as a whole". He said Knuckles' failing in boxing was that he did not have the killer instinct necessary to be a champion boxer.

Johnny Lewis, trainer of Joe Bugner and Jeff Fenech, also gave evidence. He had trained Knuckles for the 1978 Commonwealth Games at Edmonton. "He's honest and a credit to his family," Lewis said.

Jock's debut was on 13 November 1986, two years after the committal hearing had opened in the same court.

The media seats had been filled for the occasion, underlining his importance. Some of the radio reporters called in for the morning. Their trip was worth it.

Jock stood up at the bar table next to his counsel, bearded wizard-like Terry Healey, and faced the jury. He wore a pale green shirt with yellow and blue stripes and an open neck showing a white t-shirt underneath. His hair over the years in jail had grown shaggy. He had cultivated lamb chop sideburns, giving him the look of a leftover flower power man of the sixties.

Three witnesses were to be called for Jock: the police officer who investigated Jock's bike accident at West Ryde; Stephen Milligan, regarding the hiring of a van from Kennards Hire Service; and James Jackson, a nurse who had looked after him at Liverpool Hospital.

Jock began without any preamble:

Since I was shot in the brain and in the head I have lost a lot of ability of reading and writing. So I am trying to do this without any paperwork.

I was born in Glasgow on 5.8.43. I left school at fourteen and became an apprentice blacksmith. At seventeen I joined the army and served approximately six years at the Royal Engineers. I did tours of duty in Germany, a few countries in the Middle East and the Far East.

I emigrated to Australia and arrived in 1966. I then moved up to the Central Coast where my parents were living and met a few people on motor cycles and the Comanchero motor cycle club came into being . . ."

He had a receptive audience. Perhaps it was the tone of his voice—a no-nonsense sort of growl which commanded attention, or perhaps it was the controlled hand movements, almost Churchillian, he used periodically to embellish his speech. Even some of the jurors prone to be droopy-eyed sat to attention, drinking in every word.

"I will tell you why the club suffered. I was the one that split it," he spat out the last two words, "in August 1983 . . ."

Jock relayed the events leading up to the shootout. He did not hurry, like most of the men before him had, but delivered his address slowly and clearly in his modulated sing-song Scottish accent.

On the ninth of August, I got another phone call. Three of my men had been drinking at the Bull and Bush. Snoddy came in with sixteen Bandidos . . .and battered them into the ground. But I still did nothing. If I wanted to retaliate I could have done so the next day. There was a 21st birthday party only 500 yards from the clubhouse in the backyard. All of them were there. It was easy to have a shot at them at 3 to 4am when they were all blind drunk . . .

He was leading up to the declaration of war, leaning forward on the parapet like a minister addressing his congregation, emphasising his words, leaning on his hand, his head to the right, the gold wedding band on his left hand glinting under the fluorescent light.

He surveyed the jury, pausing, like a true orator, at each face, as if he was speaking to each one alone.

" . . .That Sunday afternoon, Snoddy phoned me up. He told me as far as he was concerned I was finished. I was gone. Get out of the area or he will wipe me right out . . .I argued with him. I told him he was a fool . . ."

Once he slipped up, describing "the Bandaid" clubhouse, quickly covering up the mistake.

Then he began to talk about the morning of 2 September.

"Ladies and gentlemen," he surveyed the audience seated before him. "I didn't want this conflict with the Bandidos. I didn't want it for a very good reason. When I left the club I had twelve men left. By August I had close to 36 men. The club was going well. Things were coming together good. The last thing I would want was a conflict to stuff everything up. Why should I? They mean nothing to me.

"The next day . . .excuse me, I'm a bit dry . . ." he sipped from the glass of water in front of him.

From here on my memory gets a bit fragmented with the shots in my head.

I phoned Leroy at 11 am—'Come up for a barbeque at my place at the pool.' He told me he was going to the swap meet and from there on to Mittagong. I told him 'You behave yourself', and I let it go at that.

Later on I had a phone call from Glen Eaves. His wife had an operation and was feeling pretty crook . . .He asked me if I wanted to go to the swap meet for parts . . .

He paused, reminding the jury he had $4500 of damage done to his Harley, which was not insured, when he was run off the road. He talked of the trip to the carpark, how it was their custom to travel in convoy.

"The Crown has tried to allege because people got off their bikes and looked all over the place, they were doing something wrong. I put it to you, ladies and gentlemen, you go into any carpark where there's a swap meet or anything happening—what is the first thing you do when you arrive . . ." he waited as if expecting an answer. "You get out and walk around—there's nothing sinister in that.

"They are trying to make out that we were waiting for them to come so we could make a go at them. Surely I would have kept the men together—not allowed them to scatter around the car park as the evidence says."

Three sleeping policemen sitting in the back row near the Comancheros now sat upright, their eyes drawn to the figure in the centre of the court.

"After we left the Viking Hotel, we were going to split up. As far as I knew and all the many years that I have been with bike clubs, there's no fighting at swap meets. It isn't done. I did not think this would be any different."

He spoke of Podgorski's evidence, his motives for saying certain things.

"He gave evidence he knew what Snoddy said at the meeting. Jock Ross and the Comancheros had to go. Something had to be done about the Comancheros and not just bashing, something permanent," he paused again for effect.

"I was a target," he almost whispered the fact, suspense building up around his words.

"In actual fact when he (Podgorski) said I was up the top of the carpark, I was lying on the ground near Glen Eaves' car with enough shotgun pellets in me to knock over six men."

"He's superhuman," Lard's interjection could be heard from the dock. "The only thing that could hurt him is Kryptonite and soap."

The only thing I can remember is Terry Parker hysterical. I remember the hospital. I remember not being able to breathe—the shocking pain in my side. That basically is what I remember of the first few days. Police said they took a record of interview on the fourth of September. One of my lungs had collapsed. I was on a drip. My teeth had been shot out and so had my face, my brain, my head . . .

I didn't remember the conversation . . . I had no glasses on. I was blind in the right eye for the time being. I put it to you—the words he put down . . . they are just not my words. He made most of that up. As for the sixth, and Detective Tees, I didn't believe he was even there or talked to me. He saw me there with a band around my head. I had big steel staples about five inches around the side of my head . . .

The only thing that saved me was dedicated nurses and sheer will power.

. . . Police came to see me on the eighteenth. I didn't want to talk to them. They said they'd charge me with witholding evidence and might even have a crack at the wife with some sort of conspiracy charge of some kind.

I had lost 25 kilos in weight. I was an emotional wreck. One of my best men had died. A lot more were badly injured. It was very easy to put anything over me then. I believed them.

He spoke like a beleaguered general recounting the demise of his troops.

"The police went and my mother came. My wife has asthma. My mother has cancer. I wore glasses as thick as milk bottle bottoms," he pulled the glasses he was wearing off his ears shaking them in front of the jury. "I cannot see anything without them. They say they showed me photos," he looked down to his barrister sitting at the bar table.

"Got that photo?" he spoke to him as if he was a lackey.

Justice Roden interrupted. Whether Ross heard him, it was unclear, but he gave no signs of having done so. Instead, he talked over the top of Roden, propelled by a rage that had been growing steadily over two years of sitting at the back of the court. Roden demurred.

"I was gone. I was sick. I signed my name instinctively. He took my hand and shoved it on the paper. He held it. It was my initials . . .

"I didn't go there that day to murder anybody or help anyone murder anybody. I didn't go there that day to kill anybody or help anybody to kill anybody.

"The only reason I am here as far as I can see is not for what I have done. It is for who I am.

"I'm the only leader left alive," he announced prophetically.

"The Vice-President's gone. The Sergeant's gone. The Crown and the police need somebody to hang it on. They need a scrapegoat," his voice rose to a crescendo, oblivious to the mispronunciation he had just made.

"That's why in the last six months you've heard so much garbage put on me. They want somebody to carry the can. I'm the only leader left. I'm it."

Just as suddenly, his voice dropped.

"Thanks for listening."

The trial adjourned briefly over Christmas and resumed in the first week of 1987.

A female sheriff officer wished the Bandidos a Merry Christmas. "Christmas—isn't that when the three wise men fucked the Virgin Mary." Lard's coarseness amused his mates but stung the woman to the quick.

The defence case was completed by Christmas and Viney began his final address to the jury on 5 January.

He told the jurors bullets from Spencer's .357 rifle killed three people, and the four other victims died of shotgun wounds. The crown case was that the jury could believe that Spencer had killed three of the dead.

Bystanders had found themselves in the midst of "a terrifying and bewildering gun battle . . ."

"In this trial all are either principals or accessories . . . you don't have to decide which, but must be satisfied they are either one or the other . . . Each of the accused realised guns were likely to be discharged and that anybody might be killed . . ."

Viney glanced up and down the jury as he told them nine guns and other weapons, including ten baseball bats, seven pipes and iron bars, seven clubs, nine knives, a knuckleduster and chains, were collected from the scene.

"You may think these are ferocious weapons—they are."

Before they retired to consider their verdicts, Roden had asked the jurors to consider four points in the case of each individual.

1. Was he party to the fight? If not he would be acquitted on all charges.

2. Was he unlawfully party to the fight? If so, and the jury was satisfied the nature of the fight might terrify the public, then he was guilty of affray.

3. Was he unlawfully party, not only to the fight, but to the shooting that caused death? If so, he was guilty of manslaughter.

4. The fourth point to consider was did the defendant act with the intention or state of mind necessary for his offence to be murder? "If you are satisfied, you will convict of murder, unless a manslaughter verdict is appropriate by reason of excessive self-defence or provocation," the judge said.

The jury was locked up for two months. They stayed at a motel half-an-hour from the courthouse at an undisclosed address. They lived on the top floor of the motel, eating their meals in their twin rooms—often hamburgers, salads or Kentucky Fried Chicken.

Sheriff's officers had been stationed on their floor—one sat at the end of the passageway. There was only one staircase in the middle of the walkway. The officers would sometimes play touch football with the male jurors.

The jurors were allowed a video machine after they complained of being bored in the evenings. It was placed in the common room.

At the courthouse, they would sit for hours around a large table in the jury room. There was an urn, two toilets, a sink for washing up. Comfortable chairs had been bought for them.

They had made a pact not to discuss the case unless all members were present. As the days passed tension inside the jury room mounted. Fights almost broke out.

The jurors would decide on how long they would stop for lunch. Often, some would catnap sprawled on the floor or on their chairs. Others sat over the crossword. A nerf ball materialised, which they filled with water, and they threw at each other. It helped break the tension.

On Thursday 11 June, the judge summed up against the last of the defendants, Jock Ross.

Jock was agitated, particularly as Roden read through the police record-of-interview Aarnie Tees conducted with Jock in Liverpool Hospital. For a long time he sat with his face screwed up tightly, as though to block everything out. He picked his ear, scratched his face and stared up at the ceiling above the judge.

"The Crown case is that as President of the Comancheros, Ross was primarily responsible for the decision that members of that Club go in force and armed, ready for a confrontation at the Viking Tavern . . ."

At 2.05pm, the jury retired to consider its last verdict.

Lance Wellington was munching on a red shiny apple when the Judge announced on Friday 12 June that the jury was still deliberating on a verdict for Ross. Wellington sat, legs apart, in the front row of the dock, in the seat he had occupied for the 332 days of the trial. His head was bowed over a bike magazine.

He looked up only when the judge turned to a different subject.

This is probably the last time all 31 accused will be in court together before the verdict. And there is something I feel I should say about, and to, them.

They have been kept in small enclosures at the rear of the court, day after day . . .between those daily appearances they have been transported to and from the court by means not designed primarily for comfort. All this has occurred while they are under the stress that is part and parcel of facing serious charges, and what must have been mounting tension as verdict day has approached.

If from time to time the pressure had proved too much, they could very easily have hampered and disrupted these proceedings. This has not occurred . . .

Neither the system nor the facilities were designed for a trial of these proportions . . .

I have deliberately chosen to say this before the verdict, because it applies equally to each of the accused, irrespective of whether he is about to be acquitted, or about to be convicted of affray, manslaughter or murder. In respect of any who are convicted, justice will take its course. But their difficulties to which I have referred have been experienced during the trial process, while they have been entitled to the benefit of the presumption of innocence . . ."

Roden's voice was magnified by loudspeakers in the hallway outside the courtroom where some makeshift arrangements had been made for the dozen or so members of the media who had not managed to get a seat inside the court. Instead, they sat outside, scribbling down Roden's words, heads bent in concentration. Portable partitions had been erected halfway down the hallway to cordon off the trial from the rest of the hearings within Penrith District Court. Relatives unable to be seated in the upstairs gallery craned around the screens to hear the Judge's words.

"Under our system the trial is not intended to be part of the punishment . . .cooperation has been forthcoming from these accused. For that I thank them."

Lance, his face expressionless, returned to his magazine.

Security for the verdict had been increased to ridiculous proportions. Thirty-eight uniformed police sat inside the courtroom, part of a team of 100 TRG officers brought in to patrol the building and surrounds.

Upstairs in the public gallery, the front row of seats was reserved for selected journalists who had registered their names with the police media liaison unit during the week. The relatives were seated further back, the second row of seats relegated for TRG officers and plain-clothes detectives.

Phyllis Campbell looked tired and worn as she was led protectively into the court, supported by her daughter Patricia, both eager to learn the fate of Caesar and Bull. Beverly Roberts, Bear's mother, complained bitterly when she saw the allocation for the media. Bob McElwaine and his wife sat in separate seats, Shirley in the back row, Bob immediately in front of his former wife. The rest of the relatives dutifully took their seats at the back of the gallery—Bandidos on the left, Comancheros to the right.

Lucy Hennessey, Littlejohn's wife, sat with her husband's parents, tired familiar faces who had sat through the entire proceedings in support of their son. Vanessa Ross sat in the third row on the far left. She looked like a child. Army, who had been leading her around the court, holding her hand and protecting her, remained by her side.

Lee Denholm, her blonde hair braided, accentuating high cheek bones and a strong, handsome face, stood in the corridor waiting to hear the verdict with two other Bandido women in jeans and high-heeled boots.

John Bodt, Blowwave, was also in the crowd outside the courtroom doors, dressed in a black t-shirt and loose ill-fitting jeans. He wore dark glasses, but not his Comanchero colours.

At 10am, the defendants were brought up from the cells. Most glanced upward as they climbed the steps, hoping for a friendly face. Instead they were greeted by the curious stares of the press.

At 10.23 a smiling judge re-entered the court and bowed. He had received a note indicating the jury had reached a verdict in the case of Ross, and was ready to proceed.

Eve Roden, a small woman with brown hair, sat with the judge's tip staff to the left of her husband. With hands clasped on her belly, she glanced furtively down to the dock areas, her short legs not quite reaching the floor of the court.

The jury foreman's black hair was tied back in a short ponytail. He stood up revealing blue jeans and green jumper.

Chewy was still chewing gum.

One by one, each defendant rose and walked from his coop into the dock proper, his counsel springing to his side as the judge asked the foreman how the jury found the accused.

Four minutes after the judge had returned to the bench, the first of the verdicts was read out.

Caesar was first—guilty of manslaughter.

His ol' ladies, Donna and Irene, his mother Phyllis and sister Patricia strained forward in their seats but could not see him. Patricia held her mother's arm. Relief showed on their faces.

Outside the court, the journalists concentrated on the disembodied voice from the loudspeaker.

Garry Annakin, the 25-year-old Comanchero Pee Wee, was not so lucky. Guilty of seven murders. The tall long-haired bikie gazed blankly at the jury before he was led down the steps to the holding cells.

Opey was guilty of manslaughter.

Snow was next—the second murder conviction.

Bones and Ray Denholm—manslaughter.

Glen Eaves stood and faced the judge, his cheeks flushed, a sign of anger and frustration. Murder.

He clenched, opened and clenched his fists and turned to the jury. "Now I know how Lindy Chamberlain felt!" he shouted as a policeman moved in to guide him down the stairs.

Tonka, Kraut, Bull, Roach, Dukes, Gloves, Davo, Charlie, Big Tony—all guilty of manslaughter.

"Guilty of murder."

A gasp rang through the public gallery. Lard, the baby-faced baker, was the first and only Bandido found guilty of murder.

JJ was next followed by Sunshine—both convicted of murder.

Chewy stopped chewing gum briefly to be told he was guilty of manslaughter.

Mrs Hennessey stifled a scream as her son's verdict was read out: "Guilty of murder". She wept uncontrollably as her husband tried to muffle her sobs in his jumper. Lucy, Littlejohn's wife, also broke down. John Hennessey's younger brother placed his arm around his mother. All eyes in the gallery turned to the weeping family and many began to cry in sympathy.

Littlejohn showed no reaction to his conviction. He could not see the effect of the news on his family. He turned and walked down to the cells.

Kid Rotten and Junior—both guilty of manslaughter.

There were smiles all around the Bandido side of the public gallery when Knuckles was found not guilty of murder or manslaughter, but affray only. He walked from the dock and sat by his counsel at the bar table.

Terry Parker, in a v-neck jumper and jeans, had a red nerve rash on his neck. He was found guilty of murder.

Tiny, Louie, Bear, Lance and Morts were convicted of manslaughter. Lance stood at the dock, the magazine rolled up in his hand, kept low beside his body, out of view of the judge and jury. He patted his counsel on the arm as he left the dock, as if to say well done. Greg James nodded in acknowledgement.

Jock knew what was coming. A murder conviction was inevitable. He stood in the dock, in the familiar blue shirt and jeans, his thick grey hair caught under and over his collar. A packet of Winfield cigarettes stuck out from his breast pocket.

His hands were planted firmly on the edge of the dock as he listened: "Guilty of murder."

Unlike the others, Jock took a long, calculated look along the jury before he turned slowly, leaving the court in his own time.

Outside the court, men in suits, plain clothes detectives and inquisitive barristers from other courts, their arms folded, strolled up and down while Roden's voice could be heard again on the loudspeaker.

One of the worst things was having to sit there hour after hour while I read to you from statements or transcripts . . . I appreciate the considerable difficulties under which the inadequacy of the law have forced you to operate . . .

The jury system's survival is dependent on people being prepared to serve . . . the high degree of attention and concentration throughout, even in the fourteenth month, and the third month of summing up, you have been exceptional . . . You do have every reason to feel satisfaction and pride . . .

Adam, a Bandido from Griffith, one of the few in the court to wear his colours, snorted, in disgust. "I reckon . . ." He turned on his heel and left.

The jurors stood and left the court for the last time. Roden excused them from jury service for life.

Upstairs, Mrs Littlewood, Davo's mother, crossed the public gallery to the Comanchero side and to Mrs Hennessey. Open armed, tears streaming down her face, she pulled the distraught woman to her. The two women sat together, holding each other and weeping, weeping for their sons, weeping as only a mother knows.

Knuckles was released on bail, on condition he not talk to the media, and he reside at home until he was sentenced on the charge of affray the following week.

Bob and Shirley McElwaine followed him separately down the street outside the court to the coffee shop.

"Of course I'm happy to have one son free," Shirley said to one reporter, but the family refused to comment further. Karen held Knuckles' hand as they walked out of the courthouse followed closely by four television film crews.

Mrs Hennessey collapsed and was carried down the spiral staircase from the gallery and out the side entrance of the building to escape the cameras. One photographer spotted her coming out of the side, his motor drive working steadily, attracting the attention of the television cameramen, who quickly followed his lead.

"I don't suppose you could say that you're overjoyed when anyone is convicted . . .but the main thing is that justice appears to be done," the recently-promoted Superintendent Ron Stephenson said, solemn-faced, to the media outside the courthouse.

"Yes, they behaved well during the trial, but I don't think they could achieve anything by doing otherwise. It's certainly different behaviour than on the second of September . . ."

Epilogue

On Friday 26 June at 9am, after a week-long sentence hearing, Justice Roden sentenced the 31 prisoners before him.

Before he dealt with each man, he had this to say:

. . .throughout the sentence hearing, I sought a greater understanding than I was able to obtain, of the nature of the clubs and the relationship between their respective members.

There was, I thought, very good reason for that. A number of the prisoners appeared as persons of good character. Some are in their thirties or forties, have no significant prior convictions, and have good family and work backgrounds, I felt that there had to be some explanation for the marked and perplexing difference between their behaviour in other contexts. I also wanted to know more about the clubs themselves, and what it is about the way of life that they offer that led these people, many of whom would in all other respects be regarded as law abiding, responsible citizens of commendable character, to indulge in what, on the face of it, is irresponsible, anti-social behaviour of extreme violence, bringing with it obvious danger to human life, and in the facts of this case the tragic consequences of seven deaths . . .

It is not possible to sit looking at these men for more than a year, as I have done, without feeling that there is more to them than the popular image of bikie gang members. It is unfortunate that so many of them, including all who were not convicted of murder, have chosen to play no part in the sentence hearing, although years of their lives are at stake . . .

A fierce loyalty, and a propensity for violence, which rightly or wrongly typify the popular image of such clubs, are clearly indicated by the evidence in this case . . .A need to belong, and to enjoy a close relationship and bond with others, can be readily understood. So too can a pride in physical strength and courage. But, like most admirable qualities, these can be carried to excess.

The ugly side of loyalty seems to demand enemies against whom the loyal can be united. And the ugly side of physical strength and courage is seen when violence is unleashed against those enemies.

When you have two groups like these, in conflict with one another, a Viking is always likely.

As patriotism can lead to jingoism, and mateship can lead to cronyism, so bikie club loyalty, it seems, can lead to bikie club war . . .

In July 1987, Gloves received a C2 prisoner classification and was moved to the low security Her Majesty's Training Centre at Emu Plains, at the foot of the Blue Mountains on Sydney's western outskirts.

Sandy and Jake Shadow visited him on Saturdays, Jake sitting on his father's knee under the crepe myrtal trees in the large sports-like oval where the prisoners entertained their visitors. Gloves, a black Akubra hat on his head, a present from Sandy, would read his blond haired son Little Golden Book stories.

He had been told to stop boxing by prison authorities, so he found another ambition: to break the thirteen hour *Guinness Book of Records* record for skipping.

In January 1988 he trained intensively for the event. Besides his regular running and swimming programme, he skipped at least 32 hours a week to build up his stamina for the March date, when officials from the *Guiness Book of Records* would visit to test his skill.

He still complained bitterly about the system. Sometimes wrote letters headed "Fuck'n prison" to friends.

I am working down in the piggery lookin after the boars. I take them for a walk down to the sow's pen—make sure they get a jump once a day. The last fellow who was lookin after them just got out of hospital. One of the boars tore his leg open. He received 80 stitches. Lucky I have excellent reflexes. Our release day as it stands now is Jan 89. We can earn four days a month remission if all goes well.

Lou and myself have been asked to be part in a raft race, part of a the six man team that is—it's a 14 klm race. We have visits Sats.

I am sitting in the boars yard while he's having his mornin jump. It's pissin down rain here. All the yards are just mud. What a man has to go threw for his freedom . . .

Stay cool and take it easy.

Odios.

Gloves 1%er
B.F.F.B.

Roo, Pig, Val, Zorba, Bobby Watkins, Snake, Sparksey and Stephen Hails each pleaded guilty to affray. On 19 October 1987 a sentencing hearing for the eight men was interrupted by an urgent message from Prince Henry Hospital just as evidence on behalf of Snake Campbell began.

Snake's brother, John "Whack" Campbell had died of cardiomyopathy, before the family could reach him.

The following day, the eight men fronted up at Darlinghurst's Taylor Square courthouse. Pig arrived, pushing a pram, his baby son wearing a black Harley Davidson sweatshirt. Bodor smiled warmly at the little boy.

Roo was resplendent in a long-fringed, black suede jacket. Val stood apart from the others—quiet, withdrawn and thin, in a navy suit.

Zorba, back to his job as an optical technician, was clean-shaven, flanked by his mother and father.

Bobby Watkins' wife Sylvia, wearing lace stockings, her hair dyed blonde and purple, sat with her three year-old son on her knee, the child blowing raspberries to seek attention.

They had just bought a vegetable farm at Pitt Town.

The eight men sat in the jury box.

"Which one is to be the foreman?" Justice Roden asked them, chuckling quietly, displaying a humour seldom seen during the long months at Penrith.

He sentenced them all to a two-year good behaviour bond.

The following day, Snake appeared at Penrith Police Station to collect his possessions. "I've come to get me gear," he said gruffly to Detective Demmery. Demmery unlocked the strongroom in the cell complex of the charge room and found the appropriate paper sack marked Geoffrey Campbell.

He looked inside. There was a black t-shirt and a pair of blue jeans, both blood-stained and shredded—cut by ambulance officers three years previously on the footpath outside the Viking tavern.

Among a few odd papers and letters was a brass letter opener with an elaborate eagle at the head.

The bag also contained a soft black leather long-sleeved shirt, which Snake's ol' lady had made for him. It was beautiful. Demmery held it up admiring the handiwork. There were two matching black leather wristlets into which the word "Bandidos" had been burned.

And of course, Snake's beloved Bandido colours were there in the bottom of the bag.

Snake took his time checking the list in Demmery's book, taking each item out of the bag and checking it, making sure all his rightful belongings were returned to him.

He signed the book and placed everything back in the sack.

The detective pondered the changes in the man before him. Gone was the woolley beard and unkempt appearance. Now the beard was neatly trimmed and the hair brushed back, held together behind with a leather thong.

He picked up the sack and placed it under his arm.

"I hope we've heard the last of this," the detective ventured.

Snake stared straight at Demmery, a look of disdain in his blue-grey eyes.

"This'll never be over," he returned. He pushed open the heavy glass door, turned left and disappeared into the lunchtime crowd on the main street of Penrith.

SENTENCES

Colin Campbell, 41, Caesar: manslaughter 12 years, affray 6 years, non-parole period, 7 years.

Garry Annakin, 25, Pee Wee: murder 20 years, affray 9 years, non-parole period, 12 years.

Stephen Cowan, 28, Opey: manslaughter 12 years, affray 6 years, non-parole period, 7 years.

Ian White, 34, Snow: murder life, affray 10 years.

Scott Dive, 24, Bones: manslaughter 10 years, affray 5 years, non parole period 6 years.

Raymond Denholm, 28, Ray: manslaughter 10 years, affray 5 years, non-parole period 6 years.

Glen Eaves, 25, Glen: murder life, affray 10 years.

Michael O'Keefe, 31, Tonka: manslaughter 12 years, affray 6 years, non-parole period 7 years.

Kevork Tomasian, 41, Kraut: manslaughter 12 years, affray 6 years, non-parole period seven years.

Phillip Campbell, 35, Bull: manslaughter 14 years, affray 7 years, non-parole period 8 years.

James Posar, 31, Roach: manslaughter 12 years, affray 6 years, non-parole period 7 years.

Greg McElwaine, 33, Dukes: manslaughter 12 years, affray 6 years, non-parole period 7 years.

Mark McElwaine, 27, Gloves: manslaughter 12 years, affray 6 years, non-parole period 7 years.

William Littlewood, 28, Davo: manslaughter 12 years, affray 6 years, non-parole period 7 years.

Charlie Scibberas, 27, Charlie: manslaughter 12 years, affray 6 years, non-parole period 7 years.

Tony Cain, 26, Big Tony: manslaughter 14 years, affray 7 years, non-parole period 8 years.

Tony Melville, 26, Lard: murder life, affray 10 years.

Robert Heeney, 30, JJ: murder life, affray 10 years.

Raymond Kucler, 31, Sunshine: murder life, affray 10 years.

Richard Lorenz, 32, Chewy: manslaughter 12 years, affray 6 years, non-parole period 7 years.

John Hennessy, 27, Littlejohn: murder 20 years, affray 9 years, non-parole period 12 years.

Lance Purdie, 38, Kid Rotten: manslaughter 12 years, affray 6 years, non-parole period 7 years.

Mark Shorthall, 24, Junior: manslaughter 12 years, affray 6 years, non-parole period 7 years.

Phillip McElwaine, 27, Knuckles: Acquitted of murder, affray - two year good behaviour bond.

Terrence Parker, 33, Terry: murder 18 years, affray 8 years, non-parole period 10 years.

Graeme Wilkinson, 33, Tiny: manslaughter 12 years, affray 6 years, non-parole period 7 years.

Lewis Cooper, 30, Louie: manslaughter 12 years, affray 6 years, non-parole period 7 years.

Stephen Roberts, 28, Bear: manslaughter 12 years, affray 6 years, non-parole period 7 years.

Lance Wellington, 36, Lance: manslaughter 12 years, affray 6 years, non-parole period, 7 years.

James Morton, 45, Morts: manslaughter 10 years, affray 5 years, non-parole period 6 years.

William Ross, 43, Jock: murder life, affray 10 years.

Postscript

Jock Ross is serving a life sentence at Long Bay Central Industrial Prison.

Glen Eaves was released from Long Bay's Central Industrial Prison for nine days in December 1987 while he sought leave to appeal against his conviction. His release caused a public uproar, the tabloids describing him as "Killer Freed." Eaves was returned to prison, dismissed from the Army, and transferred to the jail's Metropolitan Remand Centre where he is awaiting a date for his appeal hearing.

Ray Denholm was the first bikie to be released, having served three and a half years of a ten year sentence. He was released from Silverwater Jail on 11 March 1988, 35 days before his due remission date because his parole officers considered him to be a model prisoner.

James Arthur Morton was paroled on 17 April 1988, the first Comanchero to be released.

Scott Dive was paroled two weeks later.

Knuckles McElwaine was the only bikie to be acquitted of murder charges on 12 June 1988, and subsequently released on a good behaviour bond. He sold his story to the current affairs program *Willesee* for $5 000 and he and Karen moved to the NSW central coast where Knuckles is working as a barman in a club.

Gloves McElwaine was moved from Parklea Prison to Emu Plains Detention Centre in August 1987. On 20 March 1988, he attempted to break the world skipping record in the *Guiness Book of Records*, skipping for ten hours. The record was thirteen. He was paroled in October 1988.

Lard Melville, the only Bandido to be found guilty of murder, admitted lying to the jury at his sentencing hearing in late June 1987. In the witness box, he told Judge Roden that Lout was in Snoddy's car when they drove into the Viking Tavern on 2 September 1984, having denied Lout was in the car in his dock statement.

"... I believed I was innocent and I didn't believe I should put in another man that I believed was innocent ...," Lard told the judge.

In September 1988, Melville and five Comancheros — Ross, Kucler, Heeney, Annakin and Hennessy — began an appeal hearing against their murder convictions and sentences.

On 23 November 1988, a full bench of the Court of Criminal Appeal overturned the six mens' convictions and sentences. The judges found that Justice Roden had erred in his directions to the jury and the full bench substituted manslaughter convictions for the standing murder convictions.

Hennessey, Heeney, Annakin and Melville had their non-parole period reduced to seven years; Ross received nine years non-parole and Kucler eight years.

Comancheros Ian White and Glen Eaves are also appealing against their murder convictions and sentences. Their hearing is listed for March 1989.

Kezra Lorenz is divorced from Rick (Chewy) Lorenz and now lives in London where she has written a film script about her life with a Comanchero.

Chief Superintendent Ronald Harry Stephenson was awarded the Commissioner's commendation at the Goulburn Police Academy in NSW on 7 August 1987, in recognition of outstanding leadership and command of police resources concerned with the investigation of the Father's Day Massacre at Milperra on 2 September 1984. Detective Superintendent Stephenson showed ability in controlling and co-ordinating this inquiry, greatly contributing to the successful outcome of this matter which brought considerable merit to the NSW police force, the Commissioner said.

On 26 January 1988, Chief Superintendent Stephenson was listed in the Bicentennial Australia Day Honours List and awarded the Australian Police Medal for distinguished service.

Detective John Garvey received the Commissioner's recommendation for bravery on 7 August 1987, in recognition of outstanding courage and devotion to duty in confronting Kucler and disarming him, and in negotiations and the disarming of the bikies thus enabling medical treatment for a number of injured people.

Detectives: All of the detectives who took part in Operation Hardwalk were invited to buy a Father's Day Massacre tie. The police ran a competition for the best design. On the second anniversary of the massacre, they held A Viking Tie night, entry being by wearing one of the ties. About 80 people turned up for a smorgasbord and a few drinks. One police officer described it as "a few postmortems on the whole thing." A comedian was hired for entertainment.

The Harris Park Clubhouse was converted into a doctor's surgery. The bullet holes were still in the garage roller door at the time the doctors moved in.

No. 150 Louisa Road, Birchgrove was bought by a member of the

Penfold's family who made their name in stationery. The house was completely gutted and renovated.

Bandidos The Bandidos started a new clubhouse, resurrecting the old bar from Birchgrove and the neon sign of the Mexican Bandit from their old clubhouse being put in pride of place.

Some of the members, including those who had an early release, wore tattoos which read "Always remembered. Chopper, Snotty, Shadow"—the words around red flowers on a vine.

COST

Overall cost of court proceedings, security, legal fees, housing of the prisoners was $12.7 million. This broke down to:

Police The initial murder investigation, establishment of the six-detective Viking Taskforce and an Operation Hardwalk involving 120 detectives, dawn raids and arrests: $1 million.

Security operations: Spartan One and Two—including the salaries of police required to protect the judge, jury, courthouse, police station and the accused transported daily from jail to court—$2.9 million.

Jury: A two-day jury empanelling process cost $96 767 and from 28 April 1986 to 20 April 1987, the cost of the jury was $321 569. The figure includes jurors' allowances of $70 each per day (tax free), meals, transport, accommodation and miscellaneous expenses. Cost: $418 336.

Court Staff: A Supreme Court judge yearly salary is $102 000. For court staff, including an associate and tip staff, administrative costs of two court reporters, typists, and two court officers for one year would be $260 000.

Three Crown barristers and three solicitors for two years cost $600 000. Total cost: $962 000.

Prisoners: Housing 31 prisoners for two and a half years at $30 000 each per year cost $4.325 million. In addition, costs of keeping 11 others (released before the trial) for 18 months were $495 000.

Legal Fees: The standard amounts for Supreme Court legal officers according to Legal Aid:

A solicitor receives $275 for the first day and $215 each day thereafter with a $65 loading for each additional client.

A Queen's Counsel receives $785 for the first day and $555 each day thereafter with a $90 loading for additional clients.

A junior barrister receives $520 per day and $340 each day thereafter, with a $65 loading for the first couple of additional clients.

The trial involved the services of 17 barristers, two QCs and eight solicitors at a cost of $2.6 million. (This figure does not include legal costs for the 13 months committal hearing.)